African Primary Products
& International
Trade

*

African Primary Products & International Trade

Papers delivered at an
INTERNATIONAL SEMINAR
in the University of Edinburgh, September 1964

edited by
I.G.STEWART
and
H.W.ORD

at the University Press
Edinburgh

EDINBURGH UNIVERSITY PRESS

1 George Square, Edinburgh 8

North American Agent

Aldine Publishing Company

64 East Van Buren Street, Chicago 5

Australia and New Zealand

Hodder & Stoughton Limited

Africa

Oxford University Press

Printed in Great Britain
by T. & A. Constable Ltd., Hopetoun Street
Printers to the University of Edinburgh

Preface

*

This book contains the papers presented at an International Seminar on African Primary Products and International Trade held at the University of Edinburgh from 20 to 23 September 1964. The Seminar was organized by the Department of Political Economy in co-operation with the Centre of African Studies and was the third in a series of seminars held in the Centre since its inauguration in January 1963.

The idea of holding a Seminar devoted to academic discussion of agricultural, foreign trading, and related issues of economic development in Tropical Africa grew out of studies that had been undertaken in Nigeria and Ghana by members of the Department of Political Economy in Edinburgh. These studies, concerned with the estimation of demand for and supply of farm products, had been supported by the United States Department of Agriculture. That the Seminar took place successfully was in no small measure due to the original stimulus and material assistance provided in this way.

While the papers range over a variety of topics, their common concern is for the problems confronting African producers of commodities, many of which feature prominently in world trade. During a year that has witnessed several attempts – notably the United Nations Conference on Trade and Development in Geneva – to regulate international trade in primary products, the idea of eliciting contributions from African, American, and British economists to this subject seemed entirely appropriate.

The task of organizing the Seminar was shared by a number of colleagues both in the Centre of African Studies and in the Department of Political Economy. The thanks of the participants in the meetings are due to Professor A. J. Youngson, Head of the Department of Political Economy, for his encouragement and assistance in the publication of this book, and to Professor G. A. Shepperson, Convener of the Centre of African Studies Committee, for his support in arranging a Seminar of this kind. Among others to whom a particular debt of gratitude should be acknowledged are Miss Grace Hunter, Secretary/Librarian of the Centre, and Mrs M. Paton and Miss Eleanor Smith of the Department of Political Economy.

I. G. S.
H. W. O.

Contents

Introduction

*

For the developing countries of tropical Africa, the aim of current economic policies may be summed up as one of expansion by structural change. To achieve this at an acceptable rate most of them require to import technical skill and capital equipment. Payment for these services and commodities has to be made in foreign exchange, and there are broadly speaking three ways of acquiring foreign exchange – by exporting saleable goods and services, by borrowing, and by receiving outright aid.

The Seminar at which the papers published in this book were presented dealt, in the main, with the relationship of international trading to structural change and growth in tropical Africa. In no way, however, was this apparent emphasis on exporting primary commodities intended to suggest that members of the Seminar did not agree with Mr Dudley Seers' eloquent advocacy of aid as a vitally necessary addition to trading receipts. In the space of three busy days at Edinburgh we simply had to draw the line somewhere, and in view of the work that had been proceeding – work at Geneva for example in the United Nations Conference on Trade and Development in which some members of the Seminar had played a prominent role – the emphasis on trading relationships seemed appropriate.

As an introduction to papers whose authors properly diverge in their treatment of different problems and policies – the transformation of peasant agricultural and trading systems, estimating supply and demand responses, appraising commodity policies, or probing the larger issues of international trading principles – it may perhaps be useful if we attempt some kind of brief general statement embracing these questions in an African setting.

The most general but not necessarily the simplest dichotomy with which to open a discussion of trade in its relation to structural change is that between economic growth and economic stability. The large question to put is whether in African economic development, stability in incomes or prices or public revenues and expenditures advances or retards growth. In approaching this sort of fundamental issue, the economist trained in Anglo-Saxon modes of thought may often be hampered by classic notions of static equilibrium. As Schumpeter put it: 'Development in our sense is a distinct phenomenon, entirely

xi

foreign to what may be observed in the circular flow or in the tendency towards equilibrium. It is spontaneous and discontinuous change in the channels of the flow, disturbances of equilibrium, which for ever alters and displaces the equilibrium state previously existing'.[1] In studying the processes of change in Africa, we have to progress from the tautologies of Ricardo, Marx, and possibly Marshall to the paradoxes of Smith, Malthus, and perhaps Keynes. To consume more in the future, the African economy must first consume less; to have more income and investment at home the African economy has at present to obtain more receipts and capital from abroad. To grow faster, does the African economy benefit by having stable commodity prices abroad or fluctuating prices in the markets upon which its export earnings so much depend? Theories of growth and cyclical fluctuation have sought to bridge the interval between static and dynamic equilibrium analysis but their applicability to African economies may remain questionable in so far as they fail to take note of the Schumpeterian 'disturbances' or structural shifts that are frequently the prerequisite to dynamic thrusts forward in African productivity.

Growth may be defined in several ways; but growth in the sense of 'progress' really turns upon the maximizing of an economic surplus, subject to a variety of political, legal, social, and other constraints. An economy expands at a rate equivalent to the successive differences between the net return to factors of production and the supply prices or costs of these factors, elementarily labour, capital, land, and enterprise. If productivity is to increase, both human and physical resources have to be deployed so that returns are greater than costs of production, so that the efforts of the economy yield a surplus or net profit. It is against a fundamental criterion such as this that we have to consider the relationship between the export sector and the changing structure of domestic production, and more especially the whole question of responses to changing relative prices for different kinds of output.

The broad question of whether a nation whose principal economic activity has been agricultural benefits over the long run by continuing to concentrate on a range of primary commodities for export earnings – the classical argument for international specialisation along lines of comparative cost advantage – needs careful reconsidering in the light of present-day circumstances in Africa. It is believed that the long-term income-elasticity of demand for primary foodstuffs lies somewhere below 0·7, so that reliance on the mainly agricultural type of export suggests that a slowly diminishing share of world income will accrue to countries that take no positive steps to alter this sort of export pattern.

However, if the present allocation of resources is a profitable one,

---

[1] J. A. Schumpeter, *The Theory of Economic Development*, Oxford University Press, New York 1961, p. 64.

and there is no immediate prospect of finding a more profitable one that is less heavily dependent on the production for export of goods whose income elasticity of demand is low, then changing the allocation of resources is likely to be painful, at least for the transitional period. One must remember, of course, that the liberal case for international specialization presumes that under-employment of labour and capital is self-rectifying or need not be taken into account, and that the bargaining strength of trading nations is regulated by a competitive regimen that contains no built-in bias as between more developed and less specialized trading nations. African economies are nothing if not under-employed, and the rules of the General Agreement on Tariffs and Trade specifically recognize the imbalance in trading strength of the less-developed nations; the case, therefore, for leaving well enough alone in Africa's present productive structure cannot be said to command support on theoretical or pragmatic grounds.

On the contrary, a case can be made out for tariff protection or for other forms of government intervention as a method of bringing about *in the longer run* an allocation of productive resources that will most closely accord with the preferences of an African nation. How far off the attainment may be of the structural changes needed to bring about a more secure basis for rising real income is always extremely difficult to estimate. Set the target too low and no fundamental changes occur at all, leaving the economy as exposed to present uncertainty as ever. Pitch the horizon beyond which real consumption can rise steadily again too far ahead and confidence in the capacity of a country to transform itself from a primary producer to a diversified economic system will be lost. In the limit, the argument for radically altering the productive structure will run quite counter to the view that a nation does best if it continues producing those goods and services that *currently* earn the largest net return, or profitable surplus over costs of production.

Every African country is engaged, whether consciously or otherwise, in asking itself how far it can rely on what has come to be thought of as the traditional trading pattern as the best means of promoting long-term growth. Simultaneously it is realized – not always with sufficient clarity – that to some irreducible extent any sensible policy for growth by means of structural changes depends on the acquisition of foreign exchange by exporting primary commodities *meanwhile*. Development ultimately cannot proceed, let alone proceed rapidly, save by importing skills, knowledge, and equipment from abroad. It may be an exaggeration to describe Africa's need for imports as the Achilles' heel of its economic development, but few who have worked in African tropical countries would quarrel today with Professor Prest's comment made in 1951 that 'It is the future not the present of Nigeria which is so dependent on imports.'[1] Cut off this cord and the economy falls back upon its own internal springs of innovation, the direction, if not the force, of which it is temptingly easy to question.

If one kind of objection to reliance on the traditional trading pattern has been that it appears to perpetuate for African exporters the role of 'hewers of wood and drawers of water' for the more developed metropolitan countries, another sort of objection is that dependence on primary commodities for foreign exchange exposes producers to distressing fluctuation in prices and incomes. This brings us back to the basic problem – how may African economies reconcile growth with stability or instability in the foreign trade sector? Some will argue that a partial answer to the quest for a compromise policy may be found in the trading record over the last fifteen years. When export prices have been rising, African gross national product and incomes per head have been rising; whereas falling commodity prices have tended to bring stagnation to developmental efforts. Whether to take the simple evidence afforded by the barter terms of trade or the more pertinent relationship between the income terms of trade and expansion remains debatable, but that there is some close association between the pace of growth in African economies and the purchasing power of African exports few will deny.

Before the techniques and policies for stabilizing or supporting commodity prices or incomes are discussed later in this book, we should pause to review again the underlying issue. Smoothing out fluctuations implies the determination of a trend value that will bring and keep supplies offered for export in balance with market demands in the major importing countries. If prices are set above the trend or equilibrium value, overproduction and consequent piling up of inventories will occur; if, alternatively, the negotiations between the primary exporters and the importing nations result in contracts to purchase at prices that turn out lower than the trend, producers will have lost more than they gained. Even supposing that effective and agreeable methods of smoothing out fluctuations in prices or incomes for primary producers can be devised – and there have been numerous experiments during the last thirty years – we have still to face the question of whether stabilization is more likely on balance to assist or to retard economic development by structural change.

It may be argued that the avoidance of severe swings in export earnings facilitates planning of public works, for which the revenue is closely tied to the profitability of primary exports. Further, it may be argued that private enterprise in the developing industrial sectors of African nations requires the reassurance of a steadily expanding

---

[1] A. R. Prest and I. G. Stewart, *The National Income of Nigeria*, 1950-51, H.M.S.O., London, 1953 (Colonial Research Studies No. 11), p. 88.

domestic market to encourage new and risky ventures. For the primary producers themselves, the gains from the sudden, unexpected increases in world demand – and thus in prices – for their commodities do not overcompensate them for the distress of contracting expenditures in the unexpectedly sudden recessions – so this line of pleading runs. In the limit it would appear, therefore, that marked cyclical fluctuation is the very antithesis of that progression we have called growth. The alternative to so pessimistic a view of the economic prospects confronting African primary producers turns upon the extent to which producers' responses to price changes are rapid and large or neither – upon an estimate of the elasticities of supply. If producers can, and in fact do, react promptly to changes in commodity prices, then profitable substitutions will be made. The substitution of a more profitable for a less profitable use of resources is another way of defining economic growth, so that instability, far from being the antithesis of growth, is a means of stimulating it *provided* supply responses are positive and fairly rapid. An objection at this stage is that the elasticity of supply of most primary commodities is believed to be low, at least in the short run; and that the stimulus to growth which instability brings is apt to be excessive, bringing disruption rather than adaptation in the economic structure.

If elasticities of supply are low in the longer run then structural change is bound to take a long time to achieve unless wholly new avenues of industry can prove successful. Happily, the picture of long run supply responses seems much brighter than many observers have hitherto supposed, and the problem of selecting among stabilization policies can be treated as a policy of limited insurance against temporary deficits in export earnings. Even so, it is difficult to frame such a policy without diminishing those very responses upon which growth by structural adaptation so vitally depends.

Above all, in this, as in other realms of economic debate, we do well to recall Marshall's advice that '. . . in studying the facts of the past and in devising schemes for the future our first concern is with the things that people have wished and do wish for. . . . We must not picture to ourselves an unreal world as it might, or ought to be, and make schemes for it. That way lies social madness, leading to a failure of hot aspirations and thence to cold reaction.'[1]

---

[1] A. C. Pigou (ed.), *Memorials of Alfred Marshall*, Macmillan, London 1925, pp. 302-3.

J.A.C.BROWN

A Brief Survey of Prospects
for African Exports
of Agricultural Products

*

When I refer to Africa I follow the usage of the United Nations and include all the countries of the continent except for South Africa, which is excluded on the grounds that it is relatively developed, and for Libya, Somalia, Sudan and the U.A.R. (Egypt), which are excluded on the grounds that they are part of the Near East.[1] Defined in this way the trading problems of Africa are both as similar and as diversified as those of any of the other developing regions in Asia or South America. Africa as a whole, relies for approximately three-quarters of her exports on agricultural products, and these provide the main finance for her imports which are mainly manufactures. Very little of each country's trade is with others in the continent or even with other developing regions, but overwhelmingly with the developed countries of Western Europe and North America. As with other developing regions the agricultural component of its trade is beset with price fluctuations in the short run and with increasing competition in the long run from domestic agriculture in its main markets and from synthetic substitutes for agricultural raw materials. Together with other developing regions it shares a trade gap which grew in the 1950's to around $m1200, and which United Nations studies forecast to grow further in the 1960's. On the other hand the problems of Africa are diverse in that each of the forty or so countries of the continent is interested in a different and often fairly narrow range of the commodities exported from the whole continent. At the extreme are such countries as Mauritius, more than 90 per cent of whose exports are agricultural; these overwhelmingly consist of sugar, the production of which accounts for about a half of the gross domestic product. But in almost every commodity there are three, four or five countries which account for the majority of Africa's total exports. It is therefore difficult to attempt a unified picture and even more difficult to suggest measures which would benefit the continent as a whole.

Accordingly, in this paper, I shall begin with some orders of magni-

---

[1] Most of the trade statistics quoted in this paper include also a number of islands which are not part of Africa but whose trade is small. Cf. *Trade in Agricultural Commodities in the United Nations Development Decade, FAO Commodity Review 1964, Special Supplement*, FAO, Rome, from which most figures are taken.

A

tude for Africa as a whole, and then proceed by commodities, mentioning the main interested countries under each. In effect the survey is a brief résumé of material presented to the United Nations meeting on Trade and Development of the spring of 1964, especially by the Food and Agricultural Organization.

Recent trends

Table 1 shows the net trade picture for Africa in the second half of the 1950's compared with that for other developing regions.

Thus we see that net earnings from raw material exports remained stationary in Africa and slightly declined in all other developing regions whilst imports of manufactured goods rose. This growing deficit was only partly offset by increased earnings from fuel exports, 80 per cent of the world's exports of which come from only five countries which are thereby placed in a special position. The general deterioration in the position of the primary producers during the 1950's thus hit others (particularly in Asia) harder than it did the African countries. The reason for this was partly the stability of Africa's connexion with Western European countries, and partly some competitive gain, particularly in coffee and cocoa, from producers in other developing regions.

Of what are Africa's agricultural exports made up and what are their destinations? As much as 91 per cent go directly to developed countries, only 3 per cent going to other developing regions, 2 per cent to the communist countries and 4 per cent to other countries in Africa. As to composition, 6 per cent are products which are exported mainly by developed countries (cereals, dairy products, meat); 36 per cent compete with exports from both developed and developing countries (fats and oils, sugar, citrus, tobacco); 38 per cent are exclusively tropical products (coffee, cocoa, tea, bananas); and 20 per cent are agricultural raw materials (rubber and natural fibres). Thus, again like most other developing regions, Africa is not able, by means solely of its own production and trading policies, to exert a significant influence on the world markets in which it is mainly interested. On the other hand, internal demand for food and agricultural raw materials has been increasing under the stimulus of growing population and development plans. It is estimated by the UN that if the targets of the UN development decade are to be met, the demand for food in Africa will continue to rise by a little over 4 per cent per year. Thus not all Africa's trade problems are rooted in a sluggish world demand. Others arise from a growing internal demand combined with supply difficulties, such as animal and crop diseases and a generally low standard of agricultural technology. In some cases, for example that of grains, African trade shows a growing deficit.

To some extent a study of trends in primary commodity quantities and prices during the 1950's makes for a pessimistic bias, since the 1950's opened in post-war scarcity conditions which were presently accentuated by the Korean crisis. The terms of trade for primary producers rose to unprecedentedly high levels and it was inevitable that there would be some decline later, especially in view of the well-known time-lag between high prices and the stimulated increase in primary supplies. Indeed during 1964 primary prices have risen again, leading some authorities to suppose that much of the evidence presented to the United Nations meeting on Trade and Development at Geneva in the spring was already out of date and not necessarily indicative of a persistent trend. However, when in the next section we look at broad commodity groups we shall see that there are indeed underlying trends whose reversal, except on a temporary basis, it is difficult to contemplate in the absence of a concerted policy by developed and underdeveloped nations alike.

The main commodity groups

(a) *Cereals and livestock products.* These account for only 6 per cent of African exports and most African countries are net importers. *Wheat* is exported only by Algeria, Tunisia and Morocco, which are however often importers. Madagascar is the only exporter of rice, and Africa as a whole is a net importer of dairy products and eggs. East Africa is a favourable area for increased meat production if the problems of animal disease can be overcome. It must be expected therefore that in the next decade Africa will remain mainly an importer of those temperate zone products and again probably mainly on concessional terms. The development of production in Africa must be seen mainly as a contribution to raising the nutritional level rather than to the assistance of the foreign balance.

(b) *Sugar, citrus, and fats and oils.* Total consumption of *sugar* in the world doubled during the 1950's, but exportable supplies tended to increase faster than demand, and a precarious balance was held by the International Sugar Agreement until the development of a new source of demand from the communist countries. The African exporters are, however, confined to Mauritius, Réunion and Mozambique which rely on bilateral agreements with the United Kingdom and France. North Africa is an important exporter of *citrus* to the European market and benefited greatly from the post-war rise in continental demand. The increased plantings in the whole Mediterranean region, however, suggest that it will be difficult to maintain prices during the second half of the 1960's.

Fats and oils are of far greater importance to tropical Africa which produces annually around 3 million tons of vegetable oilseeds and oils, and accounts for about 21 per cent of world exports (though this had fallen from 24 per cent in the early 1950's). The most significant fact in the world market, however, is that the U.S. share of world exports grew from a negligible level before the war to 30 per cent of the total by the early 1960's. This was due to the development of soybean production, the meal from which is used for feeding poultry and livestock. The exportable surplus of soybean oil in the U.S. is therefore expected to continue to increase, and the share in world trade of tropical oils to decrease. A further factor tending to depress foreign exchange earnings from this source is the preferential tariff system in force in many developed countries which favours the importation of oilseeds rather than oil, thus tending to retain the value added by processing within the importing country.

(c) *Tropical foods*. These account for 38 per cent of Africa's agricultural exports, and enjoy the advantage that, apart from sugar, they do not compete with the products of developed countries using advanced agricultural techniques. As regards *coffee*, Africa's share in world trade grew during the 1950's from 17 to 23 per cent, mainly at the expense of Latin America, and perhaps more importantly, is technically better suited for the manufacture of instant coffee which has proved important especially in countries such as the U.K. which are not traditional coffee consumers. World consumption is expected to continue to grow at 3 to $3\frac{1}{2}$ per cent per year on present trends. Perhaps the most important effect on the world market would be if the U.S.S.R. and communist Europe raised their consumption to anything approaching the West European level. Although recently their imports have in fact increased sharply, consumption per head in Russia and Eastern Europe is less than a twentieth of that in most Western countries, and there seems to be no intrinsic reason against a substantial increase in demand as the standard of living rises. The average price elasticity of demand for coffee in importing countries is estimated by the FAO to be -0.34 at the retail level and -0.20 at the import level. These however are short to medium-term estimates and there is not much doubt that, in the United Kingdom for instance, a long period of lower prices would be a considerable stimulant to demand. The processing of coffee beans into instant coffee powder is commonly discriminated against by importing countries though processing industries have been successfully established in Latin America and shipments to the US have increased. The African countries most interested in coffee exports are the territories of former French West Africa, Congo and Ruanda Urundi, Uganda, Kenya and Ethiopia.

Cocoa is of course of overwhelming importance to Ghana and Nigeria, and the Ivory Coast and Cameroons are also large exporters. Total African exports account for three-quarters of world trade,

Western Europe and North America taking nearly 90 per cent of world imports. Prospects for increased demand in the traditional importing countries are not however great, since in many cases (e.g. the U.K.) saturation levels of consumption seem to have been reached. As with coffee, cocoa consumption in the communist countries is relatively low and controlled by central buying policies. I shall not attempt here to describe the recent attempts at commodity agreements either for cocoa or for coffee since my purpose is rather to describe background economic conditions. Even in the absence of discrimination there are strong technical limitations to the introduction of cocoa processing in the exporting countries except for the purpose of domestic consumption, which of course is very low in all developing countries.

Tea is important to a group of East African countries, where production increased approximately threefold during the 1950's. As is well known, world tea exports go mainly to a small group of countries, namely the U.K. and the Dominions, the Netherlands, the U.S.A. and Ireland. In all these countries there is little prospect of tea doing more than holding its own. However, the underdeveloped countries themselves, particularly Africa and the Middle East, account for as much as 18 per cent of world imports. At low levels of income, demand is fairly elastic as it is the cheapest of stimulant beverages. There are some prospects of increasing tea demand in continental Europe, where due to tariffs retail prices have been about treble those in the U.K. Recently, however, the EEC countries have suspended customs duties for a period of two years.

Although Latin America accounts for three-quarters of world *banana* exports, the second major group of exporters are the Ivory Coast, Western Cameroon, Mozambique, Somalia and the Canary Islands, each of which has substantially increased production during the 1950's. The largest importer is the U.S., where however demand is more or less stationary. Since the war a large rise in imports has taken place in EEC countries, especially in Germany. Japanese imports also trebled with the recent relaxation of controls. Imports into communist countries remain small. During the next ten years the prospects for both increased European demand and for African supply appear reasonably good, with expectations of a 30 to 50 per cent increase. These would be improved if tariffs were removed in a number of European countries, including France, the U.K and Italy.

(d) *Tobacco.* Production of *tobacco* in Rhodesia and Nyasaland has grown to about 5 times the pre-war level, being imported into the U.K. in competition with the U.S. leaf. Prospects for this market are not too optimistic in view of the cancer scare and extremely high levels of taxation which seem likely to persist. In the future the greatest opportunities will probably be in other developing countries, particularly in Africa.

(e) *Fibres and rubber.* *Cotton* is important to Chad, the Central African Republic and Uganda. In the world markets these are threatened by U.S. exports on the one hand and synthetics on the other, and world surpluses are projected. The developing countries are, however, net importers of textile manufactures, and the best prospects stem from the growth of domestic textile industries. *Hard fibres*, especially *sisal*, are exported from Tanganyika, Kenya, Angola and Mozambique, mainly to the U.K. and to Portugal. These are used mainly as baler twine and in upholstery, in both uses being subject to increased competition from synthetics. *Rubber* is important only to Liberia, where exports increased by about two-thirds during the 1950's. Future prospects depend on very narrow price margins, especially with the development of stereo regular rubbers, which have all the chemical and physical properties of the natural product.

(f) *Timber.* The most important post-war development has been the growth of European demand for timber for *veneers* and *plywood* imported from West Africa, and many African countries, particularly Gabon, Ghana, the Ivory Coast and Nigeria have benefited from this rapid development. This demand is expected to continue to increase, because of the increasing deficit in Europe of suitable woods. There would seem to be a potential further source of foreign earnings if more of the processing were carried out in the producing countries, where often the residues from veneer and plywood production can also be used to manufacture particle board and blackboard. Some of these may themselves be veneer faced. The development of this industry, too, would have an important potential in import substitution in the more highly developed African countries.

SUMMARY AND CONCLUSIONS

If the trends of the 1950's are projected over the 1960's, Africa, like other underdeveloped regions, shows an increasing tendency to trade deficit. The main cause of this is the overwhelming importance in her exports of agricultural primary products. In general, these are either subject to intense competition from the advanced and supported agriculture of developed countries, or to displacement as the result of technical advance, particularly in the production of petroleum-based synthetics, or are characteristic, tropical commodities competing against those of other underdeveloped countries, especially in Latin America, in a world market where price and income elasticities are characteristically low. In many cases too there is a substantial time-lag in either increasing or decreasing production which makes it difficult to take full advantage of a rapidly rising demand and create a strong pressure on prices. The other side of the coin is that Africa remains heavily dependent on imports for manufactures and even for processed products of agricultural origin, such as textile manufactures.

There are, however, a number of possibilities whereby this rather mechanistic projection of past trends could prove to be too pessimistic. Most of these depend at least in part on concerted action by countries other than the African countries themselves. New markets may be found for tropical products in the U.S.S.R. and communist Europe, in the Far East, especially Japan, and with more difficulty, in other underdeveloped regions especially of Asia and the Middle East. In view, too, of the diversity of exports of individual African countries, there should in the long run be great scope for increased trade within the region, which is at the moment so unimportant a part of Africa's total foreign trade. This, however, would imply the development of an adequate internal communications network in which trunk road development could play the most important part. In individual African countries domestic demand for many processed agricultural commodities provides too small a market for advantage to be taken of technically available economies of scale. A further integration of the total African market, which would of course depend on some co-ordination of individual development plans, would help to make African processed commodities more competitive on world markets. This process would be further helped by the reduction of discriminatory tariffs and quotas in the developed countries.

TABLE 1 Net trade of Africa and other developing regions[1] with the rest of the world[2] ($billion, f.o.b.)

	Africa		other developing regions	
	1956[3]	1960[4]	1956[3]	1960[4]
agricultural raw materials	2·0	2·0	6·2	5·7
fuels	0·4	0·6	3·1	4·1
other non-agricultural raw materials	0·1	0·1	0·8	1·0
manufactured goods	−2·8	−3·3	−9·8	−11·0
miscellaneous and errors	—	0·2	−0·3	−0·4
net trade balance	−0·3	−0·4	0	−0·6

[1] Other developing regions: developing countries in Latin America, Middle East, Asia and Far East.

[2] the rest of the world: the developed countries *plus* all communist countries.

[3] 1956 denotes the three-year average 1955-57.

[4] 1960 denotes the three-year average 1959-61.

H.M.A.ONITIRI

The Role of
International Organizations
in Developing African Primary Products

*

In spite of the present concern about the falling trend of world prices for primary commodities, the policy everywhere in the developing countries is generally one of expansion rather than of curtailment of output. African countries provide no exception to this statement. The expansion of staple agricultural exports is an important aspect of current development plans in the major African countries. This apparent conflict between protest and policy is only a manifestation of the problem facing the primary producers in the developing world. In spite of recent progress with industrialization, African countries are still dependent predominantly on primary commodity exports for their foreign exchange needs. And yet unless the situation on the demand side improves, the further expansion of output will be likely to curtail rather than increase their export earnings. Furthermore, as is well known, the long-term problem is complicated by short-term instability of export earnings, resulting usually but not exclusively from the instability of prices.

Although there is a wide consensus on the need to do something about the commodity problem, there are still wide differences of opinion on what should be done and how it should be done, even though the world has now had more than half a century of experience in dealing with this problem. The history of international action has gone through four fairly distinct periods – before the great depression, during the second world war, in the post-war period up to the Korean war and in the period following the Korean war. Through these periods, the scope of action has been steadily extended, particularly since the inception of the Food and Agricultural Organization in 1945.

Essentially, the problem has always been one of maintaining a proper balance between supply and demand, but it has assumed different dimensions according to the time and the circumstances. For example, although primary producers are much better off today than they were in the 1930's, concern about the commodity problem is much greater today. The reason is that the problem had assumed completely new dimensions as a result of the current interest in the rapid economic development of the developing countries.

While an analysis of the commodity problem cannot but take into account the fundamental forces of demand and supply, the emphasis in current discussion is more and more on the maintenance of earnings from primary exports at a level sufficiently high to sustain rapid economic development of the developing countries. Just as current discussions of agricultural problems in the developed countries emphasize the need to maintain producer incomes at adequate level, so discussions of the commodity problem in the international context must emphasize the development needs of the developing countries. It is in this frame of thought that a fruitful discussion of the role of international organizations in developing African primary produce can be pursued.

At present, the international agencies concerned in one way or another with the commodity problem generally, are as follows: (a) The Food and Agricultural Organization (FAO), through the *FAO Committee on Commodity Problems (CCP)*; (b) *The Interim Coordinating Committee for International Commodity Arrangements (ICCICA);* (c) *The Commission on International Commodity Trade (CICT);* (d) *General Agreement on Tariffs and Trade (GATT)* (under its Programme for Trade Expansion); (e) *The International Bank for Reconstruction and Development (IBRD)*. The staff members of the Bank have undertaken important studies on the commodity problem generally as well as on particular commodities; (f) *The International Monetary Fund (IMF)*, which has been concerned largely with compensatory financial measures to offset variation in the export incomes of primary producing countries; (g) *The Regional Economic Commissions*, particularly those for Latin America (ECLA), Asia and the Far East (ECAFE) and Africa (ECA), whose member nations are dependent predominantly on commodity exports.

What exactly can these organizations do? Or, put in another way, what can they be expected to do?

The scope for international action

The scope for international action on the commodity problem was amply reviewed at the United Nations Conference on Trade and Development. The possible measures which can be taken at the international level can be listed as follows:

1. Removal of tariff and non-tariff obstacles on the imports of primary commodities from the developing countries into the developed countries.
2. Abolition of preferential arrangements favouring some developing countries at the expense of others.
3. Abolition of differential tariffs on primary and semi-processed products.
4. Abolition of domestic support measures in the developed

countries for products competing with imports from the developing countries.

5. Stabilization of primary commodity markets at equitable and remunerative prices.

6. International compensatory financing of fluctuations in export proceeds.

The value which these measures might have would depend on the nature of the commodity and the prevailing conditions in international trade. Following the classification which has now become familiar the major African primary exports can be examined under the following heads:

(*a*) Temperate zone products exported mainly by developed countries. (African exports are wheat, barley and maize, exported mainly from North and South Africa.)

(*b*) Products originating in both temperate and tropical zones, and exported from both developed and developing countries. (African exports are oilseeds and oils, citrus fruits, tobacco, cotton and sugar.)

(*c*) Tropical products exported mainly by developing countries. (African exports are coffee, cocoa, tea, and bananas.)

(*d*) Agricultural raw materials exported from both developed and developing countries. (African exports are cotton, sisal and rubber.)

(*e*) Minerals. (African exports are copper, tin, petroleum, diamonds, bauxite and iron ore.)

The factors affecting African exports of these products can be listed as follows:

(i) Competition with exports from temperate zone developed countries. (African exports affected are those listed under (*a*) and (*b*) above.)

(ii) Protection of agricultural industries in importing countries. (African exports affected are those listed under (*a*) above, as well as sugar and oilseeds and oils lister under (*b*).)

(iii) Competition with synthetics in high-income countries. (African exports affected are rubber, oilseeds and oils and fibres.)

(iv) High revenue duties and other fiscal charges in importing countries. (African exports affected are mainly those listed under (*c*) except bananas.)

(v) Differential duties; higher for goods in processed form than for raw products. This discourages processing in the developing countries of such commodities as cocoa, coffee and tea.

(vi) Preferential arrangements such as those between the European Economic Community and the Associated States. (Almost all products under (*c*) and (*d*) are affected.)

(vii) Low supply elasticities. This applies particularly to tree crops such as cocoa, coffee and rubber. It is to be noted that low elasticity of supply of exports of a commodity may arise not only because of low elasticity of domestic output of that product but also because of the low elasticity of domestic demand for the product and, in many cases, the relatively low proportion of total output of that product consumed at home. The high elasticity of supply of exports of industrial products can be explained by three main factors: high elasticity of domestic output, high elasticity of domestic demand for the product, high proportion of domestic consumption which is imported. Given the existence of these conditions, a fall in demand for exports may be accommodated in one or more of the following ways: (1) reduction in domestic production; (2) increase in domestic consumption, and (3) reduction in imports. Not only are domestic outputs of many African products inelastic, in many cases (e.g. cocoa) the product is not consumed to any significant extent within the producing country. Added to these factors are the difficulties of holding stocks in the producing countries. For many primary commodities, better facilities for holding stocks exist in the consuming countries than in the producing countries.

(viii) Low demand elasticities. This applies to foodstuffs, beverages and agricultural raw materials.

(ix) Violent fluctuations in demand arising from (a) stock changes, (b) speculation, and (c) cyclical changes in economic activities in the importing countries. (These affect all primary commodities in varying degrees.)[1]

The bulk of African exports consists of products exported mainly by developing countries and, apart from oil-seeds which are affected by domestic support policies for competing products in the developed countries, the most significant factors influencing the market for African exports are competition with synthetics, high revenue duties and other charges in the developed countries, differential duties on primary and processed products and preferential arrangements – all these, in addition to the general factors listed under (vii), (viii) and (ix). It may be said, therefore, that all the possible measures which are listed above will be of value in dealing with the commodity problem as it affects the African countries.

What are the prospects that these measures will be taken within the existing machinery for international action? What new machinery is needed? And what are the specific forms which action might take? All these questions have been discussed extensively at the UN

[1] A comprehensive index of short-period fluctuations in quantum, unit value and export proceeds of African primary exports will be found in the UNECA document 'International Action for Commodity Stabilisation and the Role of Africa' – E/CN. 14/68.

Conference on Trade and Development, and decisions have been reached which will now provide the basis for future action. It may be useful, however, to recall some of the controversial issues which are still likely to be the subject of protracted negotiations in future deliberations on the commodity problem.

Removing obstacles

Proposals for the removal of obstacles from the trade of developing countries have been extensively discussed within the General Agreement on Tariffs and Trade, particularly since the inception of the GATT Trade Expansion Programme. However, the practical results achieved have been very small. The various resolutions and proposals have now been incorporated in the recommendations of the Conference on Trade and Development.

Although tariff obstacles still exist on several primary exports from African countries, non-tariff obstacles, especially internal fiscal charges, are now the more important. The argument for removing these obstacles is particularly strong in the case of African exports since many of these exports do not compete with domestic production in the importing countries. The industrial countries are still, however, reluctant to remove these internal charges. They argue, firstly, that this will disrupt their internal fiscal systems; secondly, that, in any case, the elasticities of demand for these products are so small that a reduction in retail prices resulting from the abolition of fiscal charges will not significantly increase their consumption; and, thirdly, that the reduction in fiscal charges on final products may not significantly increase the prices of the raw materials. These arguments are not difficult to refute. The contribution of fiscal charges (on products manufactured from African primary exports) to total revenue in the importing countries is so small that it can easily be replaced by other sources of revenue. Again, even admitting that the elasticities of demand for these products are low, it cannot be denied that some increase in demand, however modest, will result from lower prices. Furthermore, although the value of raw material inputs represents only a small proportion of the total value of the final output, an increase in demand for raw material inputs will most likely result from the expansion of demand for the final product. The removal of these obstacles will be a clear demonstration of the willingness of the developed countries to promote the trade of the developing countries.

Preferential arrangements

One of the concrete achievements of the Conference on Trade and Development was the acceptance of the principle of non-discrimination among developing countries in the commercial policies of the developed countries. It was agreed that existing preferential arrangements which embody such discrimination should be abolished as soon as international measures could be found which would give equivalent advantages to the countries now benefiting from the preferential arrangements. What these international measures should be are yet to be determined. Some of the countries benefiting from these arrangements would consider stabilization of commodity prices at adequate and remunerative levels as providing equivalent benefits; others are thinking of some form of financial compensation. Whichever it is, this seems to be an area in which international action can be extremely useful and effective within the next few years. Not only will the abolition of existing preferential arrangements – whether between the European Economic Community and the Associated Territories or between the United Kingdom and the Commonwealth countries – remove one of the obstacles to African economic unity, it will also facilitate economic co-operation between African countries and the rest of the developing world.

It has been argued that there are different degrees of underdevelopment and that there is nothing wrong in helping the less developed of the developing countries at the expense of those which are more developed. The effective answer to this argument is that if for some reasons developed countries must discriminate among the developing countries, aid rather than trade is a better instrument for such discrimination. It will help the favoured countries without hurting the others.

Higher duties on semi-processed products present particular difficulties for the trade and development of the African countries. The tropical African countries in particular are still probably the least industrialized of the developing areas of the world. Although in recent years they have endeavoured to achieve some measure of industrialization through substituting for imports, the whole process is bound to be slow unless they also have the opportunity of industrializing from the other end – that is, through processing their primary commodities for export. Economic development implies a change in the structure of trade, such that imports consist more and more of capital goods and exports consist more and more of processed rather than of primary products. If the necessary changes in the structure of exports are impeded, economic development will be seriously retarded. If developed countries are to contribute substantially to the economic development of the poorer countries through trade, they must readjust their internal production to make room for processed products from the poorer countries.

One cannot overlook the difficulty of readjusting domestic production in the developed countries in order to make room for processed products from the developing countries, but the former are in a strong position to bear the burden of such readjustment. This problem of re-adjustment in the developed countries would seem to demand more international attention than has so far been given to it. Is this not a problem in which the International Bank for Reconstruction and Development might be interested? In its early years, the Bank's operations in developed countries were concerned largely with post-war reconstruction. Perhaps we may now expect the Bank to concern itself in these countries with the readjustment of domestic production which will facilitate desirable changes in the structure of international trade.

The same argument as above can be used to support the abolition of agricultural support measures in the developed countries. Here, a major stumbling-block to progress is the political power of agricul-tural communities in the developed countries. Whatever may be the economic arguments for liberalization in this sphere, this political consideration is likely to retard action for some time yet.

Even if all the foregoing measures can be achieved, the prices of primary products may still not be high enough to sustain the economic development of the developing countries. This is certainly true of earnings from African primary exports. The abolition of tariffs and other obstacles and of domestic support measures for competing pro-ducts cannot remove the long-term tendency for demand for food to lag behind the growth of world income nor the tendency for demand for raw material inputs to lag behind the growth of world output of manu-factures.

Such measures as we have so far discussed have one thing in com-mon. They all serve to strengthen market forces. But it is now widely accepted that prices in the primary commodity markets cannot be left to market forces alone. This argument has been used in support of protective measures for agriculture in the developed countries. It now seems to be accepted in theory at the international level, but it remains to be seen whether it will be translated into practice, perhaps through new types of commodity agreements.

Commodity agreements

Commodity arrangements have been instituted since before the great depression. Sugar came under international control in 1912 and tin in 1920. During the great depression, wheat, tea and rubber were added to the list, and coffee came under control during the second world war. The inception of the FAO in 1945 brought into existence a number of study groups, the deliberations of which have helped to clarify the issues involved in dealing with particular commodities. The existing arrangements for individual commodities fall broadly into three categories. These are, control agreements, study groups and producer groups. Of the major African primary exports, control agreements exist for only coffee and tin. There are study groups for cocoa, cotton and rubber, and producer groups for petroleum and cocoa.

The relatively small number of commodities now subject to control agreements reflects the immense difficulties involved in negotiating and operating these agreements. There are three main sources of difficulties. The first arises from the usual conflict of interest between producers on the one hand and consumers on the other – the former wanting to pay as little as possible and the latter wanting to obtain as high a price as possible. The Cocoa Conference broke down partly on the failure to agree on a floor price. The second arises from the difficulty of working against the fundamental forces of supply and demand in the commodity market. The experience of tin is relevant in this connection. The Tin Council was in difficulty twice in recent years – once for shortage of money to purchase tin in order to maintain the floor price and once for shortage of tin to sell in order to maintain the ceiling price. The third source of difficulty arises from the uncertainty about the future trends of supply and demand in the primary commodity market. As already indicated, many developed countries still believe that the developing countries are exaggerating their difficulties, that the recent adverse movement in commodity prices is only a temporary phenomenon and that, sooner or later, increased demand by the industrial countries will again turn commodity prices in favour of the producing countries.

In spite of the difficulties of negotiating commodity agreements, developing countries pin much hope on this approach to the commodity problem. Indeed, more and more developed countries themselves are coming to accept the principle of using commodity agreements to stabilize commodity markets at 'equitable and remunerative' prices.

The real issue in current discussions of the subject is one of making a proper distinction between the 'allocative' and 'distributive' effects of international prices. The argument is that if international prices are to perform the allocative role efficiently, they should be determined solely by the free play of market forces – so that high prices would encourage production, and low prices discourage production. But an efficient price system in this sense may give rise to undesirable distribution of the gains from trade among producers on the one hand and consumers on the other. On the other hand, if prices are divorced from market forces in such a way that the gains from trade are distributed fairly among the trading partners, they may at the same time give rise to inefficiency in the allocation of productive resources: production may be encouraged when it should in fact be discouraged. There seems now to be general agreement that in the international commodity market, the price system cannot at one and the same time perform the two functions efficiently. Two possible solutions to this problem can be identified. The first is to leave prices alone so that they may perform the allocative function efficiently and then attempt to solve the problem of fair distribution of gain through a system of compensatory payments. If prices received by sellers fall below what are considered 'adequate' and 'fair', the buying countries will pay an appropriate sum to the selling countries. A recent exposition of this idea is to be found in the paper presented to the Conference on Trade and Development by Professor J. E. Meade.[1]

The second possible solution is to fix prices at levels which are considered fair and adequate and to ensure through a system of internal levies and subsidies in the producing countries that prices received by producers are divorced from the artificial prices ruling in international markets. This is the essence of the French Plan for the Organization of Markets presented to the Conference on Trade and Development. These alternatives or a possible combination of them are worth further study with specific reference to the major export commodities of African countries. The latter arrangement would combine very well with existing national schemes for stabilizing the income of domestic producers.

The operation of the Coffee Agreement which came into operation in 1963 will be watched carefully as it is very likely to be a model for future agreements on commodities of importance to African countries. the Coffee Agreement is notable in three important respects. In the first place it is virtually the first international agreement for a commodity of which the industrial countries are exclusively consumers. In the second place, it achieves a wide membership coverage among both producers and consumers. As of January 1964, member countries accounted for approximately 93 per cent of world exports and 93 per cent of world imports of coffee in 1961 and 1962. In the third place,
   it is the first agreement to envisage a system of price discrimination –
   dividing the world into an organized price-maintained sector on
   the one hand, comprising high-consumption countries with relatively inelastic demand, and a residual free sector on the other hand,
   in which the lower prices that could be expected to emerge as a result
   of competition among exporters might help to stimulate consumption.[2]

Compensatory finance

Even if obstacles to trade were removed, market access improved, and a measure of stabilization achieved through commodity agreements,

---

[1] 'International Commodity Agreements' – (E/CONF.36/P/1/Rev.1).
[2] See UN Document E/CONF.46/8, 19th March 1964, on 'Stabilization of International Commodity Markets'.

there would still exist a residual problem of fluctuations and short-falls in export earnings for which financial solutions would have to be sought. This is clearly illustrated by the post-war experience of the Latin American countries. Until quite recently, African countries on the whole have dealt with export fluctuations through national stabili-zation schemes. This was partly because, as dependent territories, they were not members of the International Monetary Fund and partly because the large reserves accumulated in the early post-war years enabled them to sustain national stabilization schemes in periods of falling prices. These conditions have changed. All but a few of the Afri-can countries are now full members of the international community and a majority are members of the International Monetary Fund. They have so far made little use of their drawing rights, but the current pressure on their reserves resulting from short-falls in export earnings and increasing import requirements will soon make this necessary. Of great interest to them, therefore, are current efforts to increase drawing rights, especially for dealing with fluctuations in earnings from commodity exports and to provide supplementary financial measures for dealing with long-term adverse trends in export pro-ceeds.[1]

There are many questions yet to be settled on the nature and scope of compensatory finance. The concept as it crept into international monetary discussions was essentially one of a revolving fund for dealing with short-term fluctuations in the balance of payments. The IMF is striving to keep the concept very much as it was.[2] But the urgency of the development needs of the poor countries is already giving it a new flavour. Developing countries themselves have not always been clear in their statements as to just what they want com-pensatory financial measures to achieve but it is unlikely that they will be impressed by any arrangement which does not include an element of grant. Basically, then, the questions which have to be decided in designing a system of compensatory finance are as follows:

1. What should be compensated for? Fluctuations in earnings from commodity exports (in real or monetary terms) or fluctuations in export earnings as a whole or fluctuations in the balance of payments?

2. What proportion of fluctuations should be compensated for?

3. To what extent should compensation be automatic and to what extent should it depend on the discretionary opinion of a

---

[1] The idea of 'supplementary financial measures' was introduced by the United Kingdom and Sweden at the Conference on Trade and Development.

[2] This is evident in the publication, *Compensatory Financing of Export Fluc-tuations – A Report by the International Monetary Fund*, February 1963. It is to be noted, however, that the Fund has already increased the drawing rights of the developing countries by 25 per cent of their quotas.

B

group of experts basing their judgment on development needs in relation to the trend of export earnings?

CONCLUSION

The directions which international action on the commodity problem will take in the coming years will depend very much on the reaction of the United Nations to the recommendations of the Conference on Trade and Development. Once the principle is accepted that commodity markets must be organized to support a high level of economic development in the developing countries, the most urgent need is for greater co-ordination of international action in the commodity field to realize this principle.

There are two main reasons why greater co-ordination is essential. The first is that there are now too many institutions concerned in one way or another with the problem. At the Conference on Trade and Development, the real concern of the developing countries was for the establishment not of more institutions as such but of an effective machinery for co-ordinating the activities of existing institutions. There was also a desire to have a machinery with somewhat greater authority than that of receiving resolutions or organising study groups. It is to be hoped that the new machinery which will emerge from the Conference on Trade and Development will be able to fulfil this role.

The second reason for greater co-ordination of efforts on the commodity problem is the wide dimension which the problem has now assumed. As has already been pointed out, it is now very much a development problem; and unless it is treated as such the world is likely to continue to grope from one ineffective solution to another. If the rate of economic development in the African countries can be maintained at a very high level, African economies will soon achieve such structural changes as would ease the commodity problem considerably. Efforts to improve commodity markets and efforts to increase the flow of aid for development are merely different aspects of the same policy. A strong machinery is needed to co-ordinate the efforts of the World Bank and its associates, the FAO, the GATT and the Commodity Councils, as far as they relate to the problems of developing countries.

International Trade and Development—
The Special Interests of Africa[1]

*

International economic policy is in a state of flux. The United Nations Conference on Trade and Development (1964) has put firmly on the agenda of discussion the whole question of the organization of international economic relations. This paper discusses from the point of view of Africa some of the policy questions which have been raised.

The implications of the basic trends in the world economy

Let us start by sketching with a very broad brush the trends in the world economy, considered as a unit, and then draw their implications for policy.

The determining influence on the changing structure of the world economy is the array of income-elasticities of demand. Since these elasticities are generally high for manufactures (especially metal products) while for farm products they are generally low, the elasticity of demand for manufactures as a group is higher than for primary products. Since the world economy has no external trade, and inventory fluctuations are unimportant in long-term comparisons, this difference is reflected in the changing pattern of world production. From 1928 to 1960 the production of manufactures grew at an average rate of 3·4 per cent a year, whereas that of primary products grew at 1·7 per cent (1·4 per cent if petroleum is excluded).[2]

This contrast is shown by static and dynamic research for many countries and is apparently firmly rooted in human preferences; we can presume that it will broadly continue.

Up to now, the underdeveloped countries have gained little from the rising consumption of manufactures. In the large countries of Latin America, and also in the United Arab Republic and some countries in Asia, there has been an expansion of manufacturing for the local market. Several have become in GATT's terminology 'semi-indus-

[1] This paper is a personal contribution and should not necessarily be taken to represent the views of the Economic Commission for Africa, with which I had a temporary contract when it was written. I am indebted for very useful criticisms of an earlier draft, to Mr Plessz of the ECE secretariat; Mr Ferran, Mr Nypan, and Mr Patel of the ECA secretariat; and Mr Demas, Head of the Trinidad Planning Office; I also gained greatly from discussion at the Edinburgh Seminar.

[2] *Towards a New Trade Policy for Development* (Report by the Secretary-General of UNCTAD Conference, E/CONF. 46/3), p. 19. The data exclude the communist countries, but the contrast would be if anything sharper if they were covered.

trialized'. But (apart from the special case of Hong Kong) their exports still consist very largely of primary products. During the present century, only two major countries have shifted from being mainly commodity exporters to being mainly exporters of finished manufactures – namely Japan and the United States.

The economies at present 'semi-industrialized' could, however, acquire a share in the rapidly growing world market for manufactures. This is in fact the only way in which these countries can continue to develop at a fast or even moderate pace. If they follow this path, taking advantage of the underlying trends in the world economy, they, like Japan and the United States, will become net importers of primary products.

The process of conversion is familiar. As secondary output grows, more local materials are absorbed at home, and as incomes rise, an increasing share of food output is bought by local consumers. On the supply side, the growing industrial complexes compete for the factors of production, driving up costs in primary production. One element in this process is that the surplus of unskilled labour dwindles and wage costs mount; this encourages capital-intensive forms of production, and discourages branches of activity in which the possibilities of mechanization are limited (such as the cultivation of tree crops).[1]

In practice, governments usually are compelled by political forces to slow down changes in economic structure by subsidizing and protecting local primary producers. (United States policy is the most conspicuous case here, but it can be seen in all countries, including the underdeveloped countries themselves.)

It would be very much in the interests of Africa that the exports of the semi-industrialized countries should be diversified and that the conversion of their economic structures be continued. Commodity markets would be vacated and Africa's share in these markets would grow – or, in other words, Africa's export volume would increase faster than the volume of total world trade in commodity exports. Two of these semi-industrialized countries, Brazil and Colombia, lie wholly or partly in the tropics, and produce exports directly competitive with those of Africa.

The obstacles in the way of such a process are great. In fact, the transformation of several of these economies is now blocked (notably those of Latin America); to complete it would require vigorous new policies, in both the semi-industrialized and developed economies. The semi-industrialized countries would have to develop selected manufactures competitive in price on world markets (which implies that they must be attractive in quality); in many cases this would

---

[1] It seems that urbanization is associated with a lowering of the birth rate, which in due course also tends to help make labour scarce.

involve considerable improvements in the efficiency of industries producing intermediate products such as steel.

The developed countries would need to remove tariff and quota barriers on imports from the underdeveloped countries, and in fact to adopt positive policies of encouraging such imports: for example, by technical and financial assistance to the industries of the semi-industrialized countries; the provision of import credit facilities; perhaps, even, measures to induce their own ministries and firms to purchase in such countries.

Moreover, precisely because many of the semi-industrialized countries (especially those in Latin America) have not yet broken into world manufacturing markets, they are suffering from acute balance-of-payments difficulties. If they are to afford imports of capital equipment to complete their transformation into diversified industrial economies, they need a supply of foreign exchange both rising and free from fluctuations. Their policy, therefore, emphasizes a lowering in tariff and other barriers to the exports of primary products as well as manufacturers; some of them are particularly concerned that the developed countries should cease subsidised exports of temperate-zone products. Latin American spokesmen stress the need for stretching out the repayment programmes of their short-term debt and for schemes which would stabilise commodity prices and compensate them for falls in export earnings.

Policy implications for Africa

Such schemes may seem to be of little relevance to Africa. Tables in the Report of the Secretary-General of UNCTAD show that African countries do not appear either among the leading debtors nor among those whose debt is predominantly short-term. (In fact, many of them are net creditors on short-term account.) They have little immediate prospect of exporting manufactures in quantity. Several African countries benefit from United States exports of subsidised farm products on long-term credit (or actually given away).[1] Because Africa is relatively poor, and therefore has a more pressing need of rising receipts of foreign exchange, its interest would be limited in schemes that merely compensated countries for declines in earnings from some past average.

But it would be a mistake to conclude that schemes of this sort should be opposed by African governments. Measures that help the semi-industrialized countries of other continents to change the structure of their foreign trade also benefit Africa indirectly for the reasons indicated above. There could, however, be difference in emphasis. Some schemes for stabilizing commodity prices would be inclined to

[1] Although the Nile Valley countries are harmed by subsidised exports of cotton.

freeze the structure of world commodity production (for example, schemes with production or export quotas and involving high prices), and these would tend to be against Africa's interest. She has spare land which could be moved into primary production,[1] or converted from backward agriculture to cash crops for export.

Of course, this is not to say that African countries should oppose price stabilization in principle. They, too, need a secure flow of exchange; planning development is much more difficult if the prices of leading exports fluctuate greatly; and price fluctuations encourage the development of synthetics. It should not be impossible to work out acceptable compromises over the form of stabilization schemes, especially if avenues are being opened for the semi-industrialized countries to expand their exports of manufactures, so that they can absorb resources displaced from primary production.

The implications of the distribution of world income

There is a great and well-known gap between average incomes of developed and those of underdeveloped areas. There is also a sizeable difference within the underdeveloped part of the world: Latin America is much less poor than Africa or Asia. There are also large differences within each region; some countries in Latin America are poorer than the richer countries in Africa or Asia.[2] But there are certain big Latin American countries which set the pace in policy-making – Argentina, Brazil, Chile, Colombia, and Mexico. These are all, by most indicators, more advanced economically than almost any nation in Africa or Asia. They are, on the international plane, the lower middle class rather than the proletariat.

There is another major difference: that of educational levels. Latin America suffers from shortages of engineers, agronomists, statisticians, etc., but this shortage is not comparable to the situation in Africa. (Asia is in this and other respects generally to be placed between Africa and Latin America.)

---

[1] Even if there is no such change in structure as is indicated above (i.e. thinking solely in static terms), it may be that Africa would pick up markets from Latin America at lower prices, because of the difference in labour costs. In other words, considering Africa as a whole, the demand for its output may be fairly elastic, especially in the cases of commodities such as coffee, bananas, and sugar, where its share of world exports is small.

[2] *Yearbook of National Accounts Statistics*, 1962 (United Nations), gives the latest comprehensive figures for 1958. These show $100 for Africa, a rather lower figure for Asia and about $285 for Latin America. The African figure may, however, have been somewhat inflated; later censuses have shown that the population estimates used previously have been considerably too low. To some extent, a revision of the estimated population would entail a revision of the national income estimates as well (because of the methods of estimating subsistence output), but not proportionately as great. Asia excludes China, Japan, and Turkey; Africa excludes South Africa.

This means that the problem of development is, in important respects, different for Africa. *Per capita* income would have to grow at a rate of about 3 per cent a year in Africa (and Asia) even to reach by the *end of this century* the average income levels found *today* in Latin America. Since the population of Africa is likely to increase on average by at least 2 per cent annually, the domestic product would have to grow at an average rate of more than 5 per cent a year over the next 35 years even to reach this modest target.

Development will have to be a good deal faster if Africa is to have a reasonable chance of achieving a stable political situation later in the century. (I am not falling into the naïve trap of assuming that better living conditions are a *sufficient* condition for stability, but they are certainly a *necessary* condition, if by stability we mean at the least that political processes are orderly, whatever their type.)

The same conclusion can be reached if one considers employment instead of income. Very large numbers of people are flowing from the rural areas to the towns in search of jobs, in addition to the natural growth of the urban labour force. This influx cannot be absorbed by a commercial sector which is still small, compared to subsistence production, unless growth rates of the order of 7 to 8 per cent in domestic products are achieved over the coming decades.[1]

I should emphasize at once that I am not predicting this rate of growth. The task of achieving it would be an enormous one. But I believe we should work out the economic conditions for political stability even if the task of achieving them turns out to be impossible.

The first question is whether African exports are likely to grow fast enough for, say, a 7 per cent rate of growth in domestic products (aid is ignored for the present). For this purpose, we should consider 'the purchasing power of exports',[2] which reflects two forces, the volume of exports and the terms of trade in the usual sense (that is, the relation of export prices to import prices).

Export volume depends on (i) the rate of growth of the developed countries as a whole; (ii) their consolidated income elasticity of demand for imports of primary products; and (iii) the share of Africa in these imports. Let us try to quantify these very roughly for the next three to four decades: (i) will be less than 4 per cent and 3 per cent is a more reasonable guess; (ii) is less than unity, so this is a negative influence[3]; (iii) may continue to rise, for the reasons indicated above,

---

[1] Another way of making this point would be to say that the economic structures in Africa are such that the growth process usually implies a big shift of labour from sectors with a low output per head to those where it is high, i.e. a fast rise in average productivity, taking the economy as a whole.

[2] This is the value of exports divided by an import price index.

[3] It grew more quickly in the 1950's, but this was due to the pace of growth of Continental Western Europe, largely attributable to recovery from the War.

but it would be unwise to count on great help from this positive factor, under present circumstances, until the obstacles to Latin America's development are removed.

Any prediction about the terms of trade is a hunch, at best. So far as one can judge (if we avoid the trap of basing long-term conclusions on the experience of the 1950's), they show little trend. They are today approximately what they were in the late 1920's. My own guess is that they will improve, from the viewpoint of primary producers, in the rest of the century. There is not the space here to discuss this question in detail, but briefly the explanation is the forced pace of industrialization in the world. One could hardly, however, expect this trend to be more than marginal – if it were 1 per cent either way, it would shift the terms of trade by more than 40 per cent by the end of the century, and this seems unlikely. This would therefore be a mildly positive factor.

Weighing all the negative and positive considerations, 3 per cent. a year seems a reasonable assumption of the future trend in the purchasing power of Africa's exports. (This is a very tentative estimate, since major changes in the political allegiance of underdeveloped countries have been left out of account; these could have a decisive effect on the volume of commodities entering world markets and therefore on their prices.) The trend could be 4 per cent, or even higher; but it would have to be at least 7 per cent to sustain (unaided) a growth rate of 7 per cent a year in Africa's income – and this seems impossible.

Of course Africa could theoretically enjoy an adequate rate of advance if her domestic product grew significantly faster than her exports. For an 'open' African economy, that is, one without heavy import or exchange controls or high tariffs, this is hardly possible. The income-elasticity of demand for imports into open underdeveloped countries is greater than unity, if there are no institutional developments; in other words, domestic products grow more slowly than imports. But the long-run trends of imports and exports cannot diverge (in the absence of substantial changes in invisible or capital flows). So domestic products tend to grow more slowly than exports.

It may be argued that Latin American economies which are 'closed' by controls – such as Brazil and Colombia – show that they can develop faster than their exports, through import substitution. This is true, but Latin American experience also indicates that the process of import substitution involves little or no net savings in imports, compared to what they would otherwise have been, for several decades. So the main effect is on the *composition* of imports, not on their *total*, which can in fact only be prevented from continuing to rise at a rapid rate through the use of taxation and controls. No Latin American economy has yet developed the political and administrative capacity to raise the necessary taxes or to operate the necessary controls efficiently;

so the attempt to grow faster than the purchasing power of exports has meant severe internal strains, the most conspicuous of which is chronic inflation. In view of the shortage of qualified manpower, there is no reason to expect that Africa would be more successful.

To summarize; African output needs to grow at a rate of 7 or 8 per cent a year for several decades, but the supply of foreign exchange from exports cannot be expected to rise at this rate, and under present conditions African economies cannot be expected to grow much more quickly than their exports.

CONCLUSIONS

One conclusion that inevitably follows is that Africa needs financial aid on a big scale, and that this aid will have to grow rapidly, if the necessary economic growth is to take place without severe strains. ('Trade not Aid' is a slogan which could conceivably have meaning in Latin America, but is quite inapplicable to Africa or Asia.) Another is that technical assistance is relatively more important for Africa.

Like Asia, Africa needs more than Latin America does, to be able to *rely on* both financial and technical aid over the decades ahead to back its long-term plans; it needs also more co-ordination of aid from various sources, with the various elements designed to fit the strategy of development. It is for this reason, among others, in the interests of African countries that international machinery for aid should be developed, and what might be called an international fiscal system eventually established.[1]

The levels of financial aid and technical assistance, and the machinery for supplying them, should therefore be, from Africa's point of view, the main focus of attention in the international economic debate; for example, in the main topics for the 'Prebisch secretariat' which is to be set up in 1965 to prepare for UNCTAD II. Although Latin America's main interest lies in obtaining concessions on trade (and from her point of view the discussion of these should dominate UNCTAD II as they did in UNCTAD I), reasons have been given for believing that the interests of Africa and Latin America are in essentials compatible. A world economic system could therefore be established that enabled each underdeveloped area to achieve its objectives.

[1] This is worked out in a paper for the Dar-es-Salaam Conference of the University of East Africa (September 1964), 'International Aid: The Next Steps'. Such a proposal may seem Utopian at present. The much more modest proposals of the 77 underdeveloped countries at Geneva met with a rather inflexible opposition. But the world political scene is shaping in a way that should make it possible for steps to be taken towards such a system in the reasonably near future, perhaps by 1970. My purpose here, however, is not to make predictions of what will happen to international economic arrangements, but to indicate what long-term changes are *necessary conditions* for a solution of African (and in many ways Asian) economic problems.

O. ABOYADE

A Note on External Trade, Capital Distortion and Planned Development[1]

Economists have long been intrigued by the relationship between external trade and economic growth. Recent interest in the subject has been revived by the doubt of the compatibility of the classical doctrine of comparative advantage with rapid transformation of the underdeveloped countries.[2] The structuralist-monetarist controversy historically derives in a substantial sense from the scepticism aroused concerning that classical doctrine against the background of developments in post-war world trade. As analytical technique improves and more data become available, various assertions in the controversy are being empirically tested and refuted. There seems to be a growing feeling, especially among Western economists, that the apparent belligerence of the underdeveloped countries against the existing world trade pattern derives more from political resentment than from sound objective economic facts. Specifically, proposed compensatory and counter-cyclical measures against unstable export earnings of the underdeveloped countries are now held to have very weak if any economic justification. Some recent studies have even indicated that such instability has on the contrary been accompanied by more growth of, and has certainly inflicted no damage to, the economies of those countries taken together.[3] The burden of proof is being shifted on to the structuralists and sympathetic writers of United Nations' publications on the subject. Economists from the underdeveloped areas are being put, so it appears, professionally on the defensive.

It is the purpose of this note to reformulate the crucial issue involved and to suggest a hypothesis which may reconcile both the observed facts and the anxieties of the underdeveloped countries. It will be argued that from the standpoint of economic growth it is more relevant

[1] The original draft of this note was written while on a Rockefeller Visiting Fellowship at the Economic Growth Center, Yale University. The writer wishes to thank Gerald Helleiner and Donald Mead for helpful comments.
[2] For an appraisal of the literature, see H. B. Chenery, 'Comparative Advantage and Development Policy', *American Economic Review*, March 1961.
[3] The most extensive and articulate of these studies is contained in Alasdair I. MacBean's forthcoming book, *Commodity Instability, Economic Growth and Economic Policy*. Before him and on a more general international level was J. Coppock, *International Economic Instability* (McGraw Hill, New York, 1962).

to examine the impact of external trade on the total effective productive capacity of a country rather than merely on its current investment figures or apparent growth in income. Whether or not external trade (specifically, the export of primary products) accelerates or inhibits the transformation process of an economy depends on how far it distorts the total effective productive capacity in level and composition through time, having regard to the country's factor endowment and the apparent potential for growth. By the same token, the reconciliation of the principle of comparative advantage and rapid economic growth of an underdeveloped economy can only be effected by a policy designed to eliminate such distortions in the productive capacity. It can be shown that this notion of capital distortion is in fact implicit in Chenery's plea for a dynamic view of comparative advantage and the use of accounting prices in calculating projects' relative social profitabilities in a general equilibrium planning framework.[1]

Since the relevant data for testing the hypothesis are at present unavailable, its exposition can only proceed by *a priori* theorizing and by indicating weaknesses in the main alternative empirical tests which have been advanced hitherto. The underlying argument is not that the existing tests offered are wrong, but that they are at best inadequate and at worst irrelevant for the actual problem at hand. As much as possible, the plausibility of the hypothesis presented by this note will be supported and illustrated broadly (but certainly not proved) by reference to Nigeria, with special emphasis on the cocoa economy of the Western Region since the end of the last world war.

The existing debate

The structuralist-monetarist controversy is an intellectual battle that is fought on many fronts. The major strands in the debate are well known and have been extensively discussed in the literature.[2] The main aspect of the problem that is of immediate interest to us here is the impact of primary product exports on the transformation process of the underdeveloped economies. Here, the problem can be divided into two parts which are related but in principle conceptually different. One centres around a general deficiency of export earnings by these countries, and the other around instability in the level of those earnings. The first deals with a long-term trend and the second with fluctuations around that trend. The debate has been made more complex by con-

[1] H. B. Chenery, *op. cit.*
[2] Recently, the debate has concentrated more on the inflationary aspects of trade, finance and development. The main issues are however well summed up in Albert O. Hirschman (ed.), *Latin American Issues – Essays and Comments* (The Twentieth Century Fund, New York, 1961); and Dudley Seers, 'A Theory of Inflation and Growth in Underdeveloped Economies, Based on the Experience of Latin America', *Oxford Economic Papers*, June 1962.

centrating on different aspects of the problem without clearly saying so, and more especially by moving freely between one aspect and the other. But, so far, no side has ever claimed that the growth process can be entirely explained by reference to the external trade sector or that such trade is a sufficient condition for growth. The controversy is therefore made more difficult to evaluate because it is essentially partial in nature, whereas the growth problem itself is a dynamic general equilibrium notion.

The delicate relationship between the two aspects of the problem can be seen from the way in which Prebisch himself restated the structuralists' stand some years ago.[1] He argued that the growth problem confronting the underdeveloped countries consists of how to (a) allow the growth rate to exceed the limit imposed by export earnings, and (b) achieve full employment of domestic resources without being affected by instability in those export earnings. The overall growth constraints, as opposed to specific bottlenecks, were thus seen to derive from the same source, viz. the export trade in primary products. The first element derives from demand deficiencies in the developed countries, intensified by their monopolist restrictive conditions and discriminatory protectionist practices. To avoid income contraction, this, combined with the second factor (the element of instability), generates inflationary credit expansion which weakens domestic saving capacity and may have ultimate depressive effects on overall employment, investment, income and imports. These may again result in intensified external disequilibrium, making exchange depreciation inevitable and increasing the economy's external vulnerability.

These arguments have been used to explain the nature of the postwar inflationary phenomena in the Latin American countries and to impress that this was an inescapable feature of the growth process itself. They have also been used, especially by United Nations agencies, as a professional prop for a comprehensive policy review of international trading pattern and the distritution of gains from world trade.[2] The case is advanced that, one way or another, the extra income accruing to the industrial countries as a result of the deteriorating terms of trade against the exporters of primary products must be transferred to the underdeveloped countries. This case rests on three strong presumptions. First, that the export of primary products is fully identified with the underdeveloped countries. Second, that the terms of trade are

[1] Raul Prebisch, 'Economic Development or Monetary Stability: The False Dilemma', *Economic Bulletin for Latin America* (UN Economic Commission for Latin America), Vol. VI, No. 1, March 1961.

[2] A clear testimony of this is given in the background paper for the recent UN Geneva Conference on Trade and Development, written by Raul Prebisch, *Towards a New Trade Policy for Development* (UN E/CONF.46/P/3 of 12 February 1964).

in fact significantly adverse to these countries, and especially so because the principle of comparative advantage following normal market signals imposes on them their peculiar specialization. Third, that such adverse terms of trade inhibit their growth prospects and make the process of structural transformation much more difficult. Parallel with these presumptions, and somewhat interlaced with them, is the extra vital argument that the fluctuations around the long-term average trend of export earnings from primary products deal a further blow to the growth process, either acting independently or as part of the general stream of deterrence communicated from the external sector.

In the last few years, these presumptions have been subjected to empirical verification from many sources.[1] Nurkse's 'demand deficiency' hypothesis on the export prospects of primary products was lent some credibility by Maizels' cross-sectional analysis for a number of countries, though this was nothing really definitive. Stern has shown[2] that the facts did not bear out the presumption that specialization in primary production and trade can be equated with underdevelopment. Therefore, even if it was true that the terms of trade had been adverse to primary products, it did not follow that this was coterminous with unfavourable terms of trade against the underdeveloped countries. Furthermore, the relevant measure for growth processes was in fact not the net barter terms of trade but (a) the single factoral terms of trade which reflect productivity improvement in the export sector, and (b) the income terms of trade which indicate the real purchasing power over imports. With these measures, it became far less certain that there has been a secular deterioration of terms of trade against the underdeveloped countries; and therefore unconvincing that this has inhibited their growth.

On instability, Stern pointed out that it was true that this has been a long-standing phenomenon and that its intensity has been relatively greater for the export trade of the underdeveloped than for the developed countries. But it was also true that there has been a decline in such instability in the post-war period, arising from the milder fluctuations in the general level of activities in the latter countries. In any case, there was no direct connexion between export instability and economic growth, since so much depended on whether a country was able to implement counteracting policies to stabilize domestic activities and the balance of payments. It also depended on the level of reserves as well as the availability of foreign exchange from sources other than

---

[1] The growing literature on this aspect of the problem has been recently reviewed by Robert M. Stern, *International Trade and Development* (International Conciliation, Carnegie Endowment for International Trade, 1964).

[2] Robert M. Stern, *op. cit.*

merchandise export, viz. invisible trade, foreign portfolio investment, official lending and other aid efforts.

The recent works of Coppock and MacBean have differently given quantitative dimension to the measure and effect of instability in external trade. MacBean especially has come out with exhaustive quantitative tests of various hypotheses which have been advanced by the structuralists and United Nations agencies. His results have been devastating in their implications.[1] They have shown that it is not true (as claimed by the International Monetary Fund) that those countries which experienced high export instability also had instability of real fixed investment. Capital goods imports are also very weakly, if at all, related to the current value of exports or fixed investment, except for a directional (but not statistically significant) relationship. There is little or no evidence to support the view that investment in underdeveloped countries is disrupted in any serious sense by export instability, as many other factors besides exports affect investment behaviour. In fact, there is a small *positive* association between export instability and the rate of growth of fixed capital in the underdeveloped countries. Even if the correlation is weak, it at least contradicts the United Nations' hypothesis that export instability deters investment. The positive correlation could be explained by reference to a mild ratchet mechanism in savings behaviour[2] as well as by a series of qualitative effects deriving from increased costs of capital goods or lower efficiency of investment. The effects of export instability are at worst neutral on the proportion of investment in stocks, in construction and upon the marginal capital-output ratios. Neither does any relationship exist between short-term instability in the foreign trade of underdeveloped countries and the rate of growth of their national incomes. Trade dependence is no more significantly higher for the underdeveloped countries than for the developed ones. There is no support for the view that underdeveloped countries with very unstable export earnings tend to have very unstable national incomes; which may suggest the existence of some systematic counteracting forces (e.g. the stabilizing effect of a very large subsistence sector) and/ or low values for foreign trade multiplier and accelerator effects. While there is statistical evidence for believing that instability of ex-

---

[1] These results are shown in two mimeograph papers, Alasdair I. MacBean, *Export Instability and Economic Growth*, and *The Short-Term Consequences of Export Instability to Underdeveloped Countries* (both Center for International Affairs, Harvard University, December 1963). The papers are draft chapters in Professor MacBean's forthcoming book, *op. cit.* (footnote 2).

[2] Empirical evidence cited to support this hypothesis include Michael Michaely, *Concentration in International Trade* (North-Holland Publishing Co., Amsterdam, 1959); Clark W. Reynolds, 'Domestic Consequences of Export Instability', *American Economic Review*, May 1963; and R. Galletti, K. Baldwin and I. O. Dina, *Nigerian Cocoa Farmers* (Oxford University Press, London, 1956).

port earnings is related to inflation, MacBean argues that it is really a matter of opinion whether the export fluctuations are a fundamental or only a proximate cause, or even indeed if such a causal relationship exists. His major conclusion is unequivocally stated: 'Almost every chain of reasoning in support of the view that serious damage is inflicted by instability has been found wanting when confronted with the facts.'[1] The onus of proof is thereby shifted to the proponents of the original view.

Styles in empirical verification

It probably needs to be repeated that this is only a part of the whole structuralist school of thought, although it is an important strand of the foundation on which the superstructure has been erected. It is conceivable that even if the underlying presumptions of the structuralist stand are dismissed as invalid, the case may still be strong for entirely different reasons whether or not these are recognized by the structuralists themselves.[2] Some people would rather have a good case for the wrong reason than a bad case for the right reason. And in economics, a case is not necessarily bad simply because we have not discovered the right historical evidence to support it. It is commonly recognized that there is no foolproof method of statistically separating causal influences in the social sciences. It is also slippery to move from ex-post evidence to ex-ante policy implications, because we have no means of knowing exactly what would have happened if what happened did not happen. Hence, economists often supplement their analysis of empirical evidence by *a priori* theoretical reasoning to derive policy postulates.

It has been necessary to recall these elementary propositions because we may, methodologically speaking, be killing a fly with a sledgehammer. While the advent of computer techniques has enabled us to handle more complex quantitative systems, there may be a risk in formulating research problems in such a way as to suit computer operation. We should, of course, use all available and most refined techniques to advance the frontiers of economic knowledge. But in the process we should not forget the underlying conceptual problems of deriving meaningful interpretations from our computers. The field of economic development of underdeveloped areas may be one where special restraint is needed in formulating hypotheses for computer

[1] Alastair I. MacBean, *Export Instability and Economic Growth, op. cit.*, p. 29.

[2] In a way, it is unfortunate, to have to introduce the labels of 'structuralists' and 'monetarists' in this paper. None of the critics mentioned here has used the labels and none has claimed that he is a 'monetarist' or anti-'structuralist'. Because of the pointed analytical and policy implications of their works, it is however convenient, if not inescapable, to bring in these labels as a useful anchor of discussion and for a perspective view of the literature on trade and development.

testing. The restraint is doubly necessary when the data inputs consist of cross-country materials from official statistics and when the sample of countries for which relevant data are available varies from one hypothesis being tested to another.

On this plane, some of the results of empirical verification in trade and development may not come as a big surprise after all. Before Coppock and MacBean, economists and statisticians have pointed out the bewildering variety of economic performance among the underdeveloped countries. Indeed, Simon Kuznets has been so impressed with the absence of consistent relationships between almost any two development variables one could conjure up, that he has been led to postulate that an *economic* theory of economic growth is an impossibility.[1] He was, of course, more concerned with discovering fundamental universal laws of economic growth. But the major difficulty really consists of how to derive meaningful messages from cross-country statistical evidence in a highly heterogeneous group of underdeveloped countries. Apart from the usual problems of data availability and reliability, it is doubtful if the real problem at hand is one which is best verified by aggregative cross-country official statistical data. It is here suggested that only prior analyses in depth of specific case studies can minimize the conceptual and methodological obstacles inherent in such empirical verification.

Now, there are indications that MacBean himself well appreciates this point, for he made a rather hesitant move to give us a greater insight into some case studies, especially his evidence from Uganda and Tanganyika.[2] But it may well be that if he had not stopped too soon, these case studies could have opened up a more fruitful channel for the basic structuralist hypothesis. In trying to explain the neutral effect (put at its most conservative interpretation) of export fluctuations on national incomes, MacBean hypothesized that the existence of a large subsistence sector and the dominance of expatriate concerns in the export sector was performing the function of a 'shock absorber'. In both Uganda and Tanganyika, the observed aggregate dependence on foreign trade was high. But once attention was concentrated on the exchange sector of the economy by subtracting subsistence production from the national accounts, monetary product was more correlated to exports than to total gross domestic product in Uganda; whereas in Tanganyika the correlation between monetary

[1] Simon Kuznets, 'Toward a Theory of Economic Growth', in Robert Lackman (ed.), *National Policy for Economic Welfare at Home and Abroad*, (Doubleday and Co., 1955), chapter 2. See also the series of articles under the general title 'Quantitative Aspects of Economic Growth of Nations', Vols. I-IV, *Economic Development and Cultural Change*, especially Vol. V, Supplement to July 1960, and Vol. VI, Supplement to July 1961.

[2] Alasdair I. MacBean, *The Short-Term Consequences of Export Instability to Underdeveloped Countries, op. cit.,* pp. 12-14.

product and exports disappeared. The logical sequel to this should then have been a discussion of the relative size of the subsistence sector and the relative importance of export-operating expatriate concerns in the two countries. This could lead to important differences in the effectiveness of the shock absorber in the two countries and provide a useful entry point to a consideration of the performance of each economy's total productive capacity.

MacBean was indeed hovering on the periphery of such an entry point, without actually getting to its core. He explicitly stated that he was not denying that for individual countries export instability could well adversely inhibit higher growth rates, even though this had not been so for the period examined for underdeveloped countries in general. But the basic problem can be easily assumed away both in the way the hypothesis being tested is formulated and in the type of data employed. Both these risks are real ones in the empirical tests here under review. The usual hypothesis was invariably framed as follows: If we have two countries, X and Y, with the same A phenomenon but which observedly differ with regard to B phenomenon, then we should expect X and Y to behave differently in C phenomenon if A, B and C are to be judged to have any significant relationship. Example: If X and Y have the same long-run average export trend, but X has greater short-term fluctuations about that trend than Y, then Y must have a higher growth rate than X if there is to be an admissible connection between export earnings, instability and economic growth. We can vary this by replacing the income growth rate by capital formation proportion, or the rate of increase in capital formation, or the efficiency of investment, or the level of exchange reserves, and so on.

But by framing the problem in this way, we are saying in effect that for each test, X and Y are the same in every other possibly significant sense as the common A element we have specifically recognized between them, or that none of these unmentioned non-A elements can explain the C attribute being tested. MacBean himself, of course, recognized that these unstated elements may have to be introduced to explain some deviant cases in the sample under observation; or, more interestingly, that opposite reasons may explain a common result. The existence of large expatriate firms dominating the export sector, for example, can insulate the rest of the economy from the impact of external instability, and so can its obverse of small-scale native-owned export activity units. In the one case, the expatriate firms possess sufficient financial strength to make the adjustments through stock variations and profit margins.[1] In the other, production

---

[1] MacBean assumes implicitly here that the firms will not seek to protect profit margins by cutting wages and that the stock adjustments will not reduce employment and total wage incomes.

C

probably is intermingled with the subsistence sector, which thus avoids the risks of a fully specialized producer. Even in the case of the small native producer, substantially specialized for export, they may be prudent enough (as in the observed Nigerian cocoa farmers) to save in periods of prosperity against the bad years. Above all, MacBean agreed that 'increased domestic investment is unlikely to be powerfully induced by changes in income as investment in fixed equipment is likely to be determined mainly by longer term considerations'.[1] But it is doubtful if one needed cross-country correlation analysis to establish such a hypothesis.

Reformulating the problem

In the last section, we discussed MacBean's papers at length, not because we are primarily interested in the instability of export earnings. We did so to show that the existing attempts at empirical verification of the relationship between external trade and economic development may not, in spite of their quantitative elegance, be asking the right questions. The questions that need to be asked should not be framed with a particular technique in mind; and in principle it should be neutral of any knowledge of available general statistical data for particular countries. The researcher is lucky if the available data happen to be able to handle the questions he has posed. Otherwise, he may have to build up and tailor the requisite data he needs for the particular questions to be investigated. And this may necessitate reviewing the overall problem from which the questions derive, to give the whole exercise a proper sense of focus.

No one has denied that there is *some* connexion between trade and development. Also, as long as any country freely participates in international trade, it cannot hold that all trade is bad; and there must be some sort of guiding comparative advantage principle for the country to determine what it will export and import. In an elementary fashion, the connexion between trade and development has been long illustrated by saying that the world would consist of one economy if there were no political boundaries; so that international trade is basically a study in location theory. An export surplus has the same effect conceptually as a stream of net domestic investments, as both enable the economy to consume more in a future period. Similarly, a shift in consumption propensity from domestic to foreign goods is equivalent to domestic net disinvestment. It is therefore easy to see that like any other domestic activity, external trade affects the total capacity of any participating economy. However, it no more alone accounts for total investment behaviour than the level of income itself. In the

[1] Alasdair I. MacBean, *The Short-Term Consequences of Export Instability to Underdeveloped Countries, op. cit.,* p. 18.

short-run, the rate of private investment (through entrepreneurial expectations) varies with changes in the level of income; but over a longer period, private net investment may be independent of the level of economic activity. By the same token, domestic investment may vary with the level of income, while foreign investment need not.

From this restatement of basic principles we can make two propositions. First, if we want to measure correctly the effect of external trade on income or investment in an economy, we should eliminate such autonomous influences as foreign portfolio investment and all foreign programmes. We would be hard put to it to eliminate also government fiscal intervention in the external sector through export taxes, tariffs and the manipulation of reserves; though, strictly speaking, we should also do so. The pure case is where no such intervention exists and we can follow up, say, the repercussion of export earnings in the hands of the export producers. Second, since the growth process is cumulative and since we are interested in the future time streams of income, we should consider the whole works when we are discussing the effect of one variable on growth, whether that variable be investment, export, consumption or anything else. The impact of a factor may be currently favourable, but then turn unfavourable in a relevant longer-run. Therefore, the problem of appropriate choice of time sequence comes in, so does the problem of establishing a trade-off between different time periods.

In a recent comment by Wolfgang Stolper [1] it was suggested that conflicts between comparative advantage and economic development can arise only if the economy concerned can show that as a result of external trade, the total resource available to it is decreased and that its allocation is made less efficient. In a dynamic planning framework, these conditions may not be too difficult for some underdeveloped countries to back up; and here indeed is probably the main crux of the structuralist complaint about the existing world trading relations. We do not have to look far to know that the trading patterns of colonial and semi-colonial economies fall short, in terms of potential net income, of the comparative advantage they might have had in the absence of metropolitan spheres of influence. It is also easy to appreciate that if any economy disposes its exports in virtually one market, it is that much more difficult to quickly promote alternative outlets; and it may be especially important in what currencies the prices in the transaction are in fact determined. But of greater weight still is the problem of supply elasticities. Trade economists have been interested in this problem mainly from the standpoint of price re-

[1] Wolfgang F. Stolper, 'Comment in the Discussion of Comparative Costs and Economic Development', *American Economic Review, Papers and Proceedings*, May 1964, p. 429.

sponsiveness for the export commodities,[1] whereas development economists are more interested in structural transformation to adapt and refashion a growing productive capacity to satisfy a changing demand pattern. It is in this sense that traditional comparative advantage, relying on current market indicators, can have a depressing influence on the economic development of the underdeveloped countries.

The dilemma of trade and development arises from the fact that while an underdeveloped economy must seek to improve its export prospects as the best way to earn foreign exchange for essential imports, its productive capacity that is objectively relevant for structural transformation may be rendered even more lopsided by expanding production along traditional lines. On the other hand, if it pushes further on less orthodox fronts of production, it would hit against the good old comparative advantage and more so against the restrictive-protectionist-discriminatory barriers of the advanced countries from which it needs essential imports. Therefore, whether external trade inhibits the process of development or not can be said to depend on how far it distorts or corrects the total productive capacity for transformation of the economy under consideration. Now, how far a capital structure can be judged to be distorted depends on the recent history of the economy, the nature of its current organization, its factor endowments, the future time sequence being considered, the choice of appropriate price measures and the set of internally consistent objectives of social policy given to us by the policy makers. But this is not a notion that lends itself easily to cross-country comparability tests.

This concept of capital distortion needs a little further exposition. We start by assuming that there exists a set or basket of goods and services which, through time, an economy would consume as its national income changed in level and distribution by certain policy-given magnitudes. We do not know yet whether this community preference function is a realistic one; but we still assume that the policy goals we have been objectively given are internally consistent with each other and with the factor endowments of the country. With appropriate investment leads and lags, we can perceive of a corresponding time stream of productive capacity which is necessary and most efficient to bring forth the requisite basket of goods and services in the right time sequence. In an open economy, such productive capacity would need to have taken into account what should be exported or imported, following the same rules of efficiency and economic profitability throughout the exercise. For consistency and optimality

[1] See, for example, Robert M. Stern, 'The Price Responsiveness of Primary Producers', *Review of Economics and Statistics*, May 1962.

conditions, the underdeveloped economy may find that it cannot rely on the existing structure of relative prices and the constellation of comparative costs relative to the rest of the world, because they may not achieve equilibria in the factors and products markets over the appropriate time span covered by the plan. If we assume that our planner has tremendous knowledge and ability, he will then come out with calculations which describe the time profile of the normative level and composition of capital stock and manpower requirements which are just right for the economy over the planning period, in the context of the carefully designed policy objectives. It need hardly be stated that such a solution can only in practice be approximate and that it can be approached only through an iterative process. But in principle it should not be too difficult to conceive of such a concept and to make it operational in interpretation.

Now, capital distortion arises if, at any given point in our time map, the observed set of capital stock (always in men and materials) is different from the normative set. Distortion will only be absent if both the observed total productive capacity and that of every activity unit have zero deviations at every time point from their normative specifications. A somewhat similar notion of distortion has been recently developed by Dudley Seers with special reference to consumption in some Latin American countries.[1] But apart from the difference that we are here dealing with an economy's total productive capacity, our treatment starts by assuming that the objective demand pattern is in fact already free of consumption distortions. In the development process, therefore, we can think of the brand we have briefly described here as a growth distortion of the second degree.[2] It makes sense only in the context of a particular national economy with internally consistent stated goals of social policy and with a planning machinery operating in a general equilibrium framework.

The next question is how external trade can intensify the capital distortion that is almost inherent in the very fact of underdevelopment. First, as Dudley Seers has shown, it comes in strongly on the demand side even in open underdeveloped economies, in the sense that forecasts of future demand (dynamic income-elasticities) in a planning framework cannot be directly derived from the current picture or base-year figures.[3] The most common illustration of this is that the international demonstration effects may be irrelevant to the stage of

[1] Dudley Seers, 'Normal Growth and Distortions: Some Techniques of Structural Analysis', *Oxford Economic Papers*, March 1964.

[2] The concept has been developed and more spelt out in the writer's forthcoming book, *Foundations of an African Economy: A Study of Investment and Growth in Nigeria*, Chapter 7.

[3] *Ibid.* The case of economies which are not open is probably more directly evidenced by the presence of exchange controls, queues and shortages.

the economy's development and make for inefficient utilization of its factor endowments. Second, as pointed out earlier in the note, existing operation of comparative advantage may not reflect the true growth potential of an underdeveloped economy. It means then that, following Chenery,[1] employing a notion of dynamic comparative advantage and embracing the use of accounting prices in the planning process may indicate that the economy's existing productive capacity is not 'normal'. Third, the existing trading structure of an economy may be so deep-rooted that it may conceivably make it more difficult to get on its optimum growth path if the economy had not inherited such a trading legacy in the first instance. Trade theorists are increasingly coming out with different combinations of the impact of trade on development, and we now hear of such nomenclature as growth being export-biased, export-good biased, import-biased, import-good biased, pro-trade biased, anti-trade biased, neutral and messy.[2] A particular economy may objectively need a type of trade bias which is precisely opposite to the one it has inherited or it is currently transacting. It may therefore be improper to lump all trade and all growth together as is implied in cross-country correlation analyses.

Nigeria as illustration

The stimulating influence which legitimate external trade has had on the expansion of the Nigerian exchange sector since the beginning of the century is too well known to need restatement. Specifically, we also know that the cocoa trade has contributed much to the relatively higher advance of the country's Western Region. It is a moot question whether or not the economy would have developed as fast without external trade, as no one claimed that legitimate trade (as opposed to slavery) is detrimental in an absolute sense to development. It is, however, not an irrelevant point of historical interest to speculate whether the economy was deriving the maximum possible benefit from the external trading activities, given its potential for development and taking together as one period its whole colonial history. But that is a big question by itself and we have no means of knowing the answers now. So we will concentrate only on events in the last decade or two as being more immediately pertinent to the development policy problem in hand.

The salient features of the economy relevant for our purpose can be listed as follows. Until the establishment of the Marketing Boards, the external trade was dominated by large expatriate concerns, although

---

[1] For an appraisal of the literature, see H. B. Chenery, 'Comparative Advantage and Development Policy', *American Economic Review*, March 1961.
[2] These concepts are well discussed and illustrated by Frederick L. Pryor, 'Economic Growth, the Terms of Trade and Trade Dependency', forthcoming journal article, at present in mimeographed form.

the actual production came, and still comes, from small-scale indigenous peasants. Most of the producers combine export crops with production for domestic exchange and for subsistence; although with increasing external trading prospects and social differentiation, some medium-sized farmers have become more specialized in the production for export. From all available evidence, there is a high degree of producers' responsiveness to price movements and differential price setting for quality improvement.[1] In the case of cocoa, this has been rather imperfectly so because of the longer investment lag involved in cultivated perennial crops, because there is virtually no domestic demand for the product, because other independent forces are sometimes at work (e.g. swollen shoot and black pods control), and because the area of cultivation expansion is effectively limited by geographical factors. On the policy level, the economy was, until recently, under a currency board system; so that (a) balance of payments surpluses provided the only means of expanding domestic money supply and (b) exports, imports and government revenue always moved in sympathy but with a tendency to generate both export and budget surpluses. Therefore, the monetary sector and growing points of the economy were highly subject to external vulnerability; and as long as the open and passive public policy continued, the pace of development was substantially tied to demand prospects in the metropolitan advanced countries, since Nigerians themselves do not consume cocoa.

If we look at the available national accounts data, there are no visible grounds on which anyone could complain about the impact of trade on development. One could, of course, point to the low world prices received for the export products in the last decade or so, but it should not be difficult to dismiss this. On the one hand, it could be pointed out that the immediate post-war and Korean prices against which the latter prices are being compared were artificially high and that the post-Korean movement is more in line with the long-term average trend. On the other hand, it could be argued that the country anyway couldn't even spend the foreign exchange it had, since there have been great bottlenecks in materials and manpower. In any case, the national accounts show that growth has been reasonably impressive since 1950 (when figures started to be available) in spite of any short-fall or instability in export earnings. If anything, investment was certainly favourably affected, since the capital formation proportion increased by at least one-third during the decade 1950 to 1960. It would be surprising if any correlation analysis at this aggregative level could pick up anything adverse to say against the contribution of Nigeria's external trade to its growth of income.

[1] A detailed study has been provided by G. K. Helleiner in a chapter of his forthcoming book, *The Structure and Growth of the Nigerian Economy*.

However, if we look a little more closely, at least four factors show up and tend to reduce confidence in the apparent conclusion of the last paragraph. First, we don't know if the economy's degree of trade dependence was rising or falling compared to, say, the pre-war period. It is possible that a threshold of trade dependence exists for any given economy, beyond which an ordinary degree of inadequacy or instability of export earnings will not materially affect its growth rate. The important variable here is in fact not so much the degree of trade dependence as the level of economic development already attained. So that for potential growth, exports may still impose the limit in a sense that has become irrelevant for the advanced countries.

Second, the changing economic organization in the economy may have been operating to reduce the impact of external vulnerability. In Nigeria, this was in fact so in the post-war period with the operations of the Marketing Boards. The existence of large expatriate concerns in the export trading sector did nothing to cushion off the external instability in the inter-war years. There is little reason to believe that the post-war trading position would not have resulted in more profits and dividend payments abroad by the expatriate firms and in far less protection for the producers than the Marketing Boards provided when world prices started to fall from 1954. There is no doubt that in spite of their shortcomings, the Marketing Boards were able to reduce the economy's dependence on world price fluctuations.[1] It may also be recalled that this was a time when the economy was moving away from the currency board system, and when, with the approach of political independence, government policy was becoming more self-confident, imaginative and geared to the requirements for growth as distinct from the requirements for domestic stability.[2]

Third, all the developments in the last paragraph probably have not started to make even more than a marginal impact on the process of development. Throughout the 1950's (and maybe still now) there certainly was still substantial instability of the modern sectors or growing points of the economy – and exports have always formed the largest component of the group. The role of what Onitiri has called 'primary expenditure' (marketing board payments plus payments by governments, governmental institutions, public corporations and expatriate enterprises) is likely to be greater in the development pro-

[1] For a reappraisal of the role of the Nigerian Marketing Boards in the context of growth, see Gerald K. Helleiner, 'The Fiscal Role of the Marketing Boards in Nigerian Economic Development, 1947-1961', *Economic Journal*, September 1964; and 'Marketing Boards and Domestic Stabilization in Nigeria', forthcoming journal article.

[2] A full treatment of this from the external trade standpoint is contained in H. M. A. Onitiri, *Nigeria's Balance of Payments and Economic Policy, 1946-1960* (unpublished doctoral dissertation, University of London, 1963).

cess than its size in the national accounts would suggest. And this might be a more instrumental variable for analysing the relationship between external trade and the growth of income. Certainly, one would also wish to know about the moving frontier of the subsistence sector; yet we have no means of even identifying the magnitude of the subsistence sector in the Nigerian national accounts.

Fourth, there was in fact substantial autonomous investment flowing in from the external trade sector that had little to do with either developments in that sector or with the current level of income. The capital formation proportion was rising through the period, while domestic savings ratio remained largely the same. Now, it can be assumed that most of this outside investment was going to the productive sectors of the economy, at any rate, in so far as they are from external private sources. There was not much foreign aid before 1955, and this source of investment is being increasingly tied to specific economically worthwhile projects. We also know that in spite of the publicized excesses of the Marketing Boards as a party political instrument, their questionable outlays did not amount to a large proportion of their total spending and that their allocation went substantially to directly productive efforts.[1] Yet we know from the national accounts that while the capital formation proportion was rising through the period, the growth rate achieved was in fact falling, especially since 1955; although this would not show if we take the whole period together as one block. From the foregoing, the presumption is strong that the explanation lies in shifts in investment and especially in the contribution to those shifts made by the indigenous private sector and by government activities.[2] Within the decade, the aggregate incremental capital-output ratio increased from about 1 : 1 to about 5 : 1.

A consideration of this presumption turns on the examination of changing composition of capital stock or the total productive capacity in so far as the export producers are concerned. Mention has been made of the observed savings habits of Nigerian cocoa farmers in the study by Galletti, Baldwin and Dina. Onitiri has also postulated that the marginal propensity to import of those receiving Marketing Board payments may be less than that of those receiving other 'primary expenditure'. But we do not know for certain and the Cocoa Farmers' study is now at least ten years old. We do know, however, that the overall marginal propensity to import for Nigeria is fairly high (0·37) and that practically all (99·98 per cent) of any net credit creation will

[1] Gerald K. Helleiner, 'The Fiscal Role of the Marketing Boards in Nigerian Economic Development, 1947-1961', op. cit.

[2] Further elaboration of the points in this paragraph is contained in Chapters 1 and 4 of the writer's forthcoming work, Foundations of an African Economy, op. cit.

be translated into imports within the first three years.[1] The demonstration effects are very effective, and significant distortions may exist in the revealed community demand function. Beyond that, the producers may be channelling their savings into non-directly productive investment. There was no doubt that this was so in the Western Region cocoa areas in the 1950's when the volume of residential construction increased very substantially.[2] Cocoa farmers were also probably investing in other channels like road transport and in cocoa farms (capital widening, deepening and lengthening). But it was unmistakable that most of the so-called capital formation was in the form of residential construction. Being a once-over increment generator of income, this would be bad enough for the economy if more directly productive investment opportunities existed. It was doubly serious from the standpoint of potential growth when it was sensed that a lot of irrational spending was involved even in this capital formation, as the residential buildings were either largely empty or they involved substantial wastes in the long construction time-lags. None of these facts would have shown in the capital formation estimates; yet they would affect the calculation of capital-output ratios since imputed rent is conventionally entered in the accounts for all buildings. That these facts falsify the current growth rate is, however, not even as objectionable as that they falsify the effective productive capacity for future growth. Hence the need to look at the total capital picture in any quantitative growth testing.

As rightly emphasized by Dudley Seers, to say that growth (or capital structure) is 'normal' or 'distorted' implies no value judgment. Also, it is certainly not being suggested here that the economy would be better off without trade than with trade, or that the increasing lopsidedness in private investment behaviour would not have occurred without external trade. Non-cocoa farmers would probably have behaved more irrationally if they experienced the relatively higher prosperity enjoyed by the cocoa farmers in the 1950's. Moreover, as we argued earlier, the productive capacity could still be distorted in our sense of the term, even if the cocoa farmers poured their savings into cultivating new cocoa farms. Their reading of the market prospects may be right and their investments in extending cocoa production may, by an unusual stroke of guessmanship, turn out to be perfect and well rewarded. But the current market signals may not accurately

[1] These two figures come from Clive S. Gray, 'Credit Creation for Nigeria's Economic Development: A Polak Model of Money, Income, and the Balance of Payments in Nigeria', *Nigerian Journal of Economic and Social Studies*, November 1964.

[2] The quantitative evidence for this point was developed in the writer's unpublished doctoral dissertation, *Capital Formation in Nigeria* (Cambridge University, 1960).

reflect the economy's true comparative advantage relative to the rest of the world and to its own factor endowments.

This is just another way of saying that economic growth is a study of differences between private and social profitability, and between static and dynamic equilibrium. They are the foundation in support of economic planning; and any analysis of trade and development that looks to the future should proceed in full recognition of these differences. This is the only admissible framework for reassessing the effects of trade in primary products (long-run trends as well as short-term instability) on the economic transformation of Africa. Research efforts should be directed at identifying and quantifying the capital distortions involved in each economy or in each prospective economic community, and should incorporate the two dimensions of the trade problem. It is only then that the right attention of economists interested in African problems can focus on prescribing measures for eliminating the deterrents against effective development of the continent.

GERALD K. HELLEINER

Peasant Agriculture
Development, and Export Instability:
The Nigerian Case[1]

*

The economies of tropical West Africa are sufficiently similar in structure that knowledge and experience derived from one economy are often
transferable, without major modifications, to the others. The Nigerian
economy, by far the largest in terms of population and national income of the West African group, is a useful starting-point for analysis
of the development process in the West African context. Its experiences
and its problems, while broadly typical of those of the area, are particularly deserving of study because they so frequently provide indications
of those which are likely to be faced by West Africa as a whole if or
when the much discussed plans for economic integration are finally
realized.

When world trade first made its influences strongly felt in Nigeria,
it did so by reaching directly into the very midst of the traditional
peasant economy, offering rewards directly to the peasant producer.
The staple items of export trade were palm oil and palm kernels, cocoa
and groundnuts – all capable of being produced with very little altera-
tion of existing technologies, traditions or tenure systems. Cotton,
rubber, benniseed, hides and skins, and bananas were also soon produced by peasants for export. Presented with opportunities for profit
through trade in these commodities, Nigeria's peasant producers
responded by foregoing leisure and bringing more land under cultivation. It was thus not through foreign exploitation of mining and plantation enclaves,[2] but, rather, through indigenous peasant response to
ordinary economic incentives that Nigeria entered upon the world
economy.

A very large proportion of Nigerian domestic product (over half) is
still accounted for by such 'traditional' activities as food production
and handicrafts, neither of which seem to have played a major role in
the development process. Government expenditures, at all levels,
even after their rapid expansion in recent years, remain well under half
the value of exports. Despite the doubling in their relative importance

---

[1] I would like to thank the participants in the Seminar, particularly Dr. O.
Aboyade, for their valuable comments upon an earlier draft.
[2] The tin mines at Jos and the few plantations in the south were important
exceptions.

during the previous decade, total expenditures on gross fixed capital formation also remained below the value of exports in 1960. Thus although exports themselves constituted only 16·7 per cent of gross domestic product in 1960,[1] their role is strategic. Today peasant agricultural production is still the predominant source of export earnings, accounting for 71·3 per cent of total exports in 1962 (as against 77·3 per cent in 1929).

Nigeria's development effort is based upon parlaying these principally peasant-produced primary product exports into the infrastructure and industry required for the successful operation of a modern economy. That is, it is based upon an attempt to achieve a 'structural transformation' of the economy. Greater reliance has been placed upon foreign capital in the present six-year plan than at any time previously (with the possible exception of the railway-building period in the first three decades of this century); but primary product exports remain the principal source of foreign exchange and of tax revenues for the effort.

This essay will consider, in somewhat uneven fashion, various aspects of the peasant sector's contributions both to growth and to instability in Nigeria, in order to clarify some issues and to demonstrate that, great as the role of peasant exports has been, far from the most has yet been made of the peasant agricultural base.

Peasant food production for the use of the urban-industrial population will receive scant attention, since food supply does not seem to be a major problem for the immediate future in Nigeria. Nor will this paper consider the possibilities for altering, through international action on a world-wide scale, trends in the terms of trade, commodity prices, etc.; these world conditions will be regarded as exogenously determined. The discussion is divided into two parts. Part I deals with peasant agriculture and economic development, Part II, which is of secondary importance, with peasant agriculture and export instability.

I: PEASANT AGRICULTURE AND ECONOMIC DEVELOPMENT

Peasant agriculture has contributed and will contribute to Nigerian economic development (or 'structural transformation') in four principal ways: (1) through provision of Hirschman-type linkages, (2) through provision of markets for developing industry, (3) through provision of labour for other 'modern' sectors, and, most important, (4) through the provision of tax revenues and foreign exchange for the public development effort.

[1] Throughout the 1950's, this percentage was even smaller. See Federation of Nigeria, *National Development Plan, 1962–68*, p. 13.

1. *Linkages with industry*

Peasant agricultural producers are not generally believed to contribute very much in the way of Hirschman-type 'linkages' with the rest of the economy: they neither require many intermediate inputs nor supply many intermediate outputs. Hirschman puts the case as follows:

Agriculture in general, and subsistence agriculture in particular, are of course characterized by the scarcity of linkage effects. By definition, all *primary* production should exclude any substantial degree of backward linkage although the introduction of modern methods does bring with it considerable outside purchases of seeds, fertilizers, insecticides, and other current inputs, not to speak of machines and vehicles. We may say that the more primitive the agricultural and mining activities, the more truly primary they are.

Forward linkage effects are also weak in agriculture and mining. A large proportion of agricultural output is destined directly for consumption or export; another important part is subjected to some processing in industries that can be characterized as satellite inasmuch as the value added by them to the agricultural product (milling of wheat, rice, coffee, etc.) is small relative to the value of the product itself. Only a comparatively small fraction of total agricultural output of underdeveloped countries receives elaborate processing, which usually takes place abroad.[1]

Peasant producers in Nigeria, it is true, do not individually employ significant quantities of domestic intermediate inputs. Seeds are usually self-furnished. Fertilizers and insecticides are little used, and, even where employed, are imported, only the domestic transport and distribution components of their cost therefore consituting a backward linkage; the same is true of many other inputs such as produce bags and various tools. The ratio of intermediate input purchases by this agricultural sector to the value of its total production is only 2·6 per cent,[2] far short of the already low average of 31 per cent found by Chenery and Watanabe for Italy, Japan and the U.S.[3] Still, many tools

[1] Albert O. Hirschman, *The Strategy of Economic Development* (Yale University Press, New Haven, 1958), p. 109.

[2] This figure was derived from the single existing attempt at an input-output study of Nigeria; its reliability, like that of most of the figures in the study, is not great. See Nicholas G. Carter, *An Input-Output Analysis of the Nigerian Economy, 1959-1960* (Working Paper, School of Industrial Management, Massachusetts Institute of Technology: Cambridge, 1963). I have restructured Carter's figures slightly so that 'agriculture' here includes Carter's sectors of 'agriculture', 'livestock', 'fishing', 'forestry', 'agricultural processing', and 'Food-small'. Few of the above-mentioned inputs to agriculture have been included in the derivation of this figure so that it is probably understated; but it undoubtedly can serve as a rough approximation.

[3] Hollis B. Chenery and Tsunehiko Watanabe, 'International Comparisons of the Structure of Production', *Econometrica*. Vol. 26, No. 4 (October 1958) pp. 487-521.

of a primitive nature – hoes, matchets and knives – are fashioned in local blacksmith establishments. Even the more sophisticated screw hand-presses for processing palm fruit have been manufactured locally for several years.[1] There undoubtedly exists considerable scope for expansion of domestic output and sales of intermediate products which are at present imported, and of such local tools as these.

Agriculture normally performs rather better in the production of forward linkages, the supplying of intermediate inputs for other sectors, than in that of backward ones. Chenery and Watanabe found that in Italy, Japan and the U.S., 72 per cent of total demand for the produce of agriculture and forestry went as intermediate inputs to other industries.[2] This is about midway in the range for those industries which they characterized as 'Intermediate Primary Production' because of their high forward and low backward linkages. Nigeria's corresponding figure is only 1·9 per cent, even less than that for backward dependence.[3]

This low figure includes a large element of agricultural production which moves directly to domestic food consumption. How do Nigeria's principal agricultural export commodities perform in this respect? The largest proportions of rubber, cotton lint and seed, shelled groundnuts, and palm oil move directly to final demand in the form of exports (or, in the case of the latter two, domestic consumption). Some do, however, also enter as intermediate inputs into the domestic manufacturing sector. Domestic rubber is employed in footwear, foam rubber, and tire and tire re-treading establishments, cotton in the growing number of textile plants as well as in traditional textile production, groundnuts in the four crushing mills in Kano, and palm oil in soap and margarine producing establishments. The amounts involved are still very small. Groundnuts were the only product a substantial share of which was devoted to intermediate output (19·5 per cent) in 1959-60.[4] Only 0·1 per cent of Nigerian rubber output, 7·2 per cent of palm produce output (oil and kernels, the percentage for oil alone would be nearly twice this) and 7·1 per cent of the output of cotton ginneries[5] entered as inputs into other 'higher-stage' domestic industries. Existing forward linkages of Nigeria's main agricultural

[1] These inputs may be regarded as investments rather than as current inputs without altering the argument.

[2] *Ibid.*

[3] This figure was derived in the same way as the earlier one from Carter's input-output study. It is subject to the same limitations.

[4] This and the subsequent figures have been derived from Carter's input-output study.

[5] Although 36 per cent of *total* cotton output did not reach the ginneries at all; all of this presumably constituted an input into domestic weaving and tailoring industry.

exports, while frequently stronger than those of agriculture as a whole, are thus still quite weak.

The value added in domestic manufacturing enterprises which employed these agricultural products as inputs is, however, in all cases, contrary to Hirschman's analysis, a large percentage of the value of the inputs (see Table 1). Close to 50 per cent of the value of final output of large textile and soap factories is added in these factories; that is, over 90 per cent is added to the value of domestic inputs, including non-agricultural items, in domestic processing plants. Groundnut processing adds a little over 25 per cent to the value of the groundnut and other domestic inputs. Information on rubber processing is not available but the tire retreading which was undertaken using imported material in 1959-60 was (somewhat impressionistically) estimated to add about 80 per cent to the value of inputs, and rubber footwear manufacturing contributed roughly 33 per cent to 60 per cent in value added to the input's total value.

Cocoa beans are not, at present, processed in Nigeria above the elementary level. Neither are palm kernels except for some insignificant quantities employed in soap-making. Existing forward domestic linkages from these commodities are very small; but they are already showing signs of increasing. Plans have been announced for the establishment of a palm kernel crushing plant in the Eastern Region which will produce palm kernel oil for domestic use and for export.[1] Even cocoa beans, which have long been considered unsuitable for processing under tropical conditions, are now being converted into cocoa butter in a Ghanaian plant, thus opening the possibility of similar developments in Nigeria.

Too much credence should not be lent to the linkage figures cited above because of the weakness of the data upon which they are based; nevertheless they tell a consistent story which, even allowing for a wide margin of error, gives ground for rather more hope than can be gleaned from analyses of Hirschman and others. In all these cases, not only is the percentage increase in value added through processing not as small as has commonly been believed, but the potential for the further development of processing facilities, given the quantity of unprocessed produce still exported, is also very great.

There thus exist considerable opportunities for building manufacturing industries, to supply either domestic or foreign markets,[2] upon the base of Nigerian agricultural products, which are at present exported in their raw state. Substantial 'slack' can be taken up: (a)

[1] The Belgian Congo has crushed its palm kernels domestically for many years.

[2] Tariff discrimination in the industrial nations against more processed products is here taken as given. To the extent that they hinder the development of Nigerian export markets differential import duties can be offset by offsetting differential Nigerian export duties.

in the furnishing of intermediate inputs to agriculture, principally in the forms of tools, bags, fertilizers, insecticides, containers, etc., (*b*) in the furnishing by agriculture of intermediate outputs for use in other (processing) industries.

2. *Markets for industry*

The role of peasant agriculture in final product markets is obvious enough and is frequently stressed by those who seek to establish the importance of agricultural progress to industrialization. Oshima has gone so far as to suggest that the final demand of farm workers, peasants and landlords out of agricultural income (and, for that matter, that of all other income recipients) is just as important for the calculation of meaningful 'linkages' as the agricultural sector's demands for intermediate inputs.[1]

Export farmers, besides consuming self-produced produce, also spend upon domestic consumption items furnished by Nigerian suppliers outside of their own households. The extent to which they do so, of course, varies from area to area, and from household to household, probably the most dependent in this respect today being the Yoruba cocoa farmers. The greatest share of total expenditures by peasant farmers is, of course, still accounted for by food. As incomes rise, however, increased expenditures, both absolutely and relatively, will begin to be incurred for clothing, drink, tobacco and kola, entertainment, etc., all of which are already domestically supplied. More important for increasing industrialization efforts, rising expenditures will also be incurred for manufactured products such as bicycles, tools and equipment, sewing machines, lorries, etc., which can and will be supplied domestically even if at present they must still in large part be imported. Expenditure by peasants upon non-agricultural final products which are not imported are not yet very great; but these trade-oriented peasant farmers constitute a tremendous potential market for domestically produced manufactured goods when they do appear.

Greatest advantage can be taken of these markets through maximizing their size and thus ensuring that full advantage is taken of whatever scale economies exist. This can be achieved by the freeing of intra-African trade through the formation of a common market (or at least a customs union), and the international integration of plans for industrial development to prevent the duplication of industrial facilities of less than optimum scale.

Nigeria represents a very large integrated African market. Has it been enjoying the expected benefits of economic integration? There

[1] Harry T. Oshima, 'Linkage Effects and Asian Agriculture', *Indian Journal of Economics*, October 1961, pp. 89-92.

D

has long existed considerable trade in primary products between the Northern and the Southern Regions of Nigeria, a trade based upon the Regional geographic and climatic differences. When these differences are small, as between the Eastern and Western Regions, there is very little inter-Regional trade, even in primary products, other than that of a fairly local variety analogous to trade within these Regions themselves.[1] What is most significant is that although Nigeria has now begun to industrialize there is as yet very little inter-Regional trade in Nigerian-made industrial products. Manufacturing industry in Nigeria seems to be developing as if the country were actually three separate entities. Existing manufacturing plants cater primarily either to export markets or to local or Regional markets. Plants producing textiles, beer, soft drinks, cement and metal products are among those which have been established in each Region to cater to local needs. (The sugar plant at Bacita and the Port Harcourt oil refinery, however, constitute exceptions in that they *will* serve the whole country.)

Scale economies seem, so far, to have been largely irrelevant to industrial development. This is partially attributable to the fact that, at least by African standards, each Nigerian Region is already a large economic unit. The smallest of the former three (now four) Regions, for example, was still larger in terms of population (and probably domestic product) than Ghana. Some of these industries therefore exhaust their scale economies at the Regional level. It is also attributable, in part, to the high local transportation costs.

The discouraging aspect of Nigerian experience is the scarcity of evidence that inter-Regional co-operation in industrial development planning will take place in the arising instances where it will clearly be beneficial. The most glaring case in point is that of the planned iron and steel mill. Despite the independent recommendations of an ECA team and the general knowledge of the technological and scale aspects of this industry, plans are now under way to erect three iron and steel mills in Nigeria – one in each of the old Regions, each uneconomically small. If the separate Regions of a Federation cannot agree upon such matters among themselves any more successfully, there can be little room for optimism regarding the possibilities for co-operative development planning by separate sovereign units. (It is noteworthy that in the underdeveloped areas the principal problems of economic co-operation are those having to do with manufacturing industry, whereas in Western Europe the intractable issues are those involving primary products.) The principal lesson from Nigerian experience

---

[1] East-West trade has undoubtedly been hampered by transport problems. The first East-West bridge across the Niger River is only now under construction. There is still no East-West railway.

seems to be that the mere existence or creation of a common market among primary-producing African countries is not, of itself, a very significant fact for economic development. It becomes one only if the opportunities opened thereby are seized – if, that is to say, industrialization is planned so as to make the most of scale economies wherever they are believed to exist.

3. Labour supply for industry

The labour at present employed in manufacturing and other 'modern' activities in Nigerian cities must originally have come from the agricultural sector. Peasant agriculture still competes for labour with industry and other 'urban' sectors. From the agricultural sector's point of view, labour (even of the unskilled sort) *is* a scarce factor. The development of peasant agriculture and modern industry are thus interrelated. But there has been some misunderstanding as to the nature of this interrelationship.

It is frequently argued that an agricultural revolution must precede an industrial one – that it is necessary to raise agricultural productivity so as to 'free' labour from agriculture for employment in the growing industrial sector. The agricultural sector undoubtedly did supply the labour at present employed in Nigerian industry and other 'modern' pursuits. It did so, however, not through the productivity increases which one thinks of as an agricultural revolution but, rather, through the elimination of much of the slack in the available labour force in response to price incentives; instead of raised productivity Nigeria experienced diminished leisure. Nor is an agricultural revolution a requirement for further industrialization in the immediate future.

In the first place, agricultural productivity increases are not the sole source of supply of industrial labour in Nigeria. The conventional approach assumes that food production is a bottleneck because it is the sole type of agricultural production and, apparently, that food will not be imported. But where export agriculture is also important, labour engaged in export production can shift to urban industrial pursuits if they are made sufficiently attractive, leaving food output unchanged. Indeed, food production can even quickly be increased, if necessary, in response to the usual price incentives through the mere switching of acreages from export to food crops. Thus although agriculture is linked to industry through its competition for essentially scarce labour, its ability to supply the urban sector with labour does not, in the Nigerian case, depend upon the raising of agricultural productivity.

In the second place, and at present more important, there now exist hundreds of thousands of Nigerian labourers who are either unemployed or working in the 'service' sector in the urban areas, the service sector being defined so as to include many in the distributive trades and elsewhere who are actually underemployed. Many of these are the so-called 'school-leavers' who have acquired an elementary education and are apparently unwilling to return to work upon the land.[1] It is from this pool of urban unemployed and underemployed, which is growing more rapidly than the 'modern' sector can absorb them into 'full' employment, that industrial labour will be drawn in Nigeria. Particularly is this so since urban dwellers will be far better material for factory labour than will labourers from the 'bush'. It is true that this pool originated in a flow from rural agricultural to urban areas but this flow was little related to agricultural progress. Nor, apparently, is it related to relative wage rates in urban and rural areas for it is difficult to entice members of the pool back into agriculture even with attractive earning opportunities. 'Natural' increases in urban population will certainly more than suffice to meet the labour requirements of Nigerian industry in the foreseeable future. Despite the fact that labour is a scarce factor in the agricultural sector, then, it is, given the urban unemployment and the apparently non-economic factors preventing a return flow from the cities to the land, basically free to the urban-industrial sector. Dualism in Nigeria is of a special sort: the unemployment (overt rather than disguised) is in the modern urban-industrial sector rather than in agriculture. The government is, in fact, attempting to persuade these unemployed to return to the land where their marginal productivity will be higher. Arguments for increasing investment in agriculture in order to provide the labour for industry therefore hold no water. The bottleneck in industry is not labour, but capital and entrepreneurship.

It goes without saying that there may be powerful arguments for raising agricultural productivity other than the need for urban labour. World demand for all of Nigeria's agricultural exports is of (absolutely) greater than unitary elasticity so that increased export volume will, *ceteris paribus*, raise total export earnings. With rising incomes and growing population domestic demand for agricultural produce is also growing. This increasing demand provides still another reason for increasing output. The rate of return from investment in agriculture should, of course, be compared with those obtainable elsewhere.

4. *Tax revenues and foreign exchange*

Most important of all is the role of peasant agriculture in the provision

[1] See Archibald C. Callaway, 'Unemployment Among African School Leavers', *Journal of Modern African Studies*, Vol. 1, No. 3 (September 1963), pp. 351-371; A. C. Callaway, 'School Leavers and the Developing Economy of Nigeria', *Nigerian Institute of Social and Economic Research, Conference Proceedings, December 1960*, pp. 60-72.

of savings for the development effort. Though the Nigerian economy remains fairly *laissez-faire* in character, it is the public sector which is now taking the lead as far as domestically financed net capital formation in the 'modern' sector is concerned. Moreover, the presant plan calls for a radical increase in the relative role of public capital formation. The great bulk of the tax revenues necessary for this public capital formation, as well as for current expenditures, comes from the peasant sector.

Nearly all of the export duties and a large proportion of import duties, which together accounted for 65 per cent of all federal, Regional, and local tax revenues in 1960-61, are ultimately a burden upon the peasant farmer. The trading operations of the Marketing Boards, which were originally established to protect the farmer from price or income fluctuations, have also contributed substantial revenues to the government sector at the expense of the export-producing peasant. It is difficult to assign a precise weight to the tax burden borne by peasant export producers relative to those borne by other income groups, but there can be no question as to its predominance over the others. During the post-war period, import duties and direct taxes quite apart, Nigerian governments and government boards withheld between 21 and 32 per cent of peasant gross incomes from exports controlled by the Marketing Boards. (See Table 2 for a more detailed breakdown of these government withdrawals.) Rubber exports, which are not subject to Marketing Board control, were also subjected to 10 per cent duties – or a burden of probably about 12½ per cent of gross peasant income from rubber.

Peasant export agriculture is thus consciously being squeezed through the tax system in order to finance the construction of infrastructure and industry. It will undoubtedly continue involuntarily to supply the finance for much of the development effort for a long time to come.

One can argue about the equity and, perhaps, even the efficiency of taxing export farmers heavily for development. To enter upon this debate here would lead this paper too far astray. Regardless of its rights or wrongs (and it is my opinion that the former outweigh the latter), if one is determined, as the Nigerians apparently are, to employ this method, one should seek to maximize tax revenues from this source. Such maximization has almost certainly not yet been achieved by the Nigerian authorities, largely, no doubt, because of political constraints which prevent the rate of taxation exceeding certain limits. Political constraints, which operate upon the rate of taxation, cannot be blamed, however, for lost revenue opportunities which arise through insufficient consideration of the possibilities for negative supply responses to high tax rates. Tax rates, even when the object is to maximize revenues, can be too high as well as too low. There is reason for suspicion that revenues from palm oil exports might actually be raised through the raising of the Marketing Board-set producer price (i.e. the lowering of the rate of taxation).

II: PEASANT AGRICULTURE AND EXPORT INSTABILITY

Heavy reliance upon peasant agricultural exports for the pursuit of economic development has some disagreeable implications. Export earnings from peasant-produced primary products are notoriously unstable. This instability is the product of uncontrollable fluctuations both in domestic supplies and in world prices. It is pointless to advocate autarchy as the solution to the problem of West African export instability.[1] Few would be willing to purchase stability, if indeed it were obtainable, at the cost of the decreased incomes thereby implied. Rather, one must seek in every way possible to make the best of the disagreeable facets of the international trade which is the mainspring of the economy's growth.

A great deal of attention has been devoted in recent years to the need for stabilization of the export proceeds of primary producers through international commodity agreements, compensatory finance schemes, etc. In West Africa, schemes for the stabilization of cocoa and groundnut prices come quickly to mind. (When spokesmen for the underdeveloped nations speak of 'stabilization', they frequently do not mean stabilization so much as support. Still, the stabilization of export prices, and, more broadly, export earnings, is frequently the intended aim.) Judging by the extended discussions of this problem and the many attempts at its alleviation, export instability must be presumed to have considerable and deleterious effects upon economic growth. Stabilization, for its own sake, is only of secondary interest in the underdeveloped world.

Of what benefit is reduced export instability? It has not yet been established conclusively that domestic instability is harmful to development; some, indeed, have argued the exact reverse.[2] There exists, however, a reasonable presumption that the instability of foreign exchange earnings hinders the process of orderly planning and plan implementation, whether public or private. The point of stabilization in the underdeveloped countries is the stabilization of the flow of imports which are essential for capital formation and the supplying of domestic industries. Stated a little differently, if those planning

---

[1] As seems to be done by Edward Marcus in 'Development Planning and the "Inherent" Instability of the West African Economies', *Nigerian Journal of Economic and Social Studies*, Vol. 5, No. 2 (July 1963), pp. 187-195.

[2] See, for example, Sir Sydney Caine, 'Instability of Primary Product Prices: Protest and a Proposal', *Economic Journal*, September 1954.

development efforts are to protect themselves against instability they must hold higher average foreign exchange (precautionary) reserves, with the attendant costs, when instability is great, than when it is small. No more persuasive case against instability exists. Where, as in Nigeria, a large proportion of the planned capital formation is to be undertaken by the public sector the conventional tenets of stabilization policy may have to be stood upon their heads. Government capital formation, which in the developed world is an *instrument* of stabilization policy, is now the *object* of the stabilization effort. It may even be worth while to destabilize the private sector so as to stabilize government expenditures.

Nigerian export instability

Nigeria's agricultural export products suffer from the same instability of volume and price as do the rest of the world's primary products. Fluctuations in weather, disease and pest conditions are an uncontrollable element in the determination of agricultural and other incomes and foreign exchange earnings; so are fluctuations in world demand and in the supplies offered by other major producers, both of which exert exogenous effects upon the level of world prices. The characteristics of the various crops, however, differ considerably.

These characteristics are summarized in Table 3, which shows two alternative measures of instability for each of price, volume and total receipts in the post-war period: (1) average percentage annual change; (2) average percentage deviation from a five-year moving average. The second of these measures has been calculated so as to avoid the distracting influence of trends (which, though inherently interesting, are irrelevant to the instability problem); the moving average was considered superior to a trend line because of the relevance of deviations from medium term rather than long term movements. These measures are taken with respect to exports during calendar years, not with reference to crop years, since, for our purposes, it is sufficient to get comparability at this level. Where crop years do not coincide with calendar years, the degree of instability will be understated through the use of calendar years.

It is clear from this table that rubber, groundnuts, cotton and cocoa are highly unstable earners of export receipts – their average annual deviations from the moving average of receipts ranging from 16 per cent for cocoa and cotton to 28 per cent for rubber; expressed in terms of average percentage annual change these figures are larger still and the instability of groundnut and cotton exports looms larger.

The causes of this instability vary from product to product. It turns out that, with either measure, cocoa and rubber are characterized by the greatest degree of world price instability – averaging 18 to 19 per cent deviation from the trend and 18 to 22 per cent average annual change. Palm kernels, palm oil, and groundnuts – all of which are somewhat competitive with one another on the world oilseeds market – enjoy relative stability of prices, if it is possible to call average deviations of 10 per cent from the moving average stability. In volume terms, groundnut exports are extremely volatile – averaging 21 per cent from the moving average or an average annual change of 25 per cent. Cotton export volume appears to be comparably unstable in terms of average annual percentage change, but this reflects the rapid rate of growth in volume which is eliminated in the alternative measure of deviation from the moving average. The rankings of volume instability of the other products are not affected by the measure employed. Palm kernels and palm oil enjoy relative stability of export volumes as well as of prices.

Some of the price and volume instability is mutually offsetting in the cases of cocoa, groundnuts, and, perhaps, palm oil. The instability of their receipts falls in the range between the instabilities in terms of prices and volumes. Rubber, cotton and palm kernels, on the other hand, are more unstable in terms of export receipts than in terms of either prices or volumes.

The overall instability of these earnings, measured as a percentage deviation from the moving average is less (6·8 per cent) than those of any of the components; expressed in terms of average percentage annual change, only palm kernel exports were more stable, and they were only slightly so, than the total. Table 3 illustrates clearly the advantage, from the point of view of the maintenance of stability of national export earnings, of being nationally diversified. This advantage derives from cross-commodity offsetting not only of divergent world price fluctuations but also of divergent fluctuations in export volumes.

It is worth considering what the stability advantages for each of Nigeria's component Regions are in being a part of a larger integrated economy. Each Region is, of course, far less diversified than the nation. Table 4 shows the degree of instability of each Region's agricultural exports.[1]

On the whole, intra-Regional diversification usually produces greater stability, although this is not always the case.[2] Instability of total agricultural export earnings, even with the benefits of diversifica-

---

[1] Some simplifying assumptions have been employed in the preparation of this table. See Table 4 footnotes 3, 4 and 5, p. 64.

[2] The degree of instability of agricultural export receipts in the Eastern Region is *greater* in the aggregate than it is for the component products of palm oil and palm kernels. In the Western and Northern Regions, as is to be expected, instability is reduced below those of all the individual components except palm kernels (in the West).

tion, remains substantial on a Regional level. The range of Regional instabilities varies between 14·5 per cent and 20·9 per cent when expressed as average annual changes and between 11·2 per cent and 15·4 per cent when expressed as deviations from the moving average (see Table 4). the Northern Region suffers from the greatest degree of instability and the Eastern Region enjoys the least. Each Region clearly stands to gain, from the point of view of maintaining stable foreign exchange earnings, through pooling earnings with the others; this can be seen by comparing the final column of Table 4, which gives the instability for all three Regions together, with columns (1) to (3).

Broader implications of the Nigerian experience

The point of this discussion is that considerable stabilization of export earnings can be attained through pooling of reserves by several national units. Diversification of export production, so frequently promoted as a policy objective, can be attained through thus expanding the boundaries of the economic unit to incorporate areas with different natural resources, climates, soils and peoples.

Doubt has recently been cast upon the stabilizing role of export diversification by a number of studies,[1] most recently one by B. F. Massell, which employed cross-sectional data to compare the degrees of export diversification and export instability in a large sample of economies. Massell properly qualifies his pessimistic conclusions as to the desirability of diversification by allowing that 'Ghana's decision whether or not to produce coffee in addition to cocoa should be based on the relationship between coffee and cocoa prices (among other things), rather than on generalizations based on aggregates of countries and of commodities'[2] Once this is granted, however, it is difficult to see how his study can provide 'general guidelines of some use in development planning'.[3] The results derived from the cross-country studies of Michaely, Coppock and Massell notwithstanding, diversification of the export base *has* reduced the degree of instability of export earnings in the Nigerian context. Where there exists heavy dependence on a very few types of exports, as in Ghana or in Senegal,

[1] Michael Michaely, *Concentration in International Trade* (North-Holland Publishing Company, Amsterdam, 1962), Ch. 5. Joseph D. Coppock, *International Economic Instability, the Experience after World War II* (McGraw-Hill Book Company, New York, 1962), Chs. 5-6. B.F. Massell, 'Export Concentration and Export Earnings', *American Economic Review*, Vol. LIV, No. 2, Part I (March 1964), pp. 47-63. See also L. Tarshis, 'The Size of the Economy and its Relation to Stability and Steady Progress', pp. 190-199, in E. A. G. Robinson (ed.), *Economic Consequences of the Size of Nations* (Macmillan and Company, London, 1960).
[2] Massell, *op. cit.*, p. 48.
[3] *Ibid.*

increasing their number will certainly stabilize total earnings from them. The low correlations between degree of concentration and instability found in the cross-country studies are probably largely attributable to the fact that after a certain point, increasing diversification no longer has any significant impact upon instability – there are diminishing returns to diversification.[1] This implies that some countries, those which are at present heavily concentrated in one or a few exports, will gain more than others, those already fairly diversified. Nigeria stands to gain less from reserve-pooling, as indeed from economic integration in general, than Ghana or Senegal.

This stabilization of foreign exchange earnings is only advantageous to each of the component Regions (or countries) if it is accompanied by stabilization of foreign exchange *availability*. If the full amount of foreign exchange earnings is always returned to the Region of origin the apparent reduction in instability observed in the aggregated figures is operationally meaningless (although there may remain certain other advantages from reserve-pooling.)[2] For the stabilization achieved through reserve-pooling to be effective there must exist opportunities for some countries to become temporary creditors and others temporary debtors to the pool. Thus, for example, in the event of a very favourable year for export earnings in one Region, the foreign exchange reserves which its government will probably accumulate through failure immediately to spend its increased tax revenues can be employed by the government of another Region which, having suffered a temporary decline in export earnings and taxes, would otherwise have had to postpone its plans.

It is the arrangement assuring stability of foreign exchange availability which will be the major stumbling-block in the negotiation of a pooled reserve system such as is here being suggested.[3] Member

---

[1] Michaely made essentially this same point in connection with import prices: 'A country whose imports consist . . . of four (equally important) commodities may expect considerably smaller fluctuations of import prices than a country which imports two commodities. But it is doubtful whether the same thing could be said in comparing a country which imports forty goods with one which imports only twenty' (p. 83). It is also attributable in part to the substantial differences in the volatility of particular types of exports.

[2] Others include: (1) the possibility of saving on foreign exchange transaction costs as a result of offsetting international transactions within the union. If one member is in deficit to the U.K. and in surplus to Germany while another is in deficit to Germany and enjoying a surplus with the U.K., the union as a whole may be in overall balance with both whereas individual members, had they not been union members, would have incurred the costs of exchanging the currency they had for the one they needed. This is no longer as important in a convertible world; (2) the possibility of saving on foreign exchange reserves as a result of the internalization of inter-member trading transactions; (3) the possibility of offsetting seasonal export earnings from various regions over the year, thus conserving on foreign exchange reserves held as transaction balances.

[3] Some cautious suggestions for the establishment of a payments union are advanced in Robert Triffin's *Report on the Possibilities of Establishing a Clearing*

countries must be willing to surrender some of their national sovereignty – to submit themselves to pre-arranged rules or to the discretionary authority of a 'central' bank. The political strains upon a pooled reserve system in a situation where very little trade is conducted among the members and where all the member countries are persistently short of foreign exchange for imports from the rest of the world are likely to be extreme. It might be that all that could be arranged would be the parcelling out of total export earnings, on a period by period basis, according to a pre-arranged formula; but even this would provide increased stability.

The Nigerian Federation has not taken full advantage of its diversification, from the Regions' viewpoint, but now that it has succeeded in centralizing its foreign exchange reserves its Regions do derive some of the stabilizing benefits of diversification. These benefits are provided through the operation of a single foreign exchange authority the Central Bank, for the entire Federation. An individual, firm or government has equal access to the foreign exchange reserves held by the Central Bank, regardless of which Region he or it is from. Thus, even in the event of a collapse of the cocoa market, inhabitants of the Western Region, where cocoa is grown, if they have the necesary domestic income, can obtain command over foreign exchange which has been earned in the Northern and Eastern Regions on equal terms with Northerners and Easterners. Clearly, individuals' and firms' incomes in a particular Region are likely to be greatly affected by the progress of the Region's export earnings; as far as the private sector on the first round is concerned the free access to foreign exchange may, therefore, be largely irrelevant. Under the existing revenue system, Regional and local government revenues, and therefore expenditures, are also greatly dependent upon the progress of peasant exports from the Regions in question. The Regional governments obtain some measure of freedom from this revenue constraint, however, through their participation in the federally-collected 'distributable pool' which contributes about one-quarter of total Regional revenues collected at the Federal level. Moreover, in cases of dire financial emergency (such as in the Western Region in 1962), the Federal government will lend to Regional governments; this is done, however, only on an *ad hoc* basis. Regional benefits from reserve-pooling are still not as great as they might be. If the Regional governments had the power to borrow from the Central Bank (or, if they represented independent sovereign states,

---

and Payments Union in Africa (E/CN. 14/262. Annex VI). Useful lessons could also undoubtedly be drawn from the experiences of the French-speaking African areas. The West African Monetary Union (Dahomey, Ivory Coast, Mauritania, Niger, Senegal, Togo and Upper Volta) already share one central bank, the Banque Centrale des Etats de l'Afrique de l'Ouest (BCEAO).

from their own Central Banks) they would derive far greater benefits from the centralized foreign exchange reserves than they in fact do.[1]

Through international co-operation in the use of foreign exchange reserves export instability may thus be alleviated more quickly and more efficiently than through national diversification policies or international commodity schemes.[2] It should not be too difficult to work out some sort of international reserve-pooling agreement among independent West African nations, from which all the signatories would benefit. Is one being too parallel-conscious if one also points out that payments agreements in Europe preceded the Common Market?

III: CONCLUSIONS

The lessons from the Nigerian experience and the preceding analysis are clear. The most has not yet been made of West Africa's peasant export base. There exist unexploited opportunities for further processing of peasant agricultural produce which is now exported in its raw form, both for world and for local markets. There exist substantial markets in the West African peasant sector for the building of a manufacturing sector; the greatest advantage can be taken of this potential if progress can be made not only in the formation of a customs union but also a co-ordinating industrial planning. The outlook for the latter does not yet seem to be very bright. Industrialization in West Africa does not depend upon an agricultural revolution. Investment in agriculture cannot be justified by its provision of labour supplies for the 'structural transformation' of the economy. Income from peasant export production still constitutes the most important revenue source for the public sector's development effort. Attempts should be made to maximize revenues from this source; but this does not imply maximizing rates of taxation.

The problem of export instability (whether peasant-produced or not) can be alleviated through the international pooling of foreign exchange reserves. Diversification of the export base, which in heavily

[1] The principal stabilizing element in Nigeria's public sector at present is the expenditure programme of the Federal government and the major publicly-owned utilities like the Electricity Corporation, the Ports Authority, the Coal Corporation, the Railway Corporation, the Airways, and the Niger Dams Authority. These Federal expenditures are as stable as Federal exports and Federal tax revenues permit – rather more stable, that is to say, than Regional exports or revenues, or Regional contributions to Federal revenues through the 'distributable pool', would permit. To the extent that independent states could abandon some of their sovereignty to an international 'common services' commission dealing with such matters as transport, communications, and energy sources, they too could derive the benefits of increased stability of developmental expenditures (not to speak of the more conventionally emphasized benefits of coordinated planning).

[2] This does not imply that other such policies or schemes need be abandoned. Reserve pooling is not an alternative but a complement to other stabilizing activities.

concentrated economies does diminish instability, can thus be achieved immediately without undertaking the costs of building new industries or the costs of autarchy. Some countries will derive greater benefits than others from such an arrangement, but all will benefit. The principal difficulties with such a scheme will be the reaching of international agreement on the arrangements, whether discretionary or predetermined, for the use of the pooled reserves. Present prospects for such an agreement seem brighter than those for agreements on the location of West African industry.

TABLE 1   Relationships between domestic inputs, value added, and total output in selected Nigerian manufacturing plants, 1959-60

	(1) domestic intermediate inputs as % of total output	(2) value added as % of total output	(3) value added as % of value of intermediate inputs
	%	%	%
groundnut & other oil-seed processing	75·8	20·4	25·7
textiles – large plants	46·6	48·5	93·8
soap – large plants	38·8	49·1	96·7
tire retreading	26·1	44·8	81·1
footwear	18·2	24·8	33·2
shoes – rubber	49·5	37·2	59·5

Source: Calculated from data in Nicholas G. Carter, *An Input-Output Analysis of the Nigerian Economy*, 1959-60 (Working Paper, School of Industrial Management, Massachusetts Institute of Technology: Cambridge,1963).

GERALD K. HELLEINER

TABLE 2 Government withdrawals from major agricultural export producers' incomes, 1947-62

	export duties		marketing board trading surplus		produce purchase tax		total withdrawals	
	£000's	% of potential producer income*	£000's	% of potential producer income*	£000's	% of potential producer income*	£000's	% of potential producer income*
	(1)	(2)	(3)	(4)	(5)	(6)	(7)	(8)
cocoa (1947-62)	64,481	17·8	46,638	12·8	4,553	1·3	115,672	31·9
groundnuts (1947-61)	32,154	12·9	25,743	10·4	3,998	1·6	61,895	24·9
palm kernels (1947-61)	26,997	11·1	36,978	15·2	4,327	1·8	68,303	28·1
palm oil (1947-61)	17,002	11·0	10,849	7·0	4,592	3·0	32,442	21·0
Cotton (1949-61)	8,458	12·9	5,272	8·0	792	1·2	14,522	22·1

*Potential producer income is defined as total withdrawals plus actual producers' income

Source: Gerald K. Helleiner, 'The Fiscal Role of the Marketing Boards in Nigerian Economic Development, 1947-1961', *Economic Journal*, September 1964.

TABLE 3 Measures of instability of principal Nigerian agricultural exports, 1947-62

	(1) cocoa	(2) palm kernels	(3) palm oil	(4) groundnuts	(5) cotton	(6) rubber	(7) total of six
price[1]							
% annual change[2]	22·1	11·6	12·2	14·4	16·6	18·5	—
% deviation from moving average[3]	17·9	9·7	10·0	10·1	13·2	19·3	—
volume							
% annual change[2]	14·8	7·8	10·2	24·6	24·3	15·6	—
% deviation from moving average[3]	9·5	5·3	7·5	20·8	8·2	11·4	—
receipts							
% annual change[2]	18·3	12·7	14·2	24·6	28·4	26·5	13·0
% deviation from moving average[3]	16·1	9·8	8·1	18·2	15·9	28·4	6·8

[1] Unit value of exports.
[2] Always expressed as % of the higher of the two values. Average for 1947-62 period.
[3] Deviation from 5-year moving average. Average for 1949-60 period, since two observations lost on either end of the period.

TABLE 4 Measures of instability of export earnings from Nigerian major agricultural exports by region, 1947-62

	(1) East[3]	(2) West[4]	(3) North[5]	(4) Total
% Annual Change[1]	14·5	15·0	20·9	13·0
% Deviation from the Trend[2]	11·2	13·8	15·4	6·8

[1] Average for 1947-62 period. Always expressed as % of the higher of the two values.

[2] Average for 1949-60 period since 2 observations lost on either end. Deviation from 5 year moving average.

[3] Palm oil plus half palm kernels exports.

[4] Rubber, cocoa, plus half palm kernel exports.

[5] Groundnuts plus cotton exports.

Sources: Calculated from *Trade Reports.*

ROBERT M. STERN

The Determinants of
Cocoa Supply in West Africa[1]

*

The purpose of this paper is to investigate the economic determinants of cocoa supply in the major producing nations of West Africa. These nations, particularly Ghana and Nigeria, are of course the predominant source of the world's cocoa, as is evident from Table 1. Moreover, as is further evident, they have accounted for practically the entire increase in world cocoa production in the decade since the early 1950's.

Cocoa has been singled out for special study because of its role in providing West Africa with an important means of livelihood for many people and in furnishing a major source of government revenue through controlled producer prices and export taxes. Its importance in relation to GNP and as a source of foreign exchange earnings from exports in the main producing countries can be seen from Table 2. The study of cocoa also has the particular advantages of being significantly better documented in comparison to most other West African primary products, and, furthermore, of having been treated in a fairly substantial literature.[2] Finally, because it is a perennial and not a strictly annually produced crop, cocoa presents some challenging and complex problems of economic analysis and statistical estimation.[3]

Acreage planted and harvested

The determinants of cocoa supply are complex because of the intermingling of long-run and short-run production decisions. Thus, in estimating a supply function for cocoa, data on average yields and on the total number of bearing acres in any given year are required. As far as the total number of bearing acres is concerned, it is of course changing from year to year as new acreage is coming into bearing and existing acreage is abandoned. To determine exactly the new acreage coming annually into bearing is difficult, however, since it depends upon plantings completed in a period some eight to ten years removed in the past.[4]

Unfortunately, because only fragmentary data on the acreage and new plantings of cocoa trees are available for the main producing countries, it is not possible to study the long-run planting decision directly, except in a limited way.[5] Of the main producing countries,

E

Nigeria was the only one for which annual data were available for cocoa acreage planted. These data, which are given in Table 4 of the statistical appendix, were accessible, however, only in the form of five-year moving averages centred on the middle year. The disadvantage of the measurement in this form is that it precludes study of the annual planting decision. Moreover, because of the method of centring, the averages for the centre year, t, reflect the influence of two future years, $t+1$ and $t+2$. There is, as a consequence, a certain amount of difficulty in specifying the price variable which, economically speaking, has an impact on the planting decision. For example, the use of a five-year moving average of price also centred on the middle year introduces in effect a set of expectations which are in part identical with the actual decisions made one and two years hence.

In any event, because the data were not accessible in any other form, there was no choice but to use the centred five-year moving averages. Accordingly, the relationship specified was between the five-year average acreage planted to cocoa, $\overline{AP}_t$, and the five-year average real price of cocoa, $\overline{P}_t$, both centred on the middle year, t:

$$\overline{AP}_t = a + b\overline{P}_t. \qquad (1)$$

While the acreage data were available for the period 1911-12 to 1944-1945, a scatter diagram of the relationship revealed that the early years, 1911-12 to 1918-19, lay substantially apart from the remaining years. On the assumption, therefore, that the basic relationship was inapplicable in these early years, the analysis was confined to the period from 1919-20, with the following results[6]:

1919-20 to 1944-45 – Nigeria
$$\overline{AP}_t = -5 \cdot 14 + 1 \cdot 11 \overline{P}_t, \ R^2 = \cdot 86; \ F = 152 \cdot 76.$$
$$\quad (2 \cdot 05) \quad (\cdot 09)$$

The above regression was of course highly significant and perhaps remarkably so.[7] It implies a price elasticity taken at the mean of 1.29 for acreage planted. It would be interesting of course to determine if the annual planting decision was as highly correlated with price as these results imply, and if the relationship for the years since 1944-45 was similarly close. But further research here is contingent upon the accessibility of data.

As mentioned earlier, it is necessary in considering the supply determinants of cocoa to take account of the short-run production decision which affects the size and nature of the annual harvest through devoting greater or lesser expense and attention to the maintenance and husbandry of the trees, methods of harvesting, the use of fertilizers, and the application of sprays to control disease and pests. Although data are not available for the detailed efforts and expenditures of producers in connection with the annual harvest, some isolated data do exist for the annual harvested acreage in Ghana for 1923-24 to 1937-1938.[8] This suggested the possibility of considering the annual changes in this acreage, ΔAH_t, in relation to various formulations of the current and real lagged price of cocoa. Of all the price formulations tested, only the one for price lagged one year was statistically significant:

1924-25 to 1937-38 – Ghana

$$\Delta AH_t = -18{\cdot}01 + {\cdot}24P_{t-1}, \ R^2 = {\cdot}41; \ F = 8{\cdot}18. \tag{2}$$
$$(7{\cdot}92) \ ({\cdot}08)$$

The results presented on cocoa acreage planted for Nigeria and acreage harvested for Ghana provide clear evidence of the influence of price upon long-run and short-run production decisions. Our next task is to determine whether these different time effects can be sorted out in attempting to explain the annual level of and changes in the current production of cocoa.

The level of and changes in current production

For purposes of the present analysis, it is postulated that the current annual level of cocoa production, Y_t, can be explained according to the formulation:

$$Y_t = a + b_1 A_t + b_2 P_t + b_3 t, \tag{3}$$

where a is a constant term; A_t equals the number of bearing acres in a given year, t; P_t is the current real price of cocoa; and t is a linear time trend representing the net influences of changes in productivity and other unspecified phenomena.

In order to test equation (3), data on total bearing acreage in a given year are required. Such data are unfortunately not available. It was nevertheless thought to be of interest to determine if the data on harvested acreage for Ghana might be used instead. Equation (3) was computed, accordingly, with the following results:

1923-24 to 1937-38 – Ghana

$$Y_t = -203{\cdot}16 + 1{\cdot}05AH_t + {\cdot}54P_t, \qquad R^2 = {\cdot}40; \ F = 4{\cdot}05;$$
$$(190{\cdot}64) \ \ ({\cdot}47) \qquad ({\cdot}25)$$
$$Y_t = 392{\cdot}37 - {\cdot}61AH_t + {\cdot}32P_t + 6{\cdot}52t, \ R^2 = {\cdot}65; \ F = 6{\cdot}82;$$
$$(271{\cdot}16) \ ({\cdot}70) \qquad ({\cdot}21) \quad (2{\cdot}34)$$
$$Y_t = 200{\cdot}88 \phantom{- {\cdot}61AH_t + {\cdot}32P_t} + 4{\cdot}88t, \ R^2 = {\cdot}49; \ F = 12{\cdot}55.$$
$$(1{\cdot}38)$$

While all of the foregoing regressions were statistically significant according to the F-ratio, it can be seen that the introduction of the time trend into the first formulation changed the sign for the harvested acreage from positive, which is what one would expect, to negative.

The explanation for this would appear to lie in the inadequacy of the acreage harvested measure in so far as it failed to reflect the substantial increase in the total number of bearing acres and, above all, the increase in productivity due undoubtedly to the shift towards a more favourable age distribution of these acres as a consequence of new plantings. The unquestionable importance of this latter consideration is evident in the last of the three formulations in which the time trend explained nearly one-half of the variation in the level of current production.

The results just discussed indicate clearly the point made earlier about the need for data on yields and bearing acreage in order to estimate a supply relationship for cocoa. Given the absence of such data, however, it is necessary to seek alternative and indirect procedures for cocoa supply analysis. It was stated above that it takes an estimated eight to ten years subsequent to planting for cocoa trees to come into full bearing. This would suggest, accordingly, that the annual change in the current number of bearing acres, ΔA_t, can be approximated by the average real price of cocoa eight to ten years earlier, $\bar{P}_{t-8}$:

$$\Delta A_t = a + b_1 \bar{P}_{t-8}. \tag{4}$$

Returning to equation (3) and expressing it in first differences, and substituting for ΔA_t as just noted in equation (4), we obtain our basic estimating equation for changes in the annual level of output, ΔY_t:

$$\Delta Y_t = b_1 P_{t-8} + b_2 \Delta P_t + b_3. \tag{5}$$

The influence of the planting decision made eight to ten years earlier upon the change in current production should thus be reflected by $\bar{P}_{t-8}$ if, in fact, this is a satisfactory indicator of the long-run profit expectations associated with past plantings and if the lag specified is agronomically correct.[9] The influence of short-run profitability considerations reflected in ΔP_t should thus be distinguished from the long-run considerations subsumed under $\bar{P}_{t-8}$. The constant term in the equation can be taken as representative of the average change in output due to productivity changes and other unspecified factors.

Equation (5) was estimated for the major West African cocoa producers: Ghana, Nigeria, the Ivory Coast and Cameroun. Brazil and Ecuador were also included for comparative purposes. The basic data utilized are listed with supporting notes in the appendix tables 3 through 6. Four separate regressions were computed for Ghana and Nigeria (1919-20 to 1938-39; 1919-20 to 1945-46; 1946-47 to 1963-64; and 1919-20 to 1963-64) and for Brazil (1922-23 to 1938-39; 1922-23 to 1945-46; 1946-47 to 1960-61; and 1922-23 to 1960-61). Two separate regressions were run for the Ivory Coast and Cameroun

(1931-32 to 1938-39 and 1959-60 to 1963-64) and one for Ecuador (1948-49 to 1963-64).

Out of all of these regressions, only those for Ghana for the period prior to the end of the second world war proved to be statistically significant, as noted below. Moreover, the only regression coefficients that were significant were for the change in current price[10]:

1919-20 to 1938-39 – Ghana

$$\Delta Y_t = \cdot 04 \bar{P}_{t-8} + \cdot 48 \Delta P_t, \qquad R^2 = \cdot 31; F = 3\cdot 90;$$
$$\qquad (\cdot 04) \qquad (\cdot 18)$$
$$\Delta Y_t = \cdot 003 \bar{P}_{t-8} + \cdot 48 \Delta P_t + 7\cdot 27, R^2 = \cdot 29; F = 3\cdot 49.$$
$$\qquad (\cdot 090) \qquad (\cdot 18) \qquad (14\cdot 41)$$

1919-20 to 1945-46 – Ghana

$$\Delta Y_t = \cdot 03 \bar{P}_{t-8} + \cdot 51 \Delta P_t, \qquad R^2 = \cdot 26; F = 4\cdot 25;$$
$$\qquad (\cdot 04) \qquad (\cdot 18)$$
$$\Delta Y_t = \cdot 05 \bar{P}_{t-8} + \cdot 51 \Delta P_t - 2\cdot 99, R^2 + \cdot 26; F = 4\cdot 22.$$
$$\qquad (\cdot 08) \qquad (\cdot 18) \qquad (11.98)$$

1946-47 to 1963-64 – Ghana

$$\Delta Y_t = \cdot 14 \bar{P}_{t-8} + \cdot 51 \Delta P_t, \qquad R^2 = \cdot 13; F = 1\cdot 14;$$
$$\qquad (\cdot 12) \qquad (\cdot 53)$$
$$\Delta Y_t = \cdot 30 \bar{P}_{t-8} + \cdot 64 \Delta P_t - 16\cdot 50, R^2 = \cdot 11; F = \cdot 90.$$
$$\qquad (\cdot 29) \qquad (\cdot 57) \qquad (27\cdot 18)$$

1919-20 to 1963-64 – Ghana

$$\Delta Y_t = \cdot 05 \bar{P}_{t-8} + \cdot 51 \Delta P_t, \qquad R^2 = \cdot 17; F = 4\cdot 23;$$
$$\qquad (\cdot 04) \qquad (\cdot 19)$$
$$\Delta Y_t = \cdot 07 \bar{P}_{t-8} + \cdot 51 \Delta P_t - 2\cdot 04, R^2 = \cdot 15; F = 3\cdot 74.$$
$$\qquad (\cdot 09) \qquad (\cdot 19) \qquad (10\cdot 78)$$

As is evident, equation (3) was computed both with and without a constant term. This was done in order to verify whether the constant term was picking up a substantial enough proportion of the long-run impact of past plantings so as to cause $\bar{P}_{t-8}$ to be non-significant. The results show that this apparently was not the case inasmuch as $\bar{P}_{t-8}$ remained non-significant in the two formulations. It would appear, therefore, that the average lagged real price of cocoa for eight to ten years previously is insufficiently tuned to reflect the annual *change* in output associated with the new acreage coming into bearing in a particular year. Time and resources unfortunately did not permit examination of alternative lags of longer or shorter duration. But in any event, the result suggests clearly that the proper length of the lag must be determined on empirical grounds rather than assumed *a priori*.

The findings for Ghana for the years prior to the end of the second world war are thus indicative of a positive, though relatively low, short-run price elasticity of annual production: ·17 for 1919-20 to 1938-39 and ·15 for 1919-20 to 1945-46.[11] The short-run price change was not significant in the 1946-47 to 1963-64 period. Whether this can be traced in some way to the advent of the marketing board would be interesting to determine, for it is in this period that board-controlled producer prices were introduced, and, especially in the late 1950's, a considerable amount of information and materials provided for disease and pest control.[12] The determination of whether and how marketing board policies have altered the expectations and behaviour of producers with respect to costs and returns could possibly be studied with the aid of expenditures data from board accounts. In this way, light perhaps could be shed on the output effects of different board policies.

As far as the other countries are concerned, the failure to obtain significant results may be due as much to the crudities of the available data as to the way in which the model was specified. Attention should be given, therefore, especially to the improvement of data on prices received by producers and their costs of production and of living.

Finally, it is probably worth while to experiment with differently smoothed variations of the output figures in order to reduce the influence of random factors and perhaps take more account of the agronomical characteristics that are peculiar to cocoa. Better specified models and improved data would thus hopefully produce better results and thereby add to our knowledge of cocoa supply determinants.

CONCLUSION

On balance, the findings reached in the present study provide clear evidence of the responsiveness to price of cocoa acreage planted in Nigeria in the period prior to the end of the second world war and of acreage harvested and production in Ghana in the same period. No evidence of price responsiveness was established for the producers in the other countries studied, although the fewness and quality of the data for these countries may not inspire great confidence in the results. However, even though many of the results obtained were not conclusive and therefore perhaps raise more questions than they answer, a useful purpose seems nevertheless to have been served by examining seemingly plausible relationships and finding them wanting empirically.

What is clear at any rate is that much additional research is required in order to clarify our understanding of the supply determinants of cocoa. As far as the long-run planting decision is concerned, more information is needed on the costs and returns which form the basis of long-run profit expectations and on annual plantings of new acreage. Better planting data would permit the construction of series on the total number and age distribution of bearing acres in a given year, and thus enable the current planting and production decisions to be studied more effectively. However, in the absence of such data and given the necessity therefore of resorting to indirect measurements, more experimentation with alternative data formulations and time lags for past seems imperative if we wish to obtain better explanations of the level of and changes in current cocoa production. The role of institutional and non-price factors also deserves more careful study.

As far as economic policy is concerned, the results of this study do not suggest obvious implications because these results are neither sufficiently definite nor adequately comprehensive in the sense of providing a full assessment of the responsiveness of producers to economic incentives of various kinds. We must therefore leave open such questions as the degree to which the governments of the cocoa producing countries are able to or should formulate economic policies based upon the insensitivity of producers to price.

NOTE ON SOURCES AND METHODS

1. I would like to thank Daniel B. Suits for his helpful suggestions in formulating this paper and Martin F. J. Prachowny for his research assistance. Financial assistance for the underlying research was provided through the University of Michigan's Center for Research on Economic Development and Department of Economics Ford Foundation Faculty Research Fund.

2. The world cocoa economy has been studied comprehensively in V. D. Wickizer, *Coffee, Tea and Cocoa: An Economic and Political Analysis* (Stanford: Stanford University Press, 1951), esp. pp. 261-380; FAO, Commodity Series, Bulletin No. 27, *Cacao* (November 1955); and OEEC, *The Main Products of the Overseas Territories: Cocoa* (Paris, 1956). Important current developments can be followed in the periodic reports on *Cocoa Statistics* and publications of the Cocoa Study Group of the FAO; U.S. Department of Agriculture, *Foreign Agriculture Circular* (Cocoa Beans); and in the market reports of Gill & Duffus, Ltd. Cocoa has also figured significantly in the literature on marketing boards associated especially with the work of Bauer and Paish in the 1950's, and more recently with work by Harrison G. Wehner, Jr., *The Cocoa Marketing Board and Economic Development in Ghana*: A Case Study (Ph.D. Dissertation, University of Michigan, 1963) and Gerald K. Helleiner, 'The Fiscal Role of the Marketing Boards in Nigerian Economic Development, 1947-1961', *Economic Journal* (Sept. 1964).

3. The article by Peter Ady, 'Trends in Cocoa Production', *Bulletin of the Oxford University Institute of Statistics*, Vol. II (December 1949), is noteworthy for its statistical treatment of cocoa supply factors. These factors are also considered briefly by R. Galletti *et al.*, *Nigerian Cocoa Farmers* (London: Oxford University Press for the Nigerian Cocoa Marketing Board, 1956), esp. pp. 3-4; and P. T. Bauer and B. S. Yamey, 'A Case Study of Response to Price in an Under-developed Economy', *Economic Journal*, Vol. LXIX (December 1959). The unusual problems posed by dependence on perennials, especially in Southeast Asia, have been stressed by Clifford R. Wharton, Jr., 'Monocultural Perennial Export Dominance: The Inelasticity of Southeast Asian Agricultural Trade' (University of Malaya,

Kuala Lumpur, mimeographed, October 1963). See also Robert M. Stern, 'Malayan Rubber Production, Inventory Holdings, and the Elasticity of Export Supply', *Southern Economic Journal* (forthcoming).

4. According to Peter Ady's study of Ghana, *op. cit.*, 395: 'A lag of eight to nine years was suggested by a scatter diagram on a double-log scale of export tonnages against the "real" price of cocoa.' It is stated in FAO, *op. cit.*, p. 32, that: 'Cacao trees require seven to ten years to come into substantial production . . .'; and further that a graph portraying three year moving averages of the deflated price paid to Gold Coast producers and production eight years later in the Gold Coast and in Nigeria is indicative of 'a relationship that is obviously more than coincidental'. Harrison G. Wehner, Jr., *op. cit.*, pp. 157-9, also found a close graphic relationship between three moving averages of producer prices and the output of cocoa ten years later.

5. An effective study of planting decisions would require data on the expected long-run profitability of growing cocoa, the age distribution of the existing stock of cocoa trees, and the expected profitability of alternative economic activity. Our knowledge is unfortunately rather limited when it comes to questions of profit expectations concerning production that will extend twenty or thirty years into the future. More data on costs and on the age distribution of the existing stock of trees would thus be invaluable in pursuing further research into the factors determining planting decisions. For an example of the kind of data needed and of a plausible supply model for a tree crop, see Ben C. French and Raymond G. Bressler, 'The Lemon Cycle', *Journal of Farm Economics*, Vol. XLIV (*November* 1962).

6. This same relationship was treated graphically in Galletti *et al.*, *op. cit.*, pp. 3-4, for the period 1925-26 to 1937-38, and the fit was evidently very close. The results for the longer period covered by the regression results thus extend and reinforce those reached by Galletti *et. al.*

7. This regression was also computed as follows with separate variables for the undeflated price and the price deflator:

$$\overline{AP}_t = 27 \cdot 00 + \cdot 59 \overline{P}_t{}^u - \cdot 18 \overline{P}_t{}^d, \ R^2 = \cdot 92; \ F = 127 \cdot 67.$$
$$(2 \cdot 52) \ (\cdot 06) \quad (\cdot 01)$$

8. As noted in Table 5 of the statistical appendix, some acreage data were also available for the Ivory Coast. The number of consecutive annual observations for the Ivory Coast was relatively limited.

9. In her 1949 article dealing primarily with Ghana in the inter-war period, Peter Ady *op. cit.* related both the levels and the first differences of the logarithms of current cocoa production and the real price lagged nine years. Strictly speaking, however, neither of these formulations is correct because no account is taken of other influences which could cause the levels or the first differences in both series to move together over time. If it is permissible to take lagged price as a proxy for past plantings, it should therefore be the *change* in rather than the level of current production to which the lagged price is related. As a consequence, Miss Ady's apparently good results for the long-run production effect of lagged price and her poor results for the short-run effect of current price are open to question. This would apply also to the graphic analyses cited above in note 4.

10. Equation (3) was run for all the periods and countries using the undeflated prices and price deflators as separate independent variables, but there was no improvement in the results. For Ghana, the beta co-efficients for ΔP_t were somewhat higher than those for the price deflator of ΔP_t. It may also be noted that equation (3) was computed using a first difference for P_{t-8}, and that there was little change in the results.

11. These elasticities were computed at the mean values of current production and current price.

12. Additional details can be found in Harrison G. Wehner, Jr., *op. cit.*, esp. pp. 107-221.

TABLE 1 Average annual world cocoa production, 1949/50-1953/54 to 1959/60-1963/64

countries and regions	average annual production 49/50-53/54 000 tons %		average annual production, 59/60-63/64 000 tons %		Change 49/50-53/54 to 59/60-63/64 000 tons %	
Africa	491·1	65·0	816·2	71·8	325·1	66·2
Ghana	241·4	32·0	401·5	35·3	160·1	66·3
Nigeria	106·4	14·1	185·7	16·3	79·3	74·5
Ivory Coast	54·2	7·2	87·2	7·7	33·0	60·9
Cameroun	50·8	6·7	72·4	6·4	21·6	42·5
other	38·3	5·0	69·4	6·1	31·1	81·2
South America	188·5	25·0	208·3	18·3	19·8	10·5
Brazil	124·9	16·6	136·0	12·0	11·1	8·9
Ecuador	24·4	3·2	38·7	3·4	14·3	58·5
other	39·2	5·2	33·6	2·9	−5·6	−14·1
Central America	67·2	8·9	89·9	7·9	22·7	33·7
Dom. Republic	32·8	4·3	37·2	3·3	4·4	13·5
Mexico	9·1	1·2	22·6	2·0	13·5	148·3
other	25·3	3·4	30·1	2·6	4·8	19·0
Asia	4·7	·6	6·9	·6	2·2	47·7
Oceania	3·6	·5	16·1	1·4	12·5	348·3
World total	755·1	100·0	1137·4	100·0	382·3	50·6

Sources: Derived from OEEC, *The Main Products of the Overseas Territories*: *Cocoa* (Paris, 1956) and FAO, *Cocoa Statistics*.

TABLE 2 Exports of cocoa and cocoa products in relation to gross national product and total exports in the major producing countries (Millions of U.S. Dollars)[1]

				exports of cocoa and cocoa products		
					as percentage of	
country	year	GNP	total exports	value	GNP	total exports
		$	$	$	%	%
Ghana	1962	1,484·0	290·6	173·8	11·7	59·8
Nigeria	1963	n.a.	506·5	90·7	n.a.	17·9
Ivory Coast	1963	n.a.	230·3	45·7	n.a.	19·8
Cameroun	1962	n.a.	103·2	30·1	n.a.	29·2
Brazil	1961	10,985·9	1,403·0	60·9	·6	4·3
Ecuador	1962	696·4	142·8	15·7	2·3	11·0

[1]At par values or free rates as shown in *International Financial Statistics*.

Sources: UN, *International Trade Statistics*, 1962 for Cameroun; for all other countries, IMF, *International Financial Statistics*.

General Note: The years in the tables 3 through 6 refer to a standard cocoa year ending on 30 September. Most of the price series available were based upon calendar year data. These series refer, without adjustment, to the crop year ending on 30 September in the particular calendar year.

TABLE 3 Ghana: Cocoa statistics

year	production (000 m. tons) (1)	area (000 hectares) (2)	price paid to producers (sh. per cwt.) (3)	import price index 1950-52=100 (4)	deflated price to producers (sh. per cwt.) (5)
1908-09	20·4		40·5	15·1	268·2
1909-10	23·0		39·5	15·9	248·4
1910-11	40·4		41·5	16·3	254·6
1911-12	40·6		43·5	16·8	258·9
1912-13	47·7		44·5	16·7	266·5
1913-14	56·8		46·5	16·8	276·8
1914-15	66·9		33·5	18·8	178·2
1915-16	82·9		59·5	24·2	245·9
1916-17	87·2		60·5	30·0	201·7
1917-18	71·0		39·5	39·0	101·3
1918-19	150·7		31·5	50·6	62·3
1919-20	146·9		75·5	75·0	100·7
1920-21	118·2		20·5	64·1	32·0
1921-22	164·9		23·0	42·5	54·1
1922-23	198·3		25·5	41·7	61·2
1923-24	204·0		23·0	44·5	51·7
1924-25	214·3	364·3	33·0	43·9	75·2
1925-26	210·6	356·2	29·0	41·5	69·9
1926-27	241·4	361·1	43·0	39·0	110·3
1927-28	210·3	364·3	48·5	39·1	124·0
1928-29	245·7	379·5	35·0	35·4	98·9
1929-30	235·7	380·5	32·0	30·6	104·6
1930-31	226·6	404·8	15·5	23·4	66·2
1931-32	215·4	384·6	17·0	22·6	75·2
1932-33	260·1	384·6	16·5	20·8	79·3
1933-34	223·5	386·6	10·5	19·5	53·8
1934-35	280·4	388·6	14·0	21·0	66·7
1935-36	289·6	386·0	15·5	21·3	72·8
1936-37	305·0	388·0	38·0	24·8	153·2
1937-38	235·7	405·0	12·5	22·6	55·3
1938-39	302·8		13·0	21·4	60·7
1939-40	245·6		15·0	27·7	54·2
1940-41	240·7		12·5	31·5	39·7

TABLE 3 (Continued)

year	production (000 m. tons) (1)	area (000 hectares) (2)	price paid to producers (sh. per cwt.) (3)	import price index 1950-52=100 (4)	deflated price to producers (sh. per cwt.) (5)
1941-42	254·8		14·5	38·5	37·7
1942-43	210·7		12·5	44·0	28·4
1943-44	199·2		12·5	45·5	27·5
1944-45	232·6		20·5	51·0	40·2
1945-46	212·6		25·5	59·0	43·2
1946-47	195·2		50·5	80·9	62·4
1947-48	211·0		75·5	86·7	87·1
1948-49	282·7		121·3	86·6	140·1
1949-50	251·8		84·0	86·8	96·8
1950-51	266·5		130·7	105·1	124·4
1951-52	214·3		149·0	108·1	137·8
1952-53	251·3		130·6	98·4	132·7
1953-54	225·0		134·0	93·7	143·0
1954-55	238·0		135·0	91·8	147·1
1955-56	233·0		148·5	94·6	157·0
1956-57	267·8		149·2	95·6	156·1
1957-58	209·8		134·2	94·6	141·9
1958-59	259·5		131·9	94·6	139·4
1959-60	321·9		112·2	94·6	118·6
1960-61	439·0		112·0	96·5	116·1
1961-62	416·0		100·6	96·5	104·2
1962-63	428·4		100·6	100·0	100·6
1963-64[1]	402·0		100·6	101·0	99·6

[1] Estimated.

Sources and notes:

Column (1) : Production to 1953-54 from FAO, Commodity Series, Bulletin No. 27, *Cacao* (November 1955), and thereafter from FAO, *Cocoa Statistics*.

Column (2) : Great Britain, Board of Trade, *Statistical Abstract for the British Empire*.

Column (3) : Prices to 1953-54 from FAO, Commodity Series, Bulletin No. 27, *Cacao* (November 1955), and thereafter from Harrison G. Wehner, Jr., *The Cocoa Marketing Board and Economic Development in Ghana: A Case Study* (Ph.D. Dissertation, University of Michigan, 1963) and U.S. Department of Agriculture, Foreign Agricultural Service, *Foreign Agriculture Circular* (Cocoa Beans, FCB 1-64, March 1964).

Column (4) : Import price index to 1953-54 from FAO Commodity Series, Bulletin No. 27, *Cacao* (November 1955), and thereafter, which linking for 1950-52, from IMF, *International Financial Statistics*.

TABLE 4   Nigeria: Cocoa Statistics

year	production (000 m. tons) (1)	acreage planted (000 acres) (2)	price paid to producers (sh. per cwt.) (3)	import price index 1938=100 (4)	deflated price to producers (sh. per cwt.) (5)
1908-09	2·3		32·0	53	60·5
1909-10	3·0		34·6	56	62·1
1910-11	4·5		37·4	57	65·5
1911-12	3·4	2·92	38·6	59	65·5
1912-13	3·7	3·12	43·4	58	74·2
1913-14	5·0	3·86	34·8	59	59·1
1914-15	9·3	3·70	34·4	66	52·2
1915-16	9·1	6·04	43·8	85	51·6
1916-17	15·7	6·10	32·2	105	30·6
1917-18	10·4	10·74	23·0	137	16·8
1918-19	26·1	11·08	41·6	177	23·4
1919-20	17·4	12·42	72·2	263	27·5
1920-21	18·2	11·10	24·2	225	10·8
1921-22	31·8	13·44	27·8	149	18·7
1922-23	35·1	13·36	28·2	146	19·3
1923-24	34·6	17·28	26·4	156	16·9
1924-25	40·7	20·16	32·5	149	21·8
1925-26	42·1	26·92	32·8	143	22·9
1926-27	46·4	29·78	67·3	127	53·2
1927-28	46·3	34·38	50·6	130	39·9
1928-29	54·7	32·10	43·3	130	33·3
1929-30	55·3	32·44	37·6	120	31·3
1930-31	52·4	27·52	21·4	103	20·8
1931-32	59·3	26·94	20·6	92	22·4
1932-33	73·1	20·04	16·0	93	17·2
1933-34	73·2	23·70	16·5	90	18·3
1934-35	83·6	20·20	17·2	91	18·9
1935-36	94·8	23·66	20·3	93	21·8
1936-37	103·3	20·86	38·9	100	38·9
1937-38	100·3	18·48	17·0	100	17·0
1938-39	117·5	12·88	15·4	101	15·2
1939-40	109·0	12·28	17·6	132	13·4
1940-41	102·2	7·26	14·0	145	9·7
1941-42	101·0	5·02	15·0	164	9·1
1942-43	113·0	3·00	13·0	220	5·9
1943-44	72·0	2·40	13·0	230	5·7
1944-45	86·9	1·90	23·0	218	10·5
1945-46	104·6		27·5	240	11·5
1946-47	112·7		50·0	280	17·9
1947-48	76·2		62·5	292	21·3

TABLE 4 (Continued)

year	production (000 m. tons) (1)	acreage planted (000 acres) (2)	price paid to producers (sh. per cwt.) (3)	import price index 1938=100 (4)	deflated price to producers (sh. per cwt.) (5)
1948-49	110·7		120·0	313	38·3
1949-50	100·7		100·0	298	33·5
1950-51	112·1		120·0	451	26·6
1951-52	109·6		170·0	367	46·3
1952-53	110·8		170·0	328	51·8
1953-54	99·0		166·0	345	48·1
1954-55	90·6		196·0	355	55·2
1955-56	116·1		196·0	375	52·3
1956-57	137·2		146·0	385	37·9
1957-58	82·0		146·0	361	40·4
1958-59	142·5		146·0	368	39·7
1959-60	157·1		156·0	385	40·5
1960-61	196·8		148·2	418	35·5
1961-62	199·9		96·0	451	21·3
1962-63	184·8		96·0	406	23·6
1963-64[1]	221·0		100·4	406	24·7

[1] Estimated.

Sources and notes:

Column (1) : Same as Table 3. Figures are inclusive of the British Cameroons; production in the British Cameroons for 1961-62 to 1963-64 was estimated at 6000 metric tons per annum.

Column (2) : Derived from R. Galletti *et al., Nigerian Cocoa Farmers* (London: Oxford University Press for the Nigerian Cocoa Marketing Board, 1956), p. 626. Data are 5-year moving averages centred on the year indicated.

Column (3) : Export unit value for 1908-09 to 1923-24 derived from Great Britain, Board of Trade, *Statistical Abstract for the British Empire* and for 1923-24 to 1939-40 as indicated in R. Galletti *et al.,* p. 625. Price paid to producers for 1940-41 to 1953-54 from FAO, Commodity Series, Bulletin No. 27, *Cacao* (November 1955); thereafter from Gerald K. Helleiner, 'The Fiscal Role of the Marketing Boards in Nigerian Economic Development, 1947-1961', *Economic Journal* (Sept. 1964) and the *Foreign Agriculture Circular* cited under Column (3), Table 1.

Column (4) : Ghana import price index used for 1908-09 to 1923-24 and linked at 1924 with the import price index for 1921, 1923 and 1924-38 constructed by Peter Ady and reported in her article, 'Trends in Cocoa Production', *Bulletin of the Oxford University Institute of Statistics*, Vol. 11 (December 1949), p. 402, and in R. Galletti *et al.,* p. 625. The indexes for 1939-51 reported by P. T. Bauer, *West African Trade* (Cambridge: University Press, 1954), p. 421, were linked with those given in the article by Helleiner cited above under Column (3).

TABLE 5 Ivory Coast: Cocoa statistics

year	production (000 m. tons) (1)	area (000 hectares) (2)	price paid to producers (francs per kg) (3)	import price index (4)	deflated price to producers (francs per kg) (5)
1920-21	1·5		2·60	64·1	4·06
1921-22	2·4		2·90	42·5	6·82
1922-23	3·6		3·08	41·7	7·39
1923-24	4·3		3·52	44·5	7·91
1924-25	6·3		4·80	43·9	10·93
1925-26	6·9		7·72	41·5	18·60
1926-27	9·8	40	9·42	39·0	24·15
1927-28	16·5	40	8·42	39·1	21·53
1928-29	16·3	44	6·08	35·4	17·18
1929-30	22·3	48	4·70	30·6	15·36
1930-31	19·9	50	3·10	23·4	13·25
1931-32	31·1	60	2·48	22·6	10·97
1932-33	30·9	76	1·99	20 8	9·57
1933-34	41·6	81	1·97	19·5	10·10
1934-35	43·6	83	1·93	21·0	9·19
1935-36	49·8	113	2·83	21·3	13·29
1936-37	48·1		4·84	24·8	19·52
1937-38	52·7		4·04	22·6	17·88
1938-39	55·2		3·64	21·4	17·01
1948-49	47·7		63·0	85	74·1
1949-50	53·2	158·4	79·0	88	89·8
1950-51	56·9	176·9	69·5	99	70·2
1951-52	45·0	173·2	89·0	112	79·5
1952-53	61·2	181·2	88·0	100	88·0
1953-54	53·0	171·6	167·0	93	179·6
1954-55	65·9	188·4	93·0	96	96·9
1955-56	71·4	225·6	61·3	94	65·2
1956-57	72·3	210·9	87·9	96	91·6
1957-58	45·4	212·6	87·6	107	81·9
1958-59	55·7		89·9	110	81·7
1959-60	61·8		94·8	109	87·0
1960-61	93·6		94·8	121	78·3
1961-62	81·0		69·6	119	58·5
1962-63	102·7		69·6	119	58·5
1963-64	97·0		69·6	121	57·5

[1] Estimated.

TABLE 5 (Continued)

Sources and notes:

Column (1) : Same as Table 3.

Column (2) : Pre-war data from International Institute of Agriculture, *International Yearbook of Agricultural Statistics*. Postwar data from Ivory Coast, Ministère des Finances, Des Affaires Economiques et du Plan, Service de la Statistique, *Inventaire Économique et Social de la Cote D'Ivoire, 1958*.

Column (3) : Prices for 1920-21 to 1938-39 refer to 'cours C.A.F. du cacao' for France in metropolitan francs, and are taken from France, Ministère de la France d' Outre-Mer, Service des Statistiques, *Outre-Mer, 1958*. Prices for 1948-49 to 1956-57 were taken from this same source in CFA francs and refer to 'prix nu-bascule, cacao courant' in Abidjan. This latter series was linked at 1956-57 with the series of prices paid to producers reported in the *Foreign Agriculture Circular* cited under Column (3), Table 1.

Column (4) : The Ghana import price index, with 1950-52=100, was used for 1920-21 to 1938-39. For 1948-49 to 1956-57, the import price index applicable to French West Africa was used as reported in *Outre-Mer, 1958*. The indexes for 1957-58 to 1959-60 were assumed to be identical with those for Cameroun as published in the *Economic Bulletin for Africa*. This latter index was linked beginning in 1959-60 with the African cost of living index for the Ivory Coast as reported in the IMF, *International Financial Statistics*. The postwar index shown is for 1953=100.

TABLE 6   Cameroun: Cocoa statistics

year	production (000 m. tons) (1)	price paid to producers (francs per kg) (2)	import price index (3)	deflated price to producers (francs per kg) (4)
1920-21	3·5	2·60	64·1	4·06
1921-22	3·5	2·90	42·5	6·82
1922-23	3·5	3·08	41·7	7·39
1923-24	4·5	3·52	44·5	7·91
1924-25	4·9	4·80	43·9	10·93
1925-26	5·2	7·72	41·5	18·60
1926-27	7·6	9·42	39·0	24·15
1927-28	7·3	8·42	39·1	21·53
1928-29	10·0	6·08	35·4	17·18
1929-30	10·8	4·70	30·6	15·36
1930-31	10·9	3·10	23·4	13·25
1931-32	13·8	2·48	22·6	10·97
1932-33	17·2	1·99	20·8	9·57
1933-34	19·5	1·97	19·5	10·10
1934-35	23·4	1·93	21·0	9·19
1935-36	23·8	2·83	21·3	13·29
1936-37	26·6	4·84	24·8	19·52
1937-38	31·0	4·04	22·6	17·88
1938-39	27·6	3·64	21·4	17·01
1948-49	45·4	57·0	76	75·0
1949-50	42·2	72·5	86	84·3
1950-51	48·1	78·0	94	83·0
1951-52	55·0	85·0	111	76·6
1952-53	54·3	79·0	100	79·0
1953-54	54·2	161·0	93	173·1
1954-55	56·0	82·0	96	85·4
1955-56	54·1	53·0	95	55·8
1956-57	60·0	79·2	95	83·4
1957-58	65·2	84·4	107	78·9
1958-59	60·3	75·5	110	68·6
1959-60	64·1	80·0	109	73·4
1960-61	74·0	80·0	121	66·1
1961-62	69·1	74·5	119	62·6
1962-63	76·0	69·6	119	58·5
1963-64[1]	79·0	75·0	121	62·0

[1] Estimated.

TABLE 6 (Continued)

Sources and notes:

Column (1) : Same as Table 3. Figures are exclusive of the British Cameroons, which have been included with the production of Nigeria in Table 4.

Column (2) : Prices for 1920-21 to 1938-39 same as for Ivory Coast; see Column (3), Table 5. Prices for 1948-49 to 1956-57 refer to quotations at Douala. Sources for these and later prices are the same as for the Ivory Coast: see Column (3), Table 5.

Column (3) : The Ghana import price index, with 1950-52=100, was used for 1920-21 to 1938-39. The import index for 1948-49 to 1959-60 was taken from *Outre-Mer 1958* and from the *Economic Bulletin for Africa*. The index for 1960-61 to 1963-64 was assumed to be the same as for the Ivory Coast.

TABLE 7   Brazil: Cocoa statistics

year	production (000 tons)	area (000 hectares)	average value of production ($ cr. per ton)	cost of living index 1958=100	deflated aver. value of prod. ($ cr. per ton)
	(1)	(2)	(3)	(4)	(5)
1908-09	33·7				
1909-10	29·2				
1910-11	35·0				
1911-12	30·5		545	2·23	24,453
1912-13	29·8		582	2·28	25,507
1913-14	40·8		544	2·28	23,869
1914-15	45·0		904	2·48	36,437
1915-16	43·3		834	2·66	31,359
1916-17	55·6		626	2·93	21,361
1917-18	41·9		687	3·28	20,959
1918-19	62·6		1,079	3·40	31,733
1919-20	66·9		857	3·73	22,988
1920-21	35·5		830	3·84	21,615
1921-22	58·9		1,115	4·20	26,548
1922-23	57·4		1,054	4·62	22,814
1923-24	67·9		1,027	5·41	18,983
1924-25	59·8		1,093	5·79	18,877
1925-26	72·2		1,075	5·94	18,098
1926-27	71·2		1,910	6·10	31,311
1927-28	73·3		1,685	6·01	28,037
1928-29	64·1		1,272	5·95	21,378
1929-30	68·7		1,368	5·41	25,287
1930-31	76·7	153·7	1,199	5·17	23,191
1931-32	104·4	180·0	1,096	5·23	20,956
1932-33	100·1	175·7	1,090	5·17	21,083
1933-34	107·9	175·9	992	5·59	17,746
1934-35	127·1	177·7	995	5·89	16,893
1935-36	126·7	189·1	994	6·79	14,639

F

TABLE 7 (Continued)

year	production (000 tons)	area (000 hectares)	average value of production ($ cr. per ton)	cost of living index 1958=100	deflated aver. value of prod. ($ cr. per ton)
	(1)	(2)	(3)	(4)	(5)
1936-37	118·9	187·3	998	7·33	13,615
1937-38	141·8	180·9	1,159	7·63	15,190
1938-39	134·8	205·9	1,217	7·81	15,583
1939-40	128·0	229·9	1,102	8·11	13,588
1940-41	132·3	239·4	1,659	9·08	18,271
1941-42	108·9	241·2	1,685	10·16	16,585
1942-43	148·3	239·2	1,628	11·24	14,484
1943-44	116·5	241·5	1,544	12·44	12,411
1944-45	119·7	267·9	1,850	14·51	12,750
1945-46	121·7	243·8	3,445	16·26	21,187
1946-47	119·1	257·9	6,636	20·84	31,843
1947-48	96·9	260·8	6,498	20·23	32,121
1948-49	133·4	258·0	4,616	21·89	21,087
1949-50	152·9	276·0	6,736	24·05	28,008
1950-51	121·2	291·4	8,244	29·02	28,408
1951-52	113·6	284·4	7,887	35·32	22,330
1952-53	137·0	340·5	12,530	39·80	31,482
1953-54	162·9	352·9	23,120	47·43	48,745
1954-55	157·9	368·3	20,787	57·21	36,335
1955-56	161·1	375·9	15,545	70·79	21,959
1956-57	164·6	386·7	21,253	85·90	24,741
1957-58	164·2	460·9	27,942	100·00	27,942
1958-59	177·8	466·2	40,058	126·69	31,619
1959-60	163·2	470·8	49,021	171·30	28,617
1960-61	155·9	474·3	64,082	224·37	28,561
1961-62				330·33	
1962-63				567·97	

Sources and notes:
Column (1): Production to 1945/46 from FAO, Commodity Series, Bulletin No. 27, *Cacao* (November 1955), and thereafter from *Anuário Estatístico do Brasil*.
Column (2): From *Anuário Estatístico do Brasil*.
Column (4): For 1911/12-1947/48, refers to cost of living index in Rio de Janeiro for a family of seven, as reported in Brasil, Directoria de Estatística Economica e Financeira do Thesouro Nacional, *Quadros Estatísticos* (Rio de Janeiro, 1936) and in the *Relatório* of the Banco do Brasil. This series was linked at 1947/48 with the cost of living index for the Federal District of Rio de Janeiro, as published in the *Anuário Estatístico do Brasil*.
Column (3): Average value of production for 1910/11-1918/19 estimated from export unit value on the basis of the 1919/20-1924/25 relationships. Export unit values were computed from the data given in Ivar Erneholm, *Cacao Production of South America* (Gothenburg, Sweden: C. R. Holmquists Boktryckeri AB., 1948), p. 84. Average value of production from *Anuário Estatístico do Brasil*.

J. W. F. ROWE

The Coffee Industries of East Africa in the World Market Setting

*

Traders distinguish three categories or groups of coffees on the world market – Milds, Brazils and Robustas. Milds are the fruit of the *arabica* variety of coffee tree, and the important producers are the Central and South American countries other than Brazil; also in Africa, Kenya, Tanganyika, Ethiopia, the Republic of the Congo, and some other small districts produce milds. Brazils come too from the arabica variety, but on the average command an appreciably lower price than milds owing to differences in climate (including altitude), cultivation and preparation. The third category, as its name implies, comes from the *robusta* variety, a more vigorous tree which can be grown in tropical as opposed to the sub-tropical conditions which suit the arabica variety; it bears a bigger crop but of a coarser quality with a distinctive flavour of its own, and consequently robustas are usually at a substantial discount below typical grades of Brazils. Robustas are produced in the Portuguese and formerly French territories of Africa, in Uganda and in Indonesia. Very roughly, world exports of milds have recently been around 15 to 16 million bags, of Brazils 17 to 18 million bags, and of robustas 11 to 12 million bags; but it must be added that the exportable production of milds (i.e. production minus domestic consumption) has been about 1 million bags more than the actual exports, and the exportable production of Brazils until this year has averaged about 9 million bags more. Incidentally it may be mentioned that the bag of 60 kilos (approximately 132 lb) is the universal international statistical unit for coffee, but tons are the measurement used in East Africa, roughly 17 bags making a ton.

In East Africa virtually the whole crops of Kenya and of Tanganyika other than that of the Bukoba district, are mild coffees, while Uganda's production, except in the Bugisu district of Mount Elgon, is robustas. The outstanding characteristics of each country's industries, and of the industry in different regions of each country, are very different, and it is out of the question to generalize about East Africa's coffee industries. An attempt will now therefore be made to summarize these outstanding characteristics for each main producing region.[1]

---

[1] A more detailed account can be found in my *The World's Coffee*, London: HMSO, 1963.

Kenya has a European estate industry and an African small-holders' industry. The core of the estate industry is some 250 estates of over 100 acres, mostly situated in a broad band between Nairobi and the south-eastern slopes of the Mt. Kenya massif, at an altitude of 5000 to 6000 feet. Together with a large number of smaller holdings, and with a sprinkling of estates in the Rift Valley and beyond to the west in Nyanza province, Kenya's estate production has been averaging about 25,000 tons. The estates over 100 acres are farmed intensively and at a good technical standard, but with the internal political situation of the last few years there has been very little new planting or new capital investment, except in irrigation plants. From now on, the outlook is for a slowly declining crop owing to the increasing age of the trees and the probability of wage costs continuing to rise – that is assuming that the industry carries on much as at present.

The estate industry began to develop at the beginning of this century, and in 1935-36 production was around 22,000 tons. Coffee planting by Africans was not allowed until 1937, but even in 1953-54 African production was a mere 300 tons. Then with the so-called Swynnerton plan real expansion began, and in 1960-61 African production was nearly 8000 tons. The main area is in the Meru and Embu districts on the eastern and south-eastern foothills of Mt. Kenya, though there has been substantial new planting to the south-west of the mountain round Fort Hall and Nyeri, and also in Nyanza province. Today, in 1964, the acreage in bearing is more than double that of 1961, and if new planting had not been prohibited last year as the result of the International Coffee Agreement, and the planting programmes of the Department of Agriculture had been fulfilled, by 1970 African production would probably have reached 50,000 tons, or double the production of the European estate industry. As it is, African production is likely to reach 24,000 tons in a couple of years' time, but not to increase further by reason of increasing acreage, though it may do so somewhat as the younger trees reach full bearing age. Up to 1962 the expansion of the African industry was closely controlled and supervised by the Department of Agriculture, and this ensured a high standard of cultivation and preparation. At that time the average African plot was about one-third of an acre, but the ultimate objective was about three-quarters of an acre, or say 300 to 400 trees, more than that being reckoned beyond the labour resources of the average family over and above that required for food production. In 1962 there were about 100,000 licensed coffee growers in the Central province, and the total for all Kenya was 140,000 to 150,000. They were organized in some 130 co-operative societies which operated about 180 pulperies. These societies were in turn organized into district Co-operative Unions, which undertake the transport of the parchment from the pulperies to the nearest railhead or direct to the finishing Mill at Nairobi; there each society's deliveries are treated separately, just as are the European estates, with the result that each estate and each African society receives payment from the Marketing Board according to the qualities of their coffees. The Meru and Embu districts have well nigh perfect conditions of soil and climate for coffee growing, and their crops up to 1962 fetched an average price about 10 per cent higher than the average for the whole Kenya crop, while average yields were higher than those of all but a few European estates. In the other African districts, neither yields nor quality are as high as in Meru and Embu, but the average quality of the whole African crop was higher than that of the whole European crop. It must be emphasized, however, that up to 1962 the African industry was being closely supervised by the Department of Agriculture: whether there have been substantial changes since then, I do not know. Cost of production is an entirely meaningless conception for African-grown coffee. At the 1962 price level of say £300 per ton, it is certain that coffee was by far the most remunerative cash crop, and by African standards immensely profitable. At what price level the African coffee farmer would reckon coffee unprofitable is guesswork, but it is unlikely to exceed £150 per ton, and then only after say a couple of years. A similar guess for the European estates might be £250 or even for the best not less than £200.

Tanganyika's main arabica area lies along its northern borders, and is centred on the southern slopes of Mt. Kilimanjaro and Mt. Meru. Its production averages about 16,000 to 17,000 tons, of which roughly half comes from the Kilimanjaro Native Co-operative Union which covers the slopes of that great mountain. A less important area is in the Southern Highlands and Southern Province from Mbosi to Matengo, and its production is about 4,000 to 5000 tons. Thus the total output of mild coffee in Tanganyika averages around 21,000 tons, to which must be added about 8,000 tons of robustas and some sun-dried arabicas from the Bukoba district on the west side of Lake Victoria. The KNCU is really an industry by itself. It covers a belt around the southern slopes of the mountain roughly 80 miles long and 10 miles wide between the contours 3000 and 6000 feet, and its constituent societies have a total membership of some 50,000, all of the Chagga tribe. The typical family farm consists of up to 3 acres of coffee heavily interplanted with bananas in the belt, and in addition a larger acreage in the lower lands for the other usual subsistence crops. In the belt, bananas are not only a main subsistence crop but also the largest cash crop, as much is sent to the lower areas at the eastern end of the mountain where bananas cannot be grown. If coffee was the main cash crop, as has generally been supposed until quite recently, the Chaggas might well be advised to plant pure banana stands on a scale sufficient for their subsistence, and all the rest of their land in the belt to coffee alone, thus undoubtedly very greatly increasing the yield of their coffee trees and their income; but since bananas are in fact the main cash crop, and since coffee harms bananas much less than bananas do coffee, interplanting is the right policy in view of the strictly limited area of land in the belt. Thus the Chaggas, unlike many African coffee growers in East Africa, do not rely on coffee as their main cash crop: even if coffee prices fell very low, they would still have a substantial cash income. The situation may be summed up symbolically by saying that the Chaggas produce their own bread (i.e. general subsistence), buy their butter with surplus bananas, and get their jam from their coffee crops. Cultivation has now become rather traditional, but the farmers, probably 80 per cent of whom are more or less literate, are open minded up to a point in respect of modern innovations such as chemical spraying and pruning. But with the banana interplanting, yields are low – an overall average of probably no more than around 3 cwt of clean coffee per acre – and the average family income from coffee at a price level of £300 per ton is probably not more than £40 to £50 gross. Preparation is by individual hand-pulping, and this falls far short of the standard of the co-operative pulperies of Kenya, with the result that KNCU coffees are usually priced appreciably below the Kenya crop. Opinions in 1961 differed greatly as to how much new planting had recently taken place, but it was probably not much, though a fair amount of re-planting had been going on, for about half the trees in the belt are now at least 25 years old. Improvements in husbandry may raise yields somewhat in the near future, but there will be no large increase in the KNCU crop.

Another 1500 tons of African coffee from the northern area, and some 2500 tons from the southern area, comes to market through the Tanganyika Co-operative Trading Society, or TACTA as it is commonly known, which handles all the African grown coffee outside the KNCU's domain. In the north, conditions of cultivation and preparation are much the same as on Mt. Kilimanjaro, though in 1960-61 one society on Mt. Meru started a central pulpery and got a much better price than the TACTA average price: whether it is still operating and whether this good example has yet been copied, I do not know. Not much expansion, however, is possible in this northern area. In the southern area conditions vary greatly, and there is little prospect of any large expansion, though the present output might be doubled. The industry is severely handicapped by having to send all its parchment to the one curing works in Tanganyika at Moshi, near Kilimanjaro, a distance of 800 to 1000 miles, which means a transport charge of say £12 to £15 or more per ton: even the establishment of a local mill would only save 20 per cent of the parchment weight to be transported over long distances for shipment.

The European and Asian owned estates are almost entirely in the northern area, though there are a few small ones in the south. The estates production has averaged about 4000 tons, though it reached 6000 tons in 1960-61, and most of it is handled by the Tanganyika Coffee Growers Association. Though there are a few estates which practise the most intensive cultivation, the overall standard can only be described as poor, and many of the Greeks and Asians have other commercial interests and just 'mine' their coffee estates. But the standard of preparation is very much better, and the TCGA crop normally makes a 10 per cent higher price than the KNCU. There is no prospect of any large increase in the production of estates, but equally none of decline unless prices fell heavily and remained low for some time.

Finally a brief mention must be made of the Bukoba district on the west side of Lake Victoria, which produces 6000 to 7000 tons of robustas and some 2000 tons of sun-dried arabica. Robusta has been a commercial cash crop in Bukoba for at least 80 years, and coffee culture has become traditional. Pure coffee stands are rare, and most are heavily interplanted with bananas, pruning has until quite recently been at a minimum, and spraying therefore impossible. Most of the trees are old, and some very old, though 2 million or so planted since 1954 are in relatively good order. Yields are almost incredibly low, the average being probably less than 2 cwt per acre. The co-operative societies and their Union are however reasonably well run, and the Bukoba mill has been reconditioned and is technically efficient. The Agricultural Department in 1961 claimed that production could be doubled in five years merely by pruning, spraying and better picking, but what is really wanted is a replanting programme. Neither is likely on a large scale, and production is unlikely to change much, whatever happens to prices.

Turning now to Uganda, the robusta area is a crescent, 35 to 40 miles deep, running round the northern end of Lake Victoria, which produced only some 35,000 tons in the early 1950's but today produces about 120,000 tons. In addition, the Bugisu district on the slopes of Mt. Elgon produces about 4000 tons of arabicas. Of the robusta production, non-African owned estates account for some 5000 tons: the rest is grown by over 400,000 African farmers on plots which average about $1\frac{1}{4}$ acres, though there are a few much larger holdings. Banana interplanting is rare, except temporarily for new coffee, but the average yield is probably only about $4\frac{1}{2}$ cwt per acre though some farmers get 7 to 8 cwt. Most coffee farmers employ some labour, mainly migrant, but manuring or spraying is deemed unnecessary, and pruning is apt to be erratic, so that once the trees are planted, cultivation boils down to weeding. The coffee is almost all sun-dried, much on mats raised off the ground but much on mats laid on the ground. The continuity and abundance of rainfall helps to give relatively high yields, but creates great difficulties in proper drying: hence the outstanding characteristic of the Uganda robusta industry is quantity rather than quality, and the coffee is on the whole below the average quality of the African Franc zone, especially the Ivory Coast, and definitely below that of the estate production of Angola. Hulling and marketing have been organized and controlled by the Uganda Government in a rather complicated system, and big changes have recently been made so that no summary will be attempted here. Suffice it to add that though the crop is likely to increase somewhat in the next few years, Uganda should have no great difficulty in keeping within her probable export quotas under the International Agreement. Opinions differ as to the effects on production of a substantial fall in prices below the 1962 level: some think that the farmers would lose heart, and that quantity and quality would go down and down: others think that hired labour would be replaced by the farmers themselves getting down to a real day's work, and that the crop would be maintained for at least two or three years, though after that the decline would be cumulative. Certainly, if need be, Uganda could be a low cost producer of robusta, but unless quality can be improved, the price obtained might also be very low in the event of a general excess of coffee supplies.

The Bugisu arabica industry is run by probably the most primitive tribe in Uganda. Three-quarters of the 50,000 growers on Mt. Elgon are said to be illiterate; beer drinking of a pleasant soporific sort occupies them after midday; their $\frac{1}{4}$ to $\frac{1}{2}$ acre plots of coffee are inter-planted with bananas which are exchanged for the maize posho from which their beer is made; and though coffee is the main cash crop, cash has a limited utility. The cultivation of their coffee is spasmodic; one-third of the trees need re-planting; individual hand pulping and fermentation often takes place under most primitive conditions: and improvement will be slow, though its scope is large. Troubles in the co-operative societies and the Union have not helped. The body and flavour of Bugisu coffee are intrinsically of lower quality than Kenya coffees, but up to 1962 an avoidable deterioration in Bugisu coffee was taking place. In short, the industry presents a pretty problem to the Uganda Government if the potential quantity and quality of the crop are to be realized.

These sketches of the various coffee regions of East Africa must be supplemented by some indication of the importance of coffee in the national economies of the three countries, and of their coffee industries in relation to the world's coffee production. From 1957 to 1962 Kenya's exports of coffee fetched £10·5 million annually, increased volume just balancing the decline in prices, and coffee accounted for roughly 20 per cent of Kenya's total exports, no other single export reaching £5 million. Tanganyika's exports in 1960, 1961 and 1962 averaged rather over 400,000 bags as against Kenya's 500,000 bags; the value was around £7 million, and this was 13 per cent of Tanganyika's total exports, sisal exports being double the value of coffee exports. Uganda's coffee exports averaged in the same period about £16 million, which was over 40 per cent of total exports, cotton providing rather less than another 40 per cent. But it may be observed that even Uganda's dependence on coffee exports is small compared with Brazil's 60 per cent, and Colombia's 80 per cent, not to mention such smaller countries as El Salvador and some of the other African producing countries. Turning to East Africa's position in the coffee world, Kenya and Tanganyika's exports of mild coffees, a total of say 800,000 bags, compares with world exports of milds totalling 15 million bags; and even Uganda's exports of 1·9 million bags is less than one-fiftieth of world exports of robusta. But it is only fair to add that the quality of her coffee makes Kenya a rather dangerous-looking competitor in Latin American eyes, while Angola's robusta production, and even that of the Ivory Coast, are not so far ahead of Uganda's even if they are also ahead as regards quality.

So much for the general character of East Africa's coffee industries: now let us turn to the world outside. It is impossible to present here an adequate picture of the state of affairs in the whole coffee world, and so I hope that the very sketchy outline which now follows can be regarded to some extent as being of an introductory nature. The situation in Brazil of course dominates the picture. After the end of the second world war, the price of all coffees started to rise rapidly and greatly, and finally this culminated in the great boom of 1954 when the price of Brazils touched one U.S. dollar a lb. This resulted in the planting of enormous areas in Parana, and hence by about 1957 Brazil's crop began greatly to exceed the amounts which could be exported at the current level of prices, say about 50 cents, or indeed at much lower prices, for at least in short periods demand is very inelastic. Brazil then started a policy of retention of supplies by stockpiling, and so managed to slow down the fall in the price and to avoid any market collapse. If Brazil had not taken some such defensive action, the export price would have fallen to a very low level, and this would have had two results – a severe drop in coffee's export earnings, and the financial ruin of many producers, large and small, in the older high-cost coffee areas. Brazilian industrial interests were adamant that export earnings must be at least maintained, and the ruin of large numbers of coffee farmers would have been politically and socially dangerous. With the aid of agreements, first with other Latin American producers and gradually extended to cover most of the important producing countries of the world, the price of Santos Grade 4 coffee in New York was virtually stabilized from mid-1959 to mid-1961 at around 36 cents, though it then slipped to 34 cents. This, however, was only achieved at the cost of a declining volume of Brazilian exports, mainly due to the growth of African robusta production, and of stockpiling at least 50 million bags. (It may be interjected that the world's annual consumption of all coffees was about 44 million bags, and Brazil's exports about 18 million bags.) The financial costs of the defence policy were roughly half the price per bag exported, i.e. the farmer received about half the export price. For the new farmers in Parana, and the lower-cost producers elsewhere, this was not too bad, but the higher-cost producers in the states of Sao Paulo, Southern Minas and Espirito Santo were hard pressed to make ends meet. The low-cost producers could probably produce say 20 million bags, i.e. more than Brazil's exports, at an f.o.b. price of 15 cents per lb, but Brazil could not use her position as a low-cost producer without ruining her higher-cost farmers, of whom many of the larger ones had great political influence, and almost certainly creating a big drop in her total national export earnings.

Meantime developments in the mild countries of Latin America were by comparison unimportant. Mild production there had always been slowly expanding, but the resources of land and labour have never permitted waves of large-scale expansion as in Brazil. Colombia, the second largest coffee-producing country in the world with an exportable production of 7 million bags on which she depends for 80 per cent of her total exports, joined with Brazil in restricting exports, not because the Colombian industry is relatively high cost – the reverse is the case – but because the government dared not risk a drop in coffee export earnings and the consequent hold-up to national economic development. Colombia by 1961 had stockpiled about 5 million bags. Brazil and Colombia shouldered the main burden of upholding prices; the other mild countries, as the price of joining the agreements, exacted quotas which did not mean any appreciable restriction.

Parallel with the great expansion of Brazil's crop was the expansion of Africa's total exports from less than 6 million bags in 1954 to over 11 million bags in 1961, mostly of course robustas. The first part of this expansion was the result of the great rise in coffee prices up to 1954, but it is very doubtful whether it would have continued after 1957 if the price fall of arabicas had not been checked by Brazil's retention policy, and if this had not been reinforced by a rapid increase in the world's demand for robustas for the manufacture of soluble coffee. By maintaining arabica prices, moreover, Brazil was unable to compete with robustas for a share in this rapid increase in the demand for the raw material for soluble coffees: Africa had this market to herself, and was able to sell almost her whole production at reasonable prices. If there had been less expansion of African robusta production, it is certain that the demand for lower-grade Brazils would have been much greater.

Such in broadest outline was the situation in 1961 when negotiations for a fully fledged international commodity control agreement began in earnest towards the end of that year, following the announcement that the United States was willing to join a long-term coffee agreement and regarded the stabilization of the then current price level as a desirable objective. Eventually 36 exporting countries, 22 importing countries and the representatives of 13 other nations met in New York in July and August 1962, and after six weeks' negotiations approved an Agreement, which virtually came into force almost at once, though it was not finally ratified until well into 1964. By a very strong system of regulating exports and effectively limiting the exports of non-members, the Agreement expressly sought to ensure that the 'general level of coffee prices does not decline below the general level of such prices in 1962', thus assuring the world's coffee farmers of remuneration at least on that scale, and the exporting countries of at least a maintenance of their coffee export earnings.

The truth is that this coffee agreement is a political agreement, for which the United States must bear most of the responsiblity. It is not for the economist to judge the wisdom of political decisions, but he should nevertheless point out their economic consequences. The Agreement virtually prevents any adjustment of the price level of coffee downwards towards genuine costs of production, and any adjustment of sources of supply in accordance with the demand for their particular qualities of coffee, and with their relative production costs. It does little or nothing to bring about the elimination of obsolescent high-cost capacity – indeed it really gives it a new lease of life – and it hinders the expansion of new low-cost industries, such as the African industry in Kenya; while it must seriously reduce, even if it does not completely prevent, the spread of improved techniques, which in some countries, such as Colombia, would greatly increase yields and thereby lower costs. The world's consumers of coffee are to continue to pay prices which are far above the level which would reign if demand and supply were in equilibrium. At the end of the five years of the Agreement, the problems of price adjustment, and of adjusting sources of supply in accordance with their relative costs, will remain to be solved: and the difficulties then may well be greater than they were in 1962.

These remarks may appear out of place in view of the tremendous rise in prices during the last twelve months. As the combined result of a frost in Parana and severe drought over the whole coffee regions of Brazil, the Brazilian crop for 1964 is estimated at not more than 10 million bags as compared with her export quota of about 18 million bags. One might suppose that with 50 million bags in store in Brazil, this crop failure would not have shot the Brazilian price up to 50 cents, but merchants and roasters were uncertain whether the quality of the stocks would prove to be satisfactory, and there was a panic rush to secure new crop supplies, while all consuming interests wanted to replenish stocks which they had reduced to a minimum while prices looked like falling rather than rising. The supply of robustas, as limited by the International Agreement, was also inadequate to meet the increase in market demand, and robustas price rose for this reason, and also in natural sympathy with the rise in Brazils. A small increase of about 3 per cent in export quotas, plus special concessions to Angola, Ivory Coast and Uganda to enable them to reduce the stocks which had been accumulated as a result of the Agreement, were eventually agreed upon last February by the International Coffee Council, and further concessions were made last August. There are signs that the boom has nearly spent itself, but it will very likely take another year before any considerable decline in the price gets under way, and no one can guess what the reactions of the International Coffee Council may be then. There is, however, little doubt that the Latin American producing countries at least, will be in favour of maintaining prices at the highest possible level.

This boom can only be a temporary affair. The drought in Brazil may well have weakened the bearing capacity of the trees, especially the older trees, for perhaps two or even three years, and the frost has temporarily maimed a considerable proportion of the trees in Parana. But not many trees in Parana have been killed, and not many of the older trees elsewhere have been abandoned. In due course Brazil will be producing very large crops again: fundamentally, if for a time only potentially, the problem of excess capacity remains. The future seems to me to hold two possibilities. One is that the International Agreement will be continued indefinitely, though perhaps with slowly declining prices under the pressure of excess supplies and of the interests of consuming members; and the present artificial basis of the whole industry, heavily subsidized by the consumer, will continue with little progress towards solving the problem of adjusting the general price level to costs of production, or the problem of adjusting sources of supply in accordance with their relative costs. The other possibility is that the International Agreement will not be renewed, either because of the reluctance of consuming members to continue to subsidize the producing countries by paying artificially high prices for their coffees, or because the African countries will want freedom to expand their production, and it is even possible that Colombia might come to the same point of view in order to take advantage of the new techniques of production. If this should happen, there will inevitably be a dog fight between Brazil and the robusta-producing countries of Africa. If the price of Brazils were to fall to its economic level, which for a crop of at least 20 million bags may be reckoned at somewhere around 15 cents, then at the same differential between Brazils and robustas as that ruling before the present boom, the price of robustas might be somewhere around 8 cents instead of the 20 cents of 1962. Even if the differential became smaller, and the robusta price was say 10 cents, it is very doubtful whether African farmers would continue to be interested in coffee, and unless the costs of estate production in Angola are lower than seems possible, robusta production may well shrink almost as rapidly as it has grown. Robusta has so far been the main raw material for soluble coffees, and for this it has some technical manufacturing advantages over arabica coffees, but fundamentally it is all a matter of relative prices: if Brazils become really cheap, soluble manufacturers will gradually switch, and sell a better quality product at the same sort of price as at present. I am not saying that this will happen, but it is important to realize that it is a possibility. The boom in robusta production developed primarily because of the shortage, and therefore the relatively high price, of Brazils: with the price of Brazils on a cost of production basis, robusta production in Africa may turn out to be very largely a transient phenomenon.

In this world setting, and with an eye to the uncertainties of the future, what advice should be given to the three countries of East Africa? Kenya will almost certainly have a most difficult problem of production in increasing excess of the present basic export quota during the rest of the life of the present International Agreement, but it may be supposed that she will receive special allowances and that somehow these difficulties will be surmounted. The maintenance of the high quality of Kenya's estate and African production is however an absolute essential, and this should be the overwhelming concern of the government, especially of course in respect of the African industry. Provided quality is maintained, the African industry is potentially a large very low-cost producer of high-quality mild coffee. Its expansion has been stopped by the International Agreement, and that means that the economic progress of a large part of the population has been heavily restricted. Kenya joined the International Agreement because she virtually had no option but to do so: the sooner Kenya can safely get free of any such restrictive scheme the better. On the other hand, Tanganyika's position is very different. There are nothing like the potentialities for expansion as in Kenya; much of the present production, both estate and African, is relatively high cost; and the country's export earnings from coffee are not so relatively important. Obviously anything which can be done to improve the quality of Tanganyika's coffees, and to reduce costs of production, should be done, but Tanganyika on the whole probably stands to gain by an international control scheme more than she is likely to lose. Uganda's position is different again. There should be no great difficulty in disposing of the robusta crops of the next few years, even though they will continue to increase, for some rejection of the worst produce would only help in that respect, but would also be a wise move in itself. Uganda is, if need be, a low-cost producer, but of low-quality coffees, and the most important advice that can be given both for the robusta industry and also for the little Bugisu arabica industry on Mt. Elgon is somehow to raise the average quality, even if it takes time as well as much effort. The International Agreement has this merit from Uganda's point of view that it gives a breathing space for doing this. At the same time cultivation standards, which at present leave much to be desired, should also be improved so as to reduce costs. Whether Uganda should continue to support an international control scheme if secession became a practical possibility, seems to me to depend largely on the views of the other African producers of robusta, for all would be well advised to stick together even if they cease their present alliance with the Latin American countries. Finally, all three East African countries should of course be advised to develop other export crops in case coffee lets them down, but I put this point last and not first, because it is so difficult to name other crops which at present look like being more remunerative substitutes for coffee.

Agricultural Commodity Projections, Real Growth and the Gains from Trade

*

This paper begins with a review of the general framework of agricultural commodity projections since most of the basic assumptions and general principles adopted in studies of this kind are relevant to the theme of this Seminar. Moreover, much of the discussion in subsequent sections of the paper also draws upon material assembled in Edinburgh for two studies of long-term demand for, and supply of, agricultural products in Nigeria and Ghana.[1] The special problems of measuring changes in the subsistence food sector are then examined at some length before looking at estimates of real growth in Ghana and Uganda during the past decade. Particular attention has been given to these countries which provide good case-studies of externally dependent peasant economies. The final section of the paper is concerned with movements in their terms of trade.

Agricultural commodity projections

The commodity projection studies with which we have been concerned were confined to foodstuffs and related items, drink and tobacco, for which the major end-use was personal consumption within Nigeria and Ghana respectively. On the demand side it is possible to make projections with the aid of fairly straight-forward econometric techniques. Indeed, most recent studies[2] use a simple projection model which expresses the relationship between demand and income in terms of elasticity coefficients computed from cross-section analysis of household budget studies, time-series or international comparisons. Since the unit of analysis is generally expressed in terms of households or consumption units, the projected change in aggregate demand for

---

[1] *Nigeria: Determinants of Projected Level of Demand, Supply and Imports of Farm Products in 1965 and 1975*. ERS-Foreign-32, U.S. Department of Agriculture, August 1962 and *Ghana: Projected Level of Demand, Supply and Imports of Agricultural Products in 1965, 1970 and 1975*. Report submitted to USDA, March 1964.

[2] Cf. *FAO Agricultural Commodities—Projections for 1970* E/CN.13/48. CCP 62/5. Rome, 1962; L. M. Goreux, *Income Elasticity for the Demand for Food: Household Survey Analysis* FAO AGRI/WP.7/2, 22 June 1959; and *Long Term Projections of Demand for and Supply of Selected Agricultural Commodities, 1960/61 to 1975/76*. National Council of Applied Economic Research. New Delhi, April 1962.

individual commodities or expenditure groups is obtained by combining population and income effects.

Although economic theory has long emphasized the importance of price-consumption relationships, long-term demand projections for foodstuffs are usually made under the assumption of constant prices. Neither changes in relative prices nor changes in price elasticities are considered, since it is rarely possible to make realistic assumptions about long-term price movements or obtain sufficient data on the many complex relations between price and consumption. Fortunately in dealing with broad categories of consumer expenditure such as all food, clothing, etc., it is safe to assume that price influences are less important than either income or non-economic factors. Moreover, as demand for all food is normally price inelastic, price change may be expected to influence the retail level and composition of food expenditure rather than the total volume purchased. Price effects are obviously more important where there are close substitutes within any given expenditure category, e.g. in Ghana between imported rice and locally produced grains or between different kinds of meat and fish. In low income countries price effects are usually considered to be more important than in high-income countries. (In the case of cocoa, where price appears to be a major factor influencing grindings by manufacturers in North America and Western Europe, or in the case of food products subject to major technical innovations, a price variable may have to be included in the projection model.) Usually, however, it is sufficient to consider the influence of price at the final stage of reconciliation between demand and supply projections.

The influences of non-economic factors affecting demand are more difficult to assess quantitatively than income and price and are therefore rarely introduced explicitly in demand projections. In tropical Africa the more important of these influences are probably connected with occupation, urbanization, ethnic or religious characteristics. Since occupation is closely tied to the geographical distribution of the population, and urban/rural differences in consumption patterns have long been a notable feature of family budget inquiries, some demand studies proceed on the basis of separate projections for urban and rural consumers respectively. Where the unit of analysis is the household it is also necessary to specify household size as a determining variable. Similarly it may be necessary to take account of differential growth rates as between different ethnic/religious groups. The combined influence of many of these factors which can be expected to change steadily over time may therefore be introduced in the form of a time trend.

In the case of our recent work on Nigeria and Ghana the projection models were based simply upon changes in population and income, various demand functions estimated from cross-section and time-series data and actual consumption calculated for a base period. Our limited excursion into econometric techniques may be defended on the grounds that for the data readily available and under the assumptions that we made about probable changes in population and income, the simple models provide as useful a first approximation as alternative and probably more 'scientific' calculations. Indeed, for the projection period 1960 to 1975 population growth may be expected to remain the predominant factor influencing aggregate demand for most foodstuffs consumed in West Africa.

While it is possible to project demand under various specific assumptions about the behaviour of relevant variables, projection of supply (agricultural production) presents more difficult problems. In the case of Ghana, for example, even the most simple of projection techniques – extrapolation of past trends – cannot be applied to those farm products produced for domestic consumption. Indeed, no single comprehensive census of agricultural production is yet available for Ghana, although a pilot survey is now taking place in preparation for a full census in 1964-65. Under West African peasant farming conditions it is particularly difficult to define, let alone measure, yields or acreages under mixed and successive crops, and neither FAO nor other experts have as yet much experience with large-scale censuses.

It is usual therefore for African government statisticians, concerned primarily with measuring the contribution of agriculture to total output, to estimate production not 'on the ground' or 'at the farm gate' but at some stage nearer final consumption, i.e. at organized markets, as exports f.o.b. or from sample surveys of family budgets. In Ghana, as in other Commonwealth African countries, export products are well documented by Marketing Boards or in Trade Reports. The same is true of certain cash crops sold to large domestic processing establishments; for example tobacco and limes. However, even in the case of cocoa and other tree crops grown in forest areas, it is not possible to measure acreages or tree numbers, and hence yields. It is not surprising therefore that methods of recording mixed and successive crops have still to be tested and that only the most approximate estimates of production are available, based partly on sample surveys of farms, on experimental farm records, on 'deemed' output necessary to satisfy dietary requirements or on 'impressions' of agricultural officers. Available information on production, produce movements and market prices suggest that over the decade 1951 to 1960 total Ghana domestic output of staple foods rose broadly in line with population. However, over the longer post-war period 1948 to 1962, at least three distinct phases may be discerned from movements in local market prices. First, a period of rapid increase in local food prices from 1948 to 1951,

G

which suggests that domestic food supplies were inelastic with respect
to increases in demand, arising from the expansion of cocoa farmers'
incomes especially. However, from 1951 to 1960 the annual rise in
local prices was much slower, particularly in the earlier years 1952 to
1955, despite the fact that personal cash incomes were increasing
rapidly. During this period commercialized food farming developed
rapidly, assisted partly by an improved road transport system. Cocoa
farmers are also reported to have extended their cultivation of food
crops. In 1961 adverse climatic conditions led to a serious reduction
in food production and sharp increases in urban market prices
occurred. However, in the following year supplies improved, so that
further price increases were moderate, in spite of the restrictions
placed upon imported foods towards the end of 1962.

It would appear therefore that over the post-war period as a whole
total output has risen with the expansion of the rural labour force,
which has worked a larger area of land by traditional farming methods.
There is little evidence (from price changes) of a persistent imbalance
between demand and supply of basic energy foods, roots and tubers,
plantains, etc., which can be grown easily throughout the forest zone
and the coastal areas. Acute shortages on a national scale have been
limited to years of poor harvests 1947-48, 1950-51 and 1961-62, which
through price increases had the effect of stimulating local production
as well as imports.

However, this does not mean that domestic food production, distribution and seasonal storage facilities have been adequate to avoid
widespread problems of under-nutrition in the northern part of the
country or deficient nutritional standards for the vast bulk of population. Since traditional peasant farming methods are not likely to close
either the seasonal 'hungry gap' in the north or the low level of nutrition elsewhere, the Ghana Government plans 'revolutionary' changes
in farm practices and the organization of marketing. Ambitious food
production targets have been set in the new Development Plan, aimed
at eliminating nutritional deficiencies in the present diet, reducing food
imports and providing for the growth in population. The long-run
nutritional objective provides for a daily intake of 2700 calories per
head, which is reckoned to be about 50 per cent greater than the
current intake. However, it is hoped that most of the increase in staple
foods will come from cereals, legumes and oils, which also provide
protein, rather than roots and tubers. Large-scale state farms in the
savannah areas are expected to play a leading role in supplying food
to urban areas. Another important development of food planned for
the seven years to 1970 involves a large expansion in marine fisheries,
which are expected to make up most of the deficiency in animal protein.

Since extrapolation of past trends in acreage, yields or total output of peasant farms cannot provide a sound basis for supply projections in many African countries, it is also difficult to place undue reliance on official targets included in national development plans. Where, as in Ghana, considerable emphasis in the new Seven Year Plan is also placed on large-scale state farms there are few guides available for assessing potential achievement. Experience of large-scale farming and ranching ventures in other tropical African countries over the post-war period suggests that ambitious targets, involving state-management, extensive use of machinery, fertilizers, better seed and rotations, are extremely difficult to achieve quickly. Again, replacement of shifting cultivation by 'settled' farming systems require a high degree of co-operation and the application of expensive extension services. It can be done in existing areas of close settlement, which are in any case often areas of high agricultural potential, given requisite government action or popular enthusiasm. The success of the Swynnerton Plan in the Central Province of Kenya or the development of commercialized food farming in Buganda and the Eastern Province of Uganda are cases in point. However, a great deal of experimentation with alternative crops, types of seeds and farming systems will be required before Ghana can attain rapid expansion along new lines.

While we were unable to assess how far nutritional standards could be raised from local food supplies over the next decade, we found it useful to compare various official production targets with projections of aggregate demand. In so far as demand and supply projections are determined separately, this comparison indicates the extent of discrepancies, since in the last analysis demand and supply are not independent. What is not available from domestic production plus imports cannot be consumed, and price adjustments are necessary to reconcile the two sides. In Ghana, as in other low-income countries in which agriculture is the main economic activity, there is, in addition, a close connection between the rate of growth in total output (G.D.P.) and final consumers' demand, on the one hand, and the expansion of agricultural production, on the other.

It follows therefore that a high growth rate for G.D.P. (say 5 per cent for developing countries) will require a relatively high growth rate for agricultural production (say approaching 4 per cent a year).[1] In our recent study of Ghana, in which we projected personal consumption (our demand variable) at 4·5 per cent per annum from 1960 to 1975, output of local foodstuffs would have to expand by 3·6 per cent per annum to be consistent with the increase in aggregate demand at constant prices.

The close inter-dependence between agricultural production and

[1] See *FAO Agricultural Commodities—Projections for 1970, op. cit.* p. A-50.

G.D.P. in low-income countries is reflected not only in a large agricultural component in total output and employment on the supply side but also in the major weight accorded to food consumption and primary exports in final demand. Since, however, the agricultural sector of the economy (excluding exports) is usually the most difficult to measure accurately for national income calculations, in practice estimates of domestic food consumption and food farm output are based directly or indirectly upon available population data. We have already referred to the predominant influence of population in demand projections for foodstuffs, and as the same data are also used for estimates of food farmers' output, there is some danger of assuming away a most important economic problem facing tropical countries – the availability of domestic food supplies and the pressure of population on available natural resources.

Subsistence output

With the notable exception of Nigeria where serious attempts have been made to measure the annual output of crops grown for domestic use,[1] the contribution of peasant-grown food crops to G.D.P. in most of tropical Africa is calculated on an annual basis by adjusting a base year estimate for movements in population and prices. In Ghana the current official estimates of G.D.P. rely heavily upon the preliminary findings of a comprehensive sample – the National Household Expenditure Survey, 1961-62.[2] Expenditure on local foodstuffs, including subsistence, is calculated at market prices for the years from 1955 to date by applying weighted indices of population and prices to a constant per capita quantum.[3] In East Africa a variety of methods have been employed to arrive at a base-year quantum, but here again annual changes in African-grown food crops are made dependent upon population changes.[4] Fairly arbitrary adjustments are also made

[1] See P. N. C. Okigbo, *Nigerian National Accounts 1950-1957*, Federal Ministry of Economic Development, Enugu, 1953, p. 62. These (official) estimates, based upon a product approach pioneered by A. R. Prest and I. G. Stewart, *The National Income of Nigeria, 1950-51*, HMSO, 1953, must remain independent of population weights since these are highly unreliable!
[2] See P. T. F. Golding, 'An Enquiry into Household Expenditure and Consumption and Sale of Household Produce in Ghana'. *Economic Bulletin* (Accra) Vol. VI, No. 4, 1962.
[3] See D. Walters, *Report on the National Accounts of Ghana, 1955-1961*, Accra, 1962.
[4] For a general review of the East African position, see T. A. Kennedy, H. W. Ord and David Walker, 'On the Calculation and Interpretation of National and Accounting Material in East Africa', in *African Studies in Income and Wealth* (ed. L. H. Samuels), Bowes and Bowes, 1963. In Kenya a 2 per cent compound growth rate is assumed for total African food crop production; estimated recorded cash sales for each year are then deducted to derive a subsistence residual (see East African Statistical Department, *Domestic Income and Product in Kenya*,

for nation-wide crop failures, for example the drought in 1960. However it is apparent that something like a constant *per capita* output/consumption of local foods is the basic assumption which determines the main component of G.D.P. With this as a datum, many of the conclusions drawn from analysis of movements in G.D.P. must be viewed with considerable caution.

Having issued the usual warnings about deficiencies of data, this paper offers no exception to the general practice of proceeding to measure movements in various aggregates as if they were accurate within tolerable limits. However, since improvements in statistical information on the African rural sector will obviously be a very slow process, the need to examine basic assumptions and the methodology of estimation is correspondingly greater.

There are, of course, some commentators who take the view that there is no need to measure subsistence at all. Miss Ady, for example, has recently argued that subsistence outlay is always self-balancing, has little impact on the rest of the economy, is not subject to sudden or serious year-to-year fluctuations 'except in cases of some national calamity' and is in any case a small and diminishing proportion of total G.D.P. 'Thus in the short period changes in subsistence and other rural-sector income can be taken as zero . . . the chief variable and income generating component in the tropical economies of Africa is the value of exports.'[1]

There is obviously a strong case for confining many analyses of price and income stability to the monetary economy,[2] although short-term instability in the exchange sectors may also arise from changes in subsistence output. However any discussion of long-term growth can hardly ignore the performance of subsistence activities which may account for a very large proportion of G.D.P. It may be objected that the assumption of constant subsistence output/consumption of local foodstuffs is too unrealistic even in the short run, since variations in climate, animal and plant diseases, civil strife, etc., may conspire to change physical output from year to year. On the other hand, under existing peasant farming systems, attempts to measure seasonal or short-term changes in output may be subject to even larger statistical errors.[1]

It is also difficult to assess the extent of even 'sudden and serious national calamities'. Since, by definition, subsistence output is not

[1] P. Ady, 'Uses of National Accounts in Africa', in *African Studies in Income and Wealth, op. cit.*, p. 64.
[2] E.g. the recent studies of instability in Uganda and Tanganyika by A. I. MacBean.

1954-1958, p. 19). In Tanganyika unrecorded output is adjusted for population change. In Uganda staple crops are also raised by population (East African Statistical Department, *The Gross Domestic Product of Uganda, 1954-1959*, p. 23).

marketed, price movements in rural areas may be based upon a narrow range of market transactions in 'surplus' produce. Indeed, in many countries a regular price series is in fact available only for one or two larger urban centres and it is these data that have to be used to impute a value to subsistence and unrecorded marketed output. Nevertheless, considerable use may be made of these price movements. If *per capita* subsistence consumption is assumed to be constant in real terms (nutritional intake per consumption unit?), seasonal and other short-run fluctuations in output will be reflected in movements in the volume and price level of marketed surpluses. In an open economy with a large exchange sector, Ghana for example, a rise in local food prices will stimulate imports. If these are close substitutes for local staples they will restrain local price movements and restrict a shift in the terms of trade in favour of local food producers.[1] This tendency seems to have been operating in West Africa during the past decade, and may create a ratchet effect which frustrates a rapid growth of commercialized food farming.

How this works may be seen from a closer analysis of the subsistence sector. Here we have to rely upon a number of widely held opinions rather than facts. The first is that there is no overall shortage of land in tropical Africa and thus output is largely limited by seasonal short-ages of labour for clearing, planting and harvesting. The 'effective' supply of land could therefore be increased easily by changes in pro-duction techniques which would provide additional employment between seasonal peaks and economise labour at these times (e.g. by measures to replace shifting cultivation with settled farming systems). In addition it is believed that in traditional subsistence economies a good deal of underemployment is voluntary in the sense that producers limit labour inputs rather than forego non-economic activities.[2] Once a predetermined subsistence level is attained the effort curve is in-creasingly inelastic with respect to (cash) income. In terms of price responses much will depend upon the real returns available from cash sales of surplus food. In 'bumper' crop seasons 'surplus' crops may be harvested if the extra effort can be compensated with an adequate supply of 'trade' goods. But since the 'real' price of these may also be high, because of depressed prices ruling for surplus food, the extra

[1] D. Seers, 'Normal Growth and Distortions: Some Techniques of Structural Analysis', *Oxford Economic Papers*, March 1964, p. 82 *et seq*. deals with the related problem of assessing bottlenecks in domestic food production from comparisons of time-series and cross-section demand functions. In Ghana, for example, high elasticity coefficients estimated from time-series for imported food indicate inter-nal distortions.

[2] Cf. M. Yudelman, 'Some Aspects of African Agricultural Development', *International Economic Association, Economic Development for Africa South of the Sahara* (ed. E. A. G. Robinson (Macmillan and Co., 1964, p. 571).

effort may not be forthcoming. On the other hand, since demand for food is both income and price inelastic, a fall in yields will probably induce extra efforts in harvesting and/or a reduction in food stores and sales of surpluses in order to maintain subsistence needs. In this case a rise in the real price of saleable food may not be reflected in larger cash sales. (In a 'closed' economy a persistent rise in food prices should cause some reallocation of labour in favour of food farming.) Although rarely made explicit, much of the development planning now envisaged in Africa will involve tackling this incentive aspect of peasant agriculture.

So far this discussion of the assumption of constant *per capita* subsistence consumption has been developed in terms of short-run adjustments of labour inputs, with seasonal variations in yields reflected in 'passive' movements in the size of marketable surpluses. Evidence of changes in marketable output may be appraised in some outline at least from fluctuations in market prices, produce movements and, in some cases, sales to marketing boards. Further support for the notion of stability of subsistence standards may also be drawn from the existence of different ecological zones, and the prevalence of mixed cropping over two harvesting seasons per annum will tend to cancel out variations between districts and months of the year for the larger tropical countries.

What of longer-run considerations? Constant subsistence standards obviously depend upon the continued availability of cultivable land and/or a steady improvement in yields. One manifestation of increasing population pressure in certain areas has been a reduction in the resting period for land left fallow under shifting cultivation methods, with adverse effects upon soil fertility and yields. Previously uncultivated land, e.g. far from water and roads or on less fertile soil, has been brought under permanent cultivation in populous districts, while farms have been developed in new areas of lower rainfall or poorer soils.[1] In both cases it must be expected that the average of crop yields would be decreased and thus more labour required to maintain consumption. On the other hand government investment in reclamation, tsetse clearance, etc., has tended to raise average yields and, in Uganda at least, the general opinion has been that farming families have not been called upon to work noticeably harder to provide own-food requirements.[2] Until comprehensive or detailed acreage and production statistics become available, these impressions of observers are about all the information readily at hand. Economists concerned with aggregate growth rates may, however, feel somewhat reassured that

[1] Cf. G. B. Masefield, *Agricultural Change in Uganda: 1945-1960*, Food Research Institute, Stanford, May 1962, pp. 93-94.
[2] G. B. Masefield, *op. cit.*, pp. 102-106.

in Africa at least there is little danger of excessive population pressure on limited natural resources.

There are, nevertheless, a number of important demographic issues of special relevance to economic growth projections. First, in spite of difficulties in estimating population increase from census data there is considerable evidence to suggest an acceleration in population increase over the past decade from perhaps 1 to 1½ per cent in the 1930's and 1940's to 2 to 2½ per cent. One important result of this faster growth has been a decline in the proportion of the population of working age – in many African countries 45 per cent fall into the 0 to 14 dependant age-group compared with around 30 to 35 per cent of a population growing more slowly.[1] Since the number of dependants has, been rising faster than the potential labour force, the assumption of *constant per capita consumption* requires some gradual improvement in average productivity per subsistence worker – sufficient at least to balance the fall in ratios of land/labour and labour/population. A major factor in this respect may be the increasing effectiveness of labour effort per man-hour resulting from public health measures as well as simple farm innovations such as the spread of new and 'easier' crops.

The influence of migration upon food production may be measured at least approximately from census and urban employment data. In West Africa, for example, where urban settlement has long been traditional, the population in rural areas may have risen by as little as 1 per cent per annum, compared with 7 or 8 per cent in the towns. Since opportunities for subsistence production are usually very limited in large towns, application of population growth rates weighted by geographical location provide a method of adjusting subsistence food output to take account of geographical movements in the distribution of labour and total population. While migration mainly involves adult males, who withdraw their labour from rural activities leaving dependants to be fed by the remaining rural labour force, the traditional division of farming tasks by age and sex, together with seasonal migration habits, allow many adult males to return for planting when male labour is most required.[2]

It would seem that the assumptions and methodology adopted for measuring growth in the subsistence sector are broadly consistent with the available facts and in accord with economic theory. This is reassuring since many economists and planners concerned with forecasts and predictions are not in a position to scrutinize primary data. Indeed, there is frequently a tendency to draw substantive conclusions

[1] J. J. Spengler, 'Population Movements and Problems in Sub-Saharan Africa', *I.E.A., op. cit.*, p. 302.
[2] E.g. R. W. M. Johnson, *African Agricultural Development in Southern Rhodesia: 1945-1950*, F.R.I., Stanford, May 1964, pp. 171-172.

from figures that add little to the basic components. In the case of movements in the subsistence sector, assumptions about population and price changes are combined with guesses about a base-year quantum and it is therefore important to have the right assumptions! If, as in high-income countries, subsistence or imputed transactions are relatively unimportant, there is a case for their exclusion in order to retain consistent indices. But in tropical Africa there are few countries in which subsistence activities account for less than one-quarter of total output. Moreover, where, as in East Africa, the official estimates distinguish between 'monetary' and 'unrecorded' output, there is probably a tendency to understate the weight to be assigned to peasant agriculture in any index of productive performance. The readier availability of 'income' and 'product' data for the monetary economy has encouraged this; by contrast the 'expenditure' approach adopted in Ghana keeps welfare considerations to the fore, cuts across production sector boundaries and provides the requisite categories for measuring changes in real terms by reference to the available price series.

Measurement of real growth

To date, official estimates of G.D.P. at constant prices have been calculated for Nigeria (from 1950 at 1957 prices); for Ghana (from 1955 at 1960 prices). For the East African territories various official and private calculations have been attempted with 1954 as the first year of the series.[1] Surprisingly enough, however, in view of both the relative importance of external trade and the extent of fluctuations in export prices, little attempt has so far been made to distinguish that component of real income attributable to movements in the terms of trade. Indeed, in some cases it is not clear to the general reader of published statistics whether the constant price series represents an index of production (real domestic product) or real expenditure available (domestic income received). The difference, arising from effects of shifts in the terms of trade, has been considerable in many African countries and has, of course been the subject of considerable public and academic discussion in recent years. Clearly, selection of appropriate price indices and base years influence the magnitude and, in some cases, the net effects of movements in the terms of trade. However, the year-to-year shifts have often been so pronounced in the commodity terms of trade that some effort to measure possible gains and losses appears to

[1] In particular, C. P. Haddon-Cave, 'Real Growth of the East African Territories, 1954-60', *East African Economics Review*, Vol. 8, No. 1, June 1961. See also *Real Growth in the Uganda Economy, 1954-1962*, Statistics Branch, Ministry of Economic Development, Entebbe, 1964. The calculations presented in this paper below are, however, independent of this official exercise.

be worth attempting. For this paper Ghana and Uganda have been taken as case studies. Both countries probably represent extreme examples of dependent economies. For this reason, however, the performance of their economies over the past decade is of special interest in appraising the wider question of primary exports and economic growth in tropical Africa.

Ghana's G.D.P. at current and constant (1960) market prices from 1950 to 1962 is summarized by main expenditure components in Table 1. From the constant price series, it would appear that both real product produced and real expenditure expanded over the period 1950 to 1962 at annual growth rates of 4·8 and 4·2 per cent respectively. From 1950 to 1954 the annual increase in physical output was probably only just sufficient to keep pace with a population expanding at a little over 2 per cent, whereas favourable movements in the terms of trade enabled real income available to rise by nearly 6 per cent in aggregate or 4 per cent *per capita*. By contrast, between 1955 and 1962 output in quantitative terms is officially estimated to have risen by 4·8 per cent per annum, while real income rose by only 2·8 per cent.

Although neither estimates of aggregate output nor population movements are wholly reliable, the calculations, summarized in the form of index numbers in Table 1, indicate a rapid rise in *per capita* real income available during the earlier period of the decade from about £50 at constant (1960) prices in 1950-52 to £60 in 1954-55. This rate of improvement slackened between 1955 and 1958, but during the following two years rose sharply to a peak of some £70 in 1960. Similar trends in the movement of *per capita* G.D.P. have been noted for other primary exporting countries where the reversal of export prices after 1954 retarded growth rates. However, in the case of Ghana at least, deterioration in the barter terms of trade does not seem to have had a pronounced impact on the pace of internal economic development until 1961, when a combination of unhappy circumstances, notably a poor harvest of food crops and internal trading uncertainties resulted in a sudden check to the growth in physical output. A sharp fall in cocoa prices also reduced *per capita* real income, although personal consumption continued to rise sharply as the result of record payments to cocoa farmers and substantial increases in money wages.

In drawing up a new Seven Year Development Plan, 1963 to 1970, the Ghana Planning Commission has paid particular regard to movements in real domestic product, which provides an index of the productive performance of the economy after eliminating 'windfall' gains and losses attributable to shifts in the terms of trade. A 'planned' growth rate of 5·5 per cent per annum is envisaged for real G.D.P. throughout the new planning period, compared with a rate of growth of around 5 per cent realized from 1955 to 1961. Since future movements in

Ghana's terms of trade are of course difficult to forecast, there is considerable justification for using this measure of economic growth. Moreover, if it is also assumed that there will be no significant gains or losses resulting from further movements in the terms of trade, the-projected growth in real product will also represent real income available, which is a more appropriate welfare index. However, since the planners have adopted a development model in which the rate of capital formation is the main determinant, it is surprising that little attempt has been made to integrate the main components of domestic demand in a time series showing recent trends in real income (expenditure at constant prices).

Uganda's short-term economic situation differs from that of Ghana in one major respect; aggregate domestic demand has never exceeded the level of domestic output and to date the country has not been faced with the need to pursue deflationary policies to safeguard the external balance of payments. The problem is rather one of persistently deteriorating export prices which have denied Uganda much of the potential growth in real income arising from a rapid expansion in physical output over the past decade. According to one commentator:

> Uganda represents a classic case of the Marxist 'exploitation' of
> a primary producing country 'forced' to sell to industrial countries
> despite weakening market conditions for its products. Thus the
> 'sweat' of the peasant's toil has availed him little; in the year 1960,
> for instance, more than 17 per cent of the fruits of his labours was
> 'stolen' by 'rapacious capitalists' who 'rigged' produce markets for
> their own 'profit'.[1]

This comment by Mr C. P. Haddon-Cave, an economist working in Kenya, represents perhaps an extreme view and is based upon an heroic attempt to measure real growth rates in the three East African territories during the period 1954 to 1960. The objects of his exercise were

> first, to suggest a method whereby the influence of various price
> movements in the three money series (of G.D.P. in Kenya, Tan-
> ganyika and Uganda respectively) might be extracted to yield
> estimates of (*a*) total productivity and (*b*) real income consumed . . . ;
> and secondly, to analyse the results to see to what extent prevailing
> ideas must be modified and what comparisons and contrasts can
> be drawn as regards the determinants of growth in the three terri-
> tories.[2]

The concept of real domestic product produced (calculated by the separate deflation of export and import series) provides the 'productivity' measure, while 'real income consumed' is defined by expenditure

---

[1] Haddon-Cave, *op. cit.*, p. 8.
[2] Haddon-Cave, *op. cit.*, p. 2.

on G.D.P. at constant (internal) prices. By constructing fairly simple price indices, where none existed previously, Mr Haddon-Cave concludes that many of the assertions made by the Raisman Commission,[1] by the World Bank Mission to Tanganyika and in Budget Statements, and based largely on current priced series, are 'misleading and even inaccurate'. In particular they have exaggerated the growth rate achieved by Kenya and have underestimated both the productive performance and the 'losses' from trade experienced by Uganda. According to Mr Haddon-Cave's calculations, the following annual rates of growth were achieved:

Rates of growth of East African territories, 1954-1960[2]
(Per cent)

	Kenya	Tanganyika	Uganda
G.D.P. (current prices)	6·0	4·6	2·5
Real product produced	4·8	3·8	5·9
Real income available	4·0	2·9	2·5

In spite of various criticisms of Mr Haddon-Cave's paper, which have been largely concerned with the inadequacy of the basic statistical data rather than the conceptual issues involved[3] the figures quoted above clearly emphasize the divergent movements between the measures of growth and, in particular, the extreme position of Uganda.

Table 2 reproduces estimates of Uganda's G.D.P. at market prices for the longer period 1950 to 1961. The coverage of the G.D.P. at current prices and the deflationary techniques used differ from those adopted by Mr Haddon-Cave so that the following growth rates are derived for the same period 1954 to 1960: G.D.P. at current market prices, 3·1 per cent; real domestic product, 5·6 per cent; and real income, 3·0 per cent. Since the subsistence component is calculated on the simple assumption of a population increase of 2·5 per cent per annum, the growth in the monetary sector is more illuminating: 7·0 per cent for real product and 3·4 per cent for real income. During the earlier period 1950 to 1954 the respective growth rates were 5·3 per cent and 7·0 per cent, a clear reflection of the favourable movement in the terms of trade to 1954.

A simple comparison of longer term movements over the decade 1950 to 1960 shows a remarkable 'productive performance' of the Ghana and Uganda economies; in both cases real product grew at an average annual rate of 5·2 per cent. On balance, Ghana also ex-

[1] *Report of the East African Fiscal and Economic Commission*, Cmnd. 1279 H M S O London, 1961, especially paras. 65-68.
[2] Haddon-Cave, *op.* cit., p. 7 (Table 6).
[3] Notes and Comments in *East African Economics Review* by J. Tyrrell, and by D. A. Lury (Vol. 8, No. 2); and by B. F. Massell (Vol. 9, No. 2).

perienced a net gain from trade, with real income available rising at a rate of 5·4 per cent per annum. While Uganda, on the other hand, suffered a net loss from adverse movements in her income terms of trade, the average growth of 4·1 per cent in real income was, nevertheless, a considerable achievement for an economy more heavily structured towards subsistence activities and exports of agricultural products. Since the process of structural transformation must be very long-term for these countries, it is probable that the growth rates attained during the past decade will represent upper rather than lower limits within which to establish projection lines for development planning.

African economists and statisticians are now increasingly concerned with plans extending into the 1970's, most of which involve the assessment of their countries capacity to pay for imports. In this connexion assumptions about future movements in the terms of trade are especially relevant. Having suggested that a greater appreciation of real growth rates achieved in the recent past is a useful guide in forward planning, it may be useful in the next and final section of this paper to examine briefly the extent and direction of movements in the terms of trade as experienced by Ghana and Uganda over the past decade.

The Gains from Trade

Application of a base-weighted visible terms of trade index to that component of *Ghana* output sold abroad provided approximately the same measure of the 'gains' as the separate deflation of G.D.P. time-series shown in Table 1. It will be noted that the total gain from trade takes into account not only unit prices for export and imports (as represented in a barter terms of trade index) but also the volume and relative importance of exports in G.D.P. and that apparent changes in the purchasing power of a unit of exports is not, in itself, a reliable guide to the overall gains from trade.[1] In particular an apparent deterioration in the net barter terms of trade may be consistent with an overall gain if the total volume of exports is increasing. Table 3 shows clearly the divergence between the 'net barter' and 'income' terms of trade for Ghana over the past decade.

During the early years 1949 to 1953, the aggregate increase in 'real' export income, measured in terms of imports, was severely limited by the inelasticity of supply of exports – a typical feature of primary production of both tree crops and minerals. However, in 1954 both the 'income' and 'barter' terms of trade reflected to a similar degree the gain from a fall in cocoa supply. In subsequent years the inverse correlation between supply and export prices was reflected in movements in the barter terms of trade. The gradual rise in import

[1] G. S. Dorrance, 'The Income Terms of Trade', *Review of Economic Studies*, 1949-50, XVI, p. 50·

prices after 1955 simply reinforced the trend, with export price changes as the predominant influence. Increases in supply of exports have prevented aggregate real income from falling with export prices. In other words, much of the damage to the Ghana economy that might have followed the sharp deterioration in the barter terms of trade in 1956-57 and again from 1959 to the present time (1963) has been avoided by an expansion in the volume of exports.

Before leaving this brief review of Ghana's terms of trade, two important points should be emphasized. First, although the barter terms of trade have deteriorated since 1954, and especially since 1958, taking the period as a whole the import purchasing power of a unit of exports was still greater in 1961 than in 1949 and the 'real' cost of cocoa in consuming countries (if deflated by a general whole-sale price index for primary commodities or industrial raw materials) has remained well above the pre-war level. Secondly, the import purchasing power of total Ghana exports has shown a steady if somewhat erratic upward trend. Naturally, much depends upon the period under review and the selection of 1954 as a base year for the official indices obviously presents data for subsequent years in a poorer light. However, even the years 1955 to 1961 show, on balance, a considerable gain in the purchasing power of exports.

In the case of *Uganda*, the two principal export commodities, coffee and cotton, account for a small part of world trade, and movements in Uganda's output have little influence on world price trends. The comparative stability of real exports from 1954 to 1960 may be attributed to compensating movements in prices and quanta, in particular the sharp increase in coffee production in 1955 and again in 1960, years in which prices received for many of Uganda's export commodities (but not cotton) declined sharply. The 'terms of trade effect' had, however, a major impact upon both domestic income and the external trade balance towards the end of the period, from 1959, and by 1962 represented a 'loss' of real income of as much as one-eighth of domestic output. From Table 2 it will be observed that aggregate real income changed only slightly from 1957 to 1961, while 'real exports' showed a persistent fall (see also Table 4).

While 'rapacious capitalists' abroad may have contributed to Uganda's current situation, by developing synthetic substitutes for cotton for example, part of the stagnation in real income may also be attributed to a slower rate of growth in the volume of export production. Moreover, the greater diversity of Uganda's exports does not seem to have insulated earnings from fluctuations associated with agricultural production. In Ghana, on the other hand, variations in cocoa output have led to inverse price movements. Additional stability has also been afforded by exports of minerals and timber, the prices of which have either remained infinitely stable (for gold since 1949) or experienced a longer term improvement associated with the growth of demand in industrial countries (for timber, especially).

CONCLUSION

To conclude this paper a number of points may be emphasized. First, there is an obvious need for more studies in depth of the actual situation in the agricultural sectors of African countries and a more detailed analysis of factors influencing both demand for, and supply of, basic foodstuffs. Secondly, at the macroeconomic level, there is a great deal of fairly straight-forward work that can be done on the measurement of real changes in aggregate output and expenditure. The limited statistical data presented in this paper for Ghana and Uganda indicate a high growth rate during the recent past, which may be very difficult to surpass in the present 'Development Decade'. Thirdly, it would appear to be very difficult to generalize about the advantages to be derived from diversification as opposed to specialization in exports. Ghana seems to have done better from her heavy dependence on cocoa (plus some useful non-agricultural exports) than Uganda, with a more diverse range of agricultural commodities, none of which account for a large proportion of world trade – in sharp contrast to Ghana's leading world position in cocoa.

TABLE 1 Expenditure on Ghana gross domestic product, 1950-1962 (£ million)

	1950	1951	1952	1953	1954	1955	1956	1957	1958	1959	1960	1961	1962
(a) at current market prices													
Personal consumption	146	186	194	210	212	252	262	291	279	317	339	393	405
public consumption	11	13	18	18	21	26	30	33	35	39	48	55	63
gross fixed investment	25	35	37	41	39	52	56	56	55	75	96	104	96
increase in stocks	6	1	1	−3	2	..	5	−6	−1	10	11	−14	−6
domestic expenditure	188	235	250	266	274	330	353	374	368	441	494	538	558
external balance	+26	+27	+17	+12	+45	+4	−8	−11	+15	−6	−25	−41	−23
expenditure on G.D.P.	214	262	267	278	319	334	345	363	383	435	469	497	535
(b) at constant (1960) prices													
personal consumption	193	202	209	229	233	276	275	300	292	318	339	364	335
public consumption	17	18	23	24	28	32	33	36	38	42	48	53	60
domestic investment	41	35	37	41	49	64	69	56	59	91	107	85	86
domestic expenditure	251	255	269	294	306	372	377	392	389	451	494	502	481
external balance	+30	+26	+16	+12	+48	+4	−9	−11	+16	−6	−25	−41	−24
expenditure on G.D.P.	281	281	285	306	354	376	368	381	405	445	469	461	457
trading gain	−3	+5	−1	+2	+44	+21	−8	−7	+23	+12	..	−15	−35
real domestic product	284	276	286	304	310	355	376	388	382	433	469	476	492
Indices: 1960=100													
real domestic product	61	59	61	65	66	76	80	83	81	92	100	101	105
real domestic income	60	60	61	65	75	80	78	81	86	95	100	98	97
per capita income	75	74	73	77	87	91	87	88	91	97	100	96	92
per capita personal cons.	71	73	74	79	79	92	89	95	90	96	100	105	94

TABLE 2 Expenditure on Uganda gross domestic product (£ million)

	1950	1951	1952	1953	1954	1955	1956	1957	1958	1959	1960	1961	1962
(a) at current prices													
(1) G.D.P. at factor cost					129	140	142	147	147	149	152	157	155
(2) subsistence					36	38	39	37	41	41	41	45	49
(3) monetary economy					93	102	103	109	106	108	111	112	106
(4) money product at market prices (private estimate)	57	88	92	81	97	108	108	116	113	115	119	121	
(5) external balance	10	20	19	4	11	1	4	7	8	7	8	5	(5)
(6) domestic expenditure	47	68	73	77	87	107	104	109	105	108	109	116	
(7) gross fixed investment	9	11	17	20	19	25	25	24	20	17	17	16	15
(8) public consumption	5	8	10	11	14	17	17	20	22	23	24	24	
(9) personal consumption	33	50	47	46	54	65	62	65	62	68	70	76	
(b) at 1954 prices													
(10) subsistence	32	33	34	35	36	37	39	38	39	41	42	43	44
(11) other personal consumption	47	66	60	43	54	70	64	69	64	70	75	73	
(12) public consumption	6	9	11	12	14	16	15	17	19	20	20	20	
(13) gross fixed investment	11	11	15	19	18	25	22	22	20	16	15	15	
(14) domestic expenditure	97	120	120	109	123	148	140	146	142	146	152	150	
(15) real exports	35	38	39	36	41	48	48	55	58	61	66	61	
(16) less real imports	−20	−24	−23	−27	−30	−42	−36	−40	−38	−36	−33	−34	
(17) real domestic product	112	134	136	118	133	154	152	161	162	171	185	176	
(18) trading gain	−5	−5	−3	−6	—	−5	−8	−8	−12	−18	−25	−22	
(19) expenditure on G.D.P.	107	129	133	112	133	149	144	153	150	153	160	154	

H

Notes on Sources and Methods: Tables 1 and 2

TABLE 1   *Ghana domestic product*

(i) Estimates for 1950-1954 by writer for USDA study *op. cit.*, Chapter II. From 1955 the series at current and constant prices (real product concept) are official estimates of Ghana Central Bureau of Statistics. Details of sources and methods are given in D. Walters, *Report on the National Accounts of Ghana, 1955-1961* (typescript, Accra, August 1962).

(ii) Real domestic product produced has been calculated by deflating consumption and investment components of domestic expenditure by appropriate price indices then adding real exports and substracting real imports, i.e. exports and imports deflated by their respective price indices. This aggregate represents the quantum of goods and services produced by domestic activities and excludes the effects of movements in the terms of trade. Real income available to Ghana, including the terms of trade effect, has been estimated by deflating the net balance of external trade in goods and non-factor services by the import price index and deflating domestic expenditure (as for real product produced). This approach, which expresses both 'temporary' net foreign investment and net foreign borrowing in terms of imports at constant prices, is more meaningful for a country like Ghana than alternative methods of deflating the external balance, e.g. by an implicit G.D.P. price index, by a capital goods index or by an export price index (for net export surpluses). See R. C. Geary, 'Introduction to Studies in Social and Financial Accounting', *Income and Wealth Series IX*, 1961 ; G. Stuvel, 'The Use of National Accounts in Economic Analysis', *Income and Wealth Series IV*, 1955; and J. B. D. Derksen, 'Intertemporal Comparisons of Real Income : an International Survey', *Income and Wealth Series I*, 1951.

TABLE 2   *Uganda domestic product*

Private estimate for 1950-53, see H. W. Ord, 'The Growth of Money Incomes in East Africa', *East African Economics Review*, Vol. 9, No. 1, June 1962.

Line

(1)-(3) G.D.P. at factor cost, official estimates ;

(4) Adjusted for net indirect taxes and inter-territorial transactions of EACS organizations and public enterprises ;

(5) Balance of trade external to Uganda borders in goods and non-factor services ; *net* balance of invisibles ;

(6) Line (4) less line (5) ;

(7) Fixed investment in small-scale rural sectors excluded throughout. Private estimates, 1950-58 ; official 1959-62 ;

(8) General government expenditure on goods and services ;

(9) Residual including stock changes (other than imported capital goods) ;

(10) Subsistence estimated by raising 1954 *per capita* by total African population ;

(11) Line (9) deflated by price index derived by splicing Kampala indices for upper and lower income groups in a 50 : 50 ratio throughout ;

(12) Line (8) deflated by Kampala Cost of Living Index ;

(13) Line (7) deflated by import price indices for machinery and building materials in 50 : 50 ratio ;
(14) Sum of (10) to (13) ;
(15) Domestic exports (excluding inter-territorial) f.o.b. Mombasa, etc., deflated by export price index ;
(16) Net imports retained after inter-territorial transfers plus *net* balance of inter-territorial trade in goods and overall invisible transactions. Sum deflated by net import price index (which refers to all East Africa for years, 1950-53) ;
(17) Line (14) plus balance of (15) less (16) ;
(18) $Qx . \dfrac{Px - Qx}{\overline{Pm}}$; see Note (ii) to Table 1 ; represents difference between line (17) and line (19) ;
(19) Line (5) deflated by import price index plus line (14).

TABLE 3 Indices of Ghana terms of trade
1948-54 (1948=100) and 1954-62 (1954=100)

| | Imports | | Exports | | Terms of Trade | |
	Price	Volume	Price	Volume	'Barter'[1]	'Income'[2]
1949	94	154	75	118	80	94
1950	101	152	112	123	111	137
1951	121	168	146	111	121	134
1952	127	167	141	108	111	120
1953	115	205	135	118	117	138
1954	109	208	190	108	174	188
1955	98	127	85	98	87	85
1956	101	123	68	111	67	74
1957	102	153	65	123	64	79
1958	101	118	90	102	89	91
1959	101	157	82	122	81	99
1960	107	171	70	144	65	94
1961	107	188	57	171	53	91
1962	103	161	52	189	50	95

[1] Barter terms of trade : ratio of export to import prices :
[2] Income terms of trade : barter terms of trade multiplied by export quantum index i.e. export *value* index divided by import price index.

Source : *Quarterly Digest of Statistics; Economic Survey, 1962*

TABLE 4 Indices of Uganda terms of trade
1954=100

| | Imports | | Domestic Exports | | Terms of Trade | |
	Price	Volume	Price	Volume	'Barter'	'Income'
1949	96		68	84	71	60
1950	93		82	86	88	76
1951	115		123	95	107	102
1952	123		120	97	98	95
1953	112		93	89	83	74
1954	100	100	100	100	100	100
1955	98	137	87	119	89	106
1956	101	110	84	119	83	99
1957	98	117	84	135	86	116
1958	97	111	78	143	80	114
1959	98	104	69	150	70	105
1960	103	101	63	162	61	99
1961	101	105	64	150	63	95
1962	96	107	63	147	66	97

Source: EACSO *East African Trade Indices – Revised External Trade Indices, 1954-1961 With Commentary*, January 1963; Uganda, *1961 Statistical Abstract* and E.A.S.D. *Quarterly Economic and Statistical Bulletins*.

W. D. C. WRIGHT

A Determinant of Demand for Food Imports into West Africa[1]

*

This paper seeks to examine quantitatively the relationship between export earnings from Nigerian and Ghanaian primary products and the level of imports into these two countries. Most of the calculations were carried out for two projects[2] recently completed in the Department of Political Economy at the University of Edinburgh. The analysis for Ghana was done subsequently to that for Nigeria and may be said to represent a development from the earlier work. It also helps to explain certain differences in the concepts and methods used.

The Variables

(a) *The determining variable.* Marketing Boards provide a set of data showing how much of the principal crops were purchased from the producers at what prices, how much was paid out in intermediate expenses (including export taxes and other levies) and how much was retained by the marketing boards as a surplus (or deficit). The values of the Marketing Boards' payments to the producers of groundnuts, cocoa, palm kernels, beniseed and cotton for Nigeria were totalled for the years 1950 to 1957, and this we may call our 'Income' Variable. For Ghana the procedure was slightly different because in addition to the Cocoa Marketing Board's payments to producers, a series from 1954 through 1961 was available for cash income paid to recorded employees[3] and this was added to the marketing board payments.

No attempt was made to deflate the income series for Nigeria by a price index despite the theoretical specification that the demand func-

[1] I am indebted to Messrs I. G. Stewart and H. W. Ord for their helpful advice and also to Messrs M. Bostock and Y. Yannoulis for the results of their regressions on the Ghanaian data.

[2] *Nigeria: Determinants of Projected Level of Demand, Supply and Imports of Farm Products in 1965 and 1975.* ERS-Foreign-32, U.S. Department of Agriculture, August 1962, and *Ghana: Projected Level of Demand, Supply and Imports of Agricultural Products in 1965, 1970 and 1975.* Report submitted to USDA, March 1964.

[3] See *Labour Statistics*, published annually by the Ghana Central Bureau of Statistics.

tions are independent of the monetary unit. The main reason for this was the inadequacy of price data; the size of the country for example meant that the series that did exist (entirely for the urban areas) could diverge considerably from an index which would be most appropriate to the income variable. For Ghana, however, the income series were deflated by the Accra Cost of Living Index.

(b) *The dependent variable*. The commodities selected for analysis were the individual foodstuffs with the highest c.i.f. values, and in this paper we analyse six commodities that are common to both countries, viz. wheatflour, refined sugar, unsweetened milk, canned fish, salted dried fish and total imported food. In addition to these items, salt, biscuits and confectionery were analysed for Nigeria, and rice, cattle and imported meat (excluding livestock) for Ghana.

C.i.f. values plus import duties were used for value series and quantities imported were taken for volume series. Retail values and quantities would have been desirable because some of each imported commodity would not appear as final consumer demand at the retail level; in addition, movements in relative prices at the retail stage could have been further investigated as a determining factor.

(c) *Other factors*. The influence of prices as a determining variable was investigated for Ghana; graphs were drawn of the time-series of the dependent variable, the income variable and the implicit unit value of the import. Inspection of these Ghanaian graphs revealed no lags in the relation. The price of rice fell relative to both the cost of living index and the unit import values of a close substitute (wheatflour) and this appeared to relate to the increase in consumption. Similarly, although to a lesser degree, consumption of canned meat appeared to vary with changes in the unit import value relative to the cost of living index. For the other Ghanaian imports, however, either the relative import price did not vary appreciably or the variation in consumption did not appear to correlate with them. Consumption of canned fish appeared to be influenced by unspecified factors other than income and relative price, because although income rose and relative price declined, consumption fell – implying either a Giffen good or the influence of other factors.

No allowance was made in the case of Nigerian data for changes in size and structure of the population which may be expected to be a factor determining the variation in the demand for commodities; population statistics were unreliable for Nigeria at the time the analysis was undertaken. Population data for Ghana were more reliable and the analysis was undertaken in *per capita* terms. No allowance was made for changes in the structure of the population; however it is unlikely to have changed appreciably during the eight years of the period under review.

The functions

Inspections of graphs of income against demand revealed no lags and the next stage was the fitting of functions.

The criteria for the selection of functions to fit to demand data are (*a*) theoretical, (*b*) statistical and (*c*) 'economic'. The main theoretical considerations are that demand functions should be single-valued, that total expenditure should add to income, that the proportionality condition should be satisfied, and that the substitution matrix should be symmetrical. The statistical constraint is that the function should fit the data as well as possible.[1] The third constraint is the economic one in the sense that there is a limited amount of resources available for performing the analysis and that it is desirable that they should be utilised according to some index of efficiency. Within these three sets of constraints, the additivity criterion was abandoned because we were dealing with prices not prevailing on the retail market, for which reason also the proportionality criterion no longer applied. Additional variables were excluded from the analysis because the series were of inadequate length to bear another variable and because of the extra computation involved. The forms investigated were:

(i) $y = a + bx + u$ (iii) $\text{Log}(y) = a + b \cdot \text{Log}(x) + u$

(ii) $y = a + b \cdot \text{Log}(x) + u$ (iv) $dy = a \cdot dt + b \cdot dx + u$

where y is consumption, x is income, t is time, u is the error term, a and b are parameters and d represents first differences; Logarithms are to the base e.

Equation (i) assumes a constant marginal propensity to consume b, and an elasticity of $1 - a/y$ so that as income increases, the elasticity tends to unity from above if $a < 0$ and from below if $a > 0$.

Equation (ii) assumes a marginal propensity to consume b/x which decreases to zero as income approaches infinity; so also does the income elasticity b/y.

Equation (iii) assumes a marginal propensity to consume of $b \cdot y/x$ and a constant elasticity b; this model assumes that zero income is accompanied by zero consumption.

Equation (iv) assumes a constant marginal propensity to consume (time constant) b and an elasticity of $b \cdot x/y$. It further assumes a linear relationship between consumption and time where the parameter a represents the effect of a unit increase in time on consumption with an elasticity of $a \cdot t/y$. (Income constant.)

Results

Because of the small number of observations, no attempt was made

[1] The correlation coefficients are used although they are likely to be a little biased and are also not strictly comparable as between the different forms investigated.

to deal with the problem of serial correlation in the variables beyond including the fourth equation. Elasticity estimates from the untransformed equations are sometimes therefore markedly different from those estimated by the first difference formula. Without a systematic investigation into the degree of serial correlation in the residuals, it is not possible to determine which estimate has the smaller bias; for this reason also, no standard errors have been included since they will also be biased. For projection purposes, however, these biases in the elasticity estimates are not so important because if it is not possible to disentangle the influence of other variables from the determining variable, we are forced to make the assumption that their relationship will be maintained; nevertheless, this assumption would very possibly be made even if the variables and their effects could be separated.

Table 1 shows for each of the six items the results obtained from fitting the four functions to the Nigerian and Ghanaian data. For each item, each set of four rows denotes the four functions fitted to either Nigerian data or Ghanaian data. The first column is the country name, the second column is the parameter a (shown only for the first difference equation), the third column shows parameter b, the fourth column the value of R^2 and the fifth column is the end period elasticity so that it represents the elasticity for 1957 for Nigeria and 1961 for Ghana.

In spite of the obvious similarities of climate, level and pattern of economic development, etc., the two countries are different in many ways with population and sheer geographical size as obvious factors. Ethnic, religious and occupational characteristics may also be prominent. Apart from these differences, which are possibly not so important in determining differences in the consumption patterns of the countries, the methods of analysis will affect the result in a number of ways: the non-deflation of the Nigerian data by population or price indices means that the elasticities for Nigeria will be lower than if the figure had been so adjusted. The inclusion of cash income from employment in the Ghanaian income variable will lower the Ghanaian elasticity because of the persistent upward trend of wages and salaries relative to producer receipts during the period under review. Because of all these factors and the imperfections of the data (i.e. the short time series and error in observing and measuring the variables), it is difficult to deduce much from the comparisons but some points do appear to be relevant.

For example, there is considerable agreement between the Ghanaian and the Nigerian estimates of demand for canned fish which is generally inelastic with a poor fit of the equation. Salted/dried fish is more elastic and this is especially marked in the first difference equation. The elasticity for total food for Ghana is similar to the Nigerian elasticity, as are the results for wheatflour. Sugar is partly an intermediate good and the elasticity will reflect the demand for some final commodities such as beer and confectionery. The milk estimates are remarkably similar as between countries. The elasticity for salt, as might be expected, is less than unity as is generally the demand for biscuits, which largely consists of cabin bread.

As mentioned above, the declining price of rice (relative to close substitutes and to other prices generally) is a factor that will have reinforced the income variable and will help to explain the very high apparent income elasticity in Ghana. The divergence between the elasticities for cattle and imported meat (other than livestock) may be partly due to the composition of the latter category. Frozen meat and meat preparations other than canned meats are consumed mainly by high-income groups and are therefore less likely to be affected by variations in the income variable that we have used; however, canned meats are already consumed in fairly large quantities by the income group we are considering. Livestock on the other hand is generally prized as a source of fresh meat, particularly by this sector of the population.

CONCLUSIONS

The inadequate length and scope of the series of observations has meant that the analysis has been restricted to two variables; a further result is that a rigorously theoretical interpretation of the elasticity estimates has not been possible. Also it was not possible to test hypotheses such as that relating cross-section income elasticities for food items to those computed for close substitutes from time series.[1] The results have, however, proved of value for their primary purpose of predicting the future movements in demand for selected foodstuffs.

[1] D. Seers, 'Normal Growth and Distortion: Some Techniques of Structural Analysis', *Oxford Economic Papers*, Vol. 16, No. 1, March 1964, p. 82, *et. seq.*

TABLE 1   Elasticities of demand and regression coefficients

		a	*b*	R^2	*e*
		wheatflour			
Nigeria	(i)		0·029	0·65	1·24
	(ii)		2·740	0·67	1·17
	(iii)		2·27	0·78	2·27
	(iv)	24·1	0·001	0·00	0·04
Ghana	(i)		1·8553	0·71	1·42
	(ii)		23·6850	0·73	1·19
	(iii)		1·5073	0·71	1·51
	(iv)	0·30	1·3544	0·26	1·04

TABLE 1 (Continued)

refined sugar

		a	b	R^2	e
Nigeria	(i)		0·046	0·74	1·78
	(ii)		427·0	0·73	1·66
	(iii)		2·85	0·80	2·85
	(iv)	19·8	0·018	0·52	0·70
Ghana	(i)		2·3799	0·89	1·81
	(ii)		30·3304	0·89	1·52
	(iii)		2·1535	0·86	2·15
	(iv)	1·11	0·7859	0·51	0·62

unsweetened milk

		a	b	R^2	e
Nigeria	(i)		0·008	0·61	1·27
	(ii)		72·0	0·61	1·14
	(iii)		2·20	0·72	2·20
	(iv)	5·6	0·002	0·19	0·32
Ghana	(i)		0·322	0·83	1·71
	(ii)		4·079	0·82	1·43
	(iii)		2·147	0·81	2·15
	(iv)	0·18	0·082	0·13	0·15

canned fish

		a	b	R^2	e
Nigeria	(i)		0·004	0·23	0·67
	(ii)		42·0	0·26	0·70
	(iii)		1·55	0·35	1·55
	(iv)	9·0	−0·006	0·25	−0·99
Ghana	(i)		0·226	0·25	0·77
	(ii)		2·909	0·26	0·65
	(iii)		0·849	0·27	0·85
	(iv)	0·219	0·089	0·01	0·13

salted dried fish

		a	b	R^2	e
Nigeria	(i)		0·121	0·70	1·57
	(ii)		1143·0	0·73	1·48
	(iii)		4·54	0·83	4·54
	(iv)	95·7	0·017	0·15	2·20
Ghana	(i)		0·346	0·65	1·94
	(ii)		4·277	0·51	1·58
	(iii)		2·297	0·64	2·30
	(iv)	0·01	0·272	0·24	1·51

TABLE 1 (Continued)

total imported food

		a	b	R^2	e
Nigeria	(i)		0·274	0·68	1·37
	(ii)		2577·0	0·70	1·29
	(iii)		2·73	0·81	2·73
	(iv)	215·4	0·026	0·38	0·13
Ghana	(i)		0·424	0·91	1·64
	(ii)		5·409	0·91	1·38
	(iii)		1·904	0·89	1·90
	(iv)	0·041	0·397	0·54	0·93

salt

		a	b	R^2	e
Nigeria	(i)		0·012	0·52	0·74
	(ii)		113·0	0·26	0·69
	(iii)		0·96	0·55	0·96
	(iv)	10·9	0·003	0·02	0·02

biscuits

		a	b	R^2	e
Nigeria	(i)		0·005	0·31	0·78
	(ii)		46·0	0·30	0·72
	(iii)		1·10	0·28	1·10
	(iv)	5·9	−0·002	0·19	−0·32

confectionery

		a	b	R^2	e
Nigeria	(i)		0·005	0·52	1·43
	(ii)		28·0	0·55	0·80
	(iii)		1·09	0·54	1·09
	(iv)	2·1	0·001	0·04	0·29

rice

		a	b	R^2	e
Ghana	(i)		2·899	0·82	2·95
	(ii)		37·089	0·82	2·49
	(iii)		6·846	0·76	6·85
	(iv)	1·0	1·538	0·24	0·35

cattle

		a	b	R^2	e
Ghana	(i)		0·0018	0·48	1·37
	(ii)		0·0235	0·56	1·17
	(iii)		1·6149	0·77	1·61
	(iv)	0·0004	0·0013	0·24	0·31

imported meat (excl. livestock)

		a	b	R^2	e
Ghana	(i)		0·0116	0·56	0·59
	(ii)		0·1476	0·56	0·50
	(iii)		0·5533	0·54	0·55
	(iv)	−0·0029	0·0207	0·40	0·63

TABLE 2a NIGERIA Table showing values of imported foodstuffs (including import duty) and exports of the 'Marketing Board' crops valued at producer prices. All figures are in £0.000

	total food	canned fish	dry fish	wheat flour	sugar	salt	condensed unsweetened milk	biscuits	confectionery	export values
1950	409	15	51	63	67	80	18	28	17	6,990
1951	613	42	146	81	83	145	21	39	33	7,700
1952	826	20	295	106	102	146	22	21	29	9,100
1953	1092	43	402	128	137	138	33	37	37	10,090
1954	1344	37	523	174	211	141	43	34	29	10,760
1955	1448	50	478	177	244	153	39	50	34	9,720
1956	1772	42	627	200	305	167	55	60	39	12,250
1957	1996	60	771	233	258	163	63	64	35	9,990

TABLE 2b GHANA Table showing volume and deflated value of imported foodstuffs per capita and per capita deflated cash income

	wheat flour	sugar	unsweetened milk	rice	canned meat	cattle	canned fish	dried/salted fish (excl. stockfish)	imported meat	total imported food	cash income
	lb.	lb.	lb.	lb.	lb.	No.	lb.	lb.	lb.	£	£
1954	11·87	8·72	1·26	1·02	0·70	0·012	2·56	1·43	0·23	1·90	10·81
1955	12·52	10·59	1·27	1·63	0·75	0·009	4·25	1·40	0·26	2·23	10·86
1956	12·70	11·39	1·40	3·20	0·82	0·013	3·78	1·00	0·25	2·33	11·84
1957	17·78	12·62	1·70	6·52	1·23	0·013	3·65	1·28	0·30	2·75	12·86
1958	15·35	12·45	1·81	4·86	0·93	0·013	3·04	1·07	0·25	2·43	11·36
1959	19·86	15·23	2·12	11·34	0·84	0·014	4·57	1·13	0·26	3·19	12·48
1960	18·67	18·41	2·17	9·52	0·78	0·015	3·67	2·49	0·26	3·41	13·96
1961	19·85	19·95	2·85	14·94	0·84	0·020	4·48	2·71	0·30	3·93	15·18

IAN LIVINGSTONE

The Marketing of Crops
in Uganda and Tanganyika

*

Broadly speaking there are in East Africa, superimposed on one another, two patterns of trade. The dominant one is the export-import trade, funnelling on Mombasa and Dar es Salaam, and certain smaller ports, with Nairobi and Kampala acting as entrepôts in Kenya and Uganda respectively. In this trade the marketing of the main African-grown cash crops, cotton and coffee, which are produced in distinct geographical regions of Uganda and Tanganyika, is quite differently organized and can be treated separately.[1] In addition to this export trade, an important inter-regional trade in foodstuffs exists within each country and between countries, although inter-territorial trade in the principal foodcrop, maize, is restricted. This trade between surplus and deficit areas each season may be carried on over vast distances and despite difficult transport conditions, particularly in Tanganyika. There is, of course, a substantial overlap between these two categories with cereals, beans, groundnuts and cassava both exported and consumed locally.

Statistics of the internal trade in foodstuffs are not available and this fact may be responsible in discussions for some neglect of food production for sale. There is a danger also that the 'fragility' of the economy may be somewhat exaggerated by stressing the dominance in exports of two or three crops. Moreover, the relatively high income elasticity of demand for food which has been estimated in tropical Africa, as well as improvements in internal transport, is likely to increase the volume and relative importance of internal trade in foodstuffs. The World Bank Mission to Tanganyika made some brave estimates for 1958 of the percentage of foodcrops actually sold[2] (See Table, p 126).

The percentages are not large, apart from those for maize and beans of the more important crops, but large enough to support an important volume of trade. Moreover, the percentages are likely to vary within certain limits, for there is plenty of evidence that foodcrops originally intended for self-consumption may be sold on the market if conditions turn out to be particularly favourable, and vice versa. Thus the customary division of the economy into 'subsistence' and 'cash' sectors, underlined by the manner in which national product statistics are

[1] As can non-African estate production (of coffee, sisal, tea and sugar).
[2] IBRD, *The Economic Development of Tanganyika*, 1960, p. 231, Table 47.

Estimates of values of sales of food crops, Tanganyika, 1958

	value produced (£'000)	value of sales (£'000)	percentage sold (%)
cassava	7,280	730	10
other root crops	1,590	160	10
maize	8,920	2,230	25
millet	10,850	1,085	10
sorghum	7,820	1,175	15
beans and peas	5,360	1,610	30
bananas	6,700	670	10
fruits and vegetables	5,040	1,370	25
mission's estimates	53,560	9,030	17

presented, is liable to give a misleading impression. Self-provision of a large part of the household's food supply may well be economic in some circumstances, and very little definite is known concerning the rationality of the choice commonly made between production for use and production for the market. It is interesting to note the view of the recent World Bank Mission to Uganda who stated that:

It is accepted that, as long as the principal goal of many producers is to provide for self-subsistence, a large proportion of resource allocation is automatic and impervious to price change; however, it is our view that while there are many interdependent factors at work, relative prices do have a pronounced effect on the use of land and labor between competing crops ... and so are a significant factor in directing resource use ... [1]

At the same time prospects in the world market for the main African-grown cash crops in Uganda and Tanganyika, cotton and coffee, for which marketing is highly organized throughout East Africa, are comparatively bleak. Interest is thus stronger in developing local and export trade in other crops and in considering the efficiency with which their marketing is organized. There are major differences within the three East African territories in respect of marketing policy for these crops, and if the recommendations of the recent World Bank Reports to the Territories were to represent future policy, these differences may be intensified rather than the reverse.

Marketing policies

In Tanganyika there has been rather a remarkable reversal of government attitudes towards regulation and control in the post-war period. Controls over the marketing of general produce were imposed around 1935, after widespread criticism and fears regarding the quality of

[1] IBRD, *The Economic Development of Uganda*, October 1961, p. 150.

Tanganyikan export produce. Sales outside the produce markets that were set up all over the country were made illegal. During the war and immediate post-war periods controls over the marketing movement and prices were intensified, essentially as emergency measures, under the Department of Economic Control. Up till 1949, when the Grain Storage Department was set up, arrangements for the marketing and distribution of staple foodstuffs formed part of the general system of wartime economic controls, directed by the Department of Economic Control. The new Department was part of more permanent arrangements aimed at self-sufficiency in staple grains and pulses, to prevent local and territorial shortages and famines and avoid the periodic need to import maize. These involved guaranteed prices and assured markets, controls over the distribution and movement of produce, and year by year self-sufficiency obtained through a programme of expanding storage facilities all over the country. Losses made by the Grain Storage Department were disastrous, but other factors also contributed to a remarkable reverse of policy. In mid-1953 controls over groundnuts and *simsim* (sesame) were removed, followed in 1955 by white *mtama* (sorghum) and gunny bags; in 1955, maize, in 1956, paddy and rice, and finally at the end of 1957, wheat. Since that time also, supervision of the produce markets has been substantially relaxed, and there is evidence that illegal marketing outside officially organized markets has been taken progressively less seriously by administrators and traders alike. This change in attitude is increasing as alternatives to the produce cess levied at the markets are being devised for the provision of local authority revenue. Compulsory planting of cassava has been abandoned, regulation over the movement of produce from potential famine areas made less strict, and growers encouraged to grow high-priced crops in preference to food. Currently, therefore, the situation is essentially one of a free enterprise system with government control comparatively limited. The position in Uganda is broadly similar.

While the World Bank Mission to Tanganyika has comparatively little to say about these developments, the reports of the Missions to Uganda and Kenya provide an interesting contrast of recent views. Following in the footsteps of the McGillivray Report, which recommended the setting up of further Boards in Kenya to handle marketing of foodstuffs, the Mission to Kenya assert that:

> To ensure sufficient supplies at reasonable prices is a national responsibility.... To fulfil these requirements, some system of organized marketing is essential; an organization is essential; and to fulfil national objectives, government intervention is also essential. Although modifications to the present arrangements may be necessary, and we envisage that there would still be a role

for the private trader, Kenya should continue to exert control over the production and distribution of major foodstuffs.[1]

The most important elements in these suggested arrangements are the fixing of prices by the Ministry of Agriculture and the provision of storage in support of this. They state that:

> At this stage of very imperfect development of a private marketing system, and with the resultant uncertainties regarding both price and the difficulties of moving produce into markets at all, the case for government utilities to perform this function is very strong indeed.... [1]

And again, ... Production is in the hands of a very large number of farmers, many of them unused to producing for the market.

> A guaranteed market needs to be assured at remunerative price levels, to provide the incentive and to ensure the reward of increasing effort.[3]

The Uganda Mission state, in contrast, that:

> ... there should be greater reliance on the market, and we do not recommend the setting of fixed prices for commodities that are uncontrolled at present.... [4]

And in the particular case of groundnuts:

> It has been suggested that a fixed price for groundnuts would encourage an increase in the amounts marketed, since present price fluctuations deter marketing. The Mission saw no evidence to lead it to subscribe to this view. Price uncertainty is not, in our opinion, a major deterrent to increased output and marketing. Furthermore, a fixed price programme would involve a considerable amount of government intervention which we believe undesirable.[5]

There would thus appear to be a major difference of opinion regarding the effect on the grower of the occurrence of the price fluctuations and associated uncertainty, the effect particularly stressed by the Kenya Mission. Elsewhere the Uganda Mission make further recommendations aiming at a freer system. They do not on the other hand consider the present system to be free from serious deficiencies, but these are due to the undercapitalization of small traders which hindered their effective operation as middlemen. The main proposal for alleviating this situation is, however, the continued encouragement of co-operatives to take over the bulking of produce, within a free system.

While, therefore, the Uganda Mission proposes, if anything, some relaxation of what regulation exists in Uganda, the Kenya Mission regrets the differences of policy between territories and suggests in-

---

[1] IBRD, *The Economic Development of Kenya*, 1963, p. 106.
[2] *Ibid.*, p. 113.
[3] *Ibid.*, p. 106.
[4] IBRD, *The Economic Development of Uganda*, p. 150.
[5] *Ibid.*, p. 145.

quiry into the possibility of closer co-ordination, in the direction of the Kenya model. They consider that:

Problems have arisen from different systems of marketing in operation in parts of Tanganyika and Uganda contiguous with areas of Kenya in which the provincial marketing boards operate. We suggest that this matter should be discussed....[1]

... There now appears to be a stronger case than ever for very close East African collaboration in trade with as near an approach to a common trading policy as can be achieved, to include the extension of organized marketing arrangements for key commodities....[2]

There is a good deal of literature on the Kenya marketing board system, and it is not proposed to discuss this directly. We shall try to throw some light, however, on the marketing system as it operates in Uganda and Tanganyika with a view to furthering a rational assessment of the validity of the differing opinion and policies referred to above. This will centre on whether the operation of the marketing systems in Uganda and Tanganyika are such as to inhibit the expansion of production in those territories. The aim will be not so much to reach very definite conclusions as to present critically various arguments that have been made and to discuss as closely as possible their implications.

Market structure and trade finance

We now turn specifically to the description of the system of produce-buying in Tanganyika. We can distinguish three levels of marketing in Tanganyika: there are large numbers of primary buyers ('traders') purchasing directly from growers, the wholesale buyers ('merchants') located in the up-country marketing towns, and the comparatively small group of large import-export firms situated mainly in Dar es Salaam. The number of intermediaries will not of course always be the same, even apart from the speculation in produce which goes on after bulking and arrival in the ports, but this represents the broad pattern.

The most interesting feature of this structure is the system of trade advances which operates through it. Credit is advanced by exporters at the main ports to up-country merchants, and by the merchants in turn to a vast number of traders buying direct from farmers or other minor intermediaries. It is very difficult to estimate the volume of trade credit passing from exporter to merchant, as policies vary considerably between firms. The amounts involved, however, may be large: one merchant in Tabora, Western Province, stated that he regularly received advances amounting to some 50 per cent of that required for

---

[1] IBRD, *The Economic Development of Kenya*, p. 113.
[2] *Ibid.*, p. 302.

I

financing turnover during the produce-buying season, which might go up to 80 per cent according to the volume of business to be handled.

The system of advances is most developed at the primary level of trading, and here, while the amount lent varies, large numbers of traders used little or no capital of their own. Another Tabora merchant, for example, stated that he had supplied 100 per cent advances to over a hundred buyers at the height of the season. These advances are usually of an extremely short-run nature and specifically for the immediate purpose of obtaining produce, perhaps just the days required for the collection of minimum economic consignments. Somewhat more elasticity might be accorded to reputable buyers of longer standing, but not sufficient for this to be described as general trade credit. The African traders who have gained entry into the trade tend to do the buying only in the very small and remote settlements and markets, where there is less competition from Asians and Arabs. Often they are actually paid employees, sent out by the merchant to collect produce. This practice appears to be particularly common in Kigoma, for example. In all cases, of course, there is a tendency for primary traders to become little more than agents of the merchant on whom they are dependent for credit.

It is largely through their control over the supply of credit, therefore, that the large merchants maintain their control over purchases of produce. The strong position of the middleman in underdeveloped countries is, of course, well known.

In this context it is interesting to note the declaration of a firm in the Western Province of Tanganyika that:

We don't know any firm in any district (of Western Province) that supplies such a big amount (of money) daily for the purchase of produce, and from this you will also appreciate that if we stop buying and supplying money only one day, all the markets of this district come to a standstill.

While control of trade credit is a source of monopoly, there is no question of its restriction. Reliance on it might be diminished by the provision of credit institutions catering more specifically for the small trader and willing to take somewhat greater risks than the banking system can afford to do. Unfortunately this type of loan is very risky without close personal knowledge of the character and business of the would-be borrower; and the person in the best position to assess the trader's credit-worthiness is the one doing business with him. Hence, as has been stated with reference to Nigeria:

It is difficult to see what other system could be adopted when the farmers and middlemen have insufficient capital of their own, banks generally consider it too risky to advance money to middlemen, and even money-lenders will not advance direct to farmers.

The advances have thus become an integral part of the whole credit structure of the country.[1]

There is also a certain amount of extension of aid to farmers, but this appears to be extremely limited. It would appear that the marketing system is far from playing a proper role in the extension of productive finance to the grower. Traders in fact can obtain high rates of return from the purchase and resale of produce to growers within one season,[2] suggesting rather that links between grower and trader, with exceptions, are not strongly developed. Responsibility for this is two-sided, but racial differences that raise problems of communication may well be an aggravating factor. Co-operatives have a tremendous *potential* advantage as a possible means of distributing short-term finance to growers, as well as storage to reduce the need for this finance. This is specifically recognized in the report of the World Bank Mission to Uganda, which recommends that 'the co-operative movement . . . should become the major instrument for providing credit to producers'.[3] It is unwise to expect any great transformation however until the present risks of making loans to small farmers in East Africa are diminished.

The distributive trade appears to rely even more heavily on credit than the produce trade, from the importer through to the small dealer. The standard period of credit is ninety days, though a sixty-day period may be adopted, particularly in better years when turnover is quicker. Since retail credit is easier to obtain, both in terms of volume and period of loan, considerable use is made of it for the purchase of produce. Instead of repaying retail credit at once, cash receipts may be used to purchase produce, for which the rate of turnover is very much faster.

In West Africa the term 'Gold Coasting' has been applied to the practice of buying retail goods with rapid turnover, on credit, with the aim of obtaining cash, even where the goods have to be sold at a loss.[4] The difference between the actual return on the goods and a 'normal' return is a concealed interest payment. If the 'Gold Coaster' can re-lend the cash at a higher rate of interest or use it in other enterprises showing a higher rate of return, the practice is profitable. It implies imperfection of the credit market such that the 'Gold Coaster' can perform intermediary functions not done by other intermediaries and can borrow goods more easily than he can cash, goods being more

[1] K. D. S. Baldwin, *The Marketing of Cocoa in Western Nigeria*, O.U.P., 1954.

[2] Cf. Anne Martin, *The Marketing of Minor Crops in Uganda, A Factual Study*, Department of Technical Co-operation, Overseas Research Publications, No. 1 1963.

[3] IBRD, *The Economic Development of Uganda*, p. 155.

[4] United Africa Company, *Statistical and Economic Review*, No. 3, March 1949, p. 24, and No. 6, September 1950, p. 39.

easily retrieved if necessary. This is, of course, merely an extreme case of the general interdependence of distributive and produce-buying trades which we are stressing – an extreme case where the purchase of goods for resale is incidental. In Tanganyika sugar is a major item of distribution and even large merchants may make important use of wholesale credit on this commodity in produce-buying activities.

Discussion of the system of trade finance is revealing of the structure of the market. The situation in the Western Province of Tanganyika is fairly typical, outside the main cash-cropping regions. In Tabora, it is probably true to say that perhaps 95 per cent of produce for export passes through the hands of five or six large merchants. Membership of this oligopsony group would be extremely static, and entry would be more likely to occur through a large firm (in Dar es Salaam or else-where) setting up a branch, than through the expansion of small busi-nesses on the spot. It is a situation that might perhaps be described as 'spatial oligopsony'. At the primary level, the situation is, of course, highly competitive. Entry is usually via the retail side, and seldom direct. Produce-buying is a more skilled and certainly more risky occupation than retailing – some participants described it as 'pure gambling' – and requires more capital. A retail business can help a trader to start in produce-buying, by allowing him to accumulate funds of his own, by helping him to secure cash loans through acquir-ing a reputation for honesty as a retail trader and, as just outlined, by his use of retail credit.

One must be very wary of drawing parallels between Tanganyika and Uganda, but Miss Martin, in her study, after observing a similar general marketing structure and system of advances, finds that:

Trading in minor crops in Uganda does seem to be an essentially 'open' industry in that there are fewer barriers to enter. Licences are not required to trade in minor produce. Asian would-be entrants find it reasonably easy to raise the small capital required to start business (although Africans find it less so) and there is seldom a monopolistic ownership of sites for shops and produce stores within townships and Trading Centres.[1]

This would accord with our own findings *at the primary level:* but if our description is correct the monopolistic element occurs at the *wholesaling and export* levels, and entry here is another matter. In Tanganyika the up-country merchant is sometimes a branch of a large firm in Dar es Salaam or other port, or has more or less direct family ties with exporting or processing firms. Miss Martin comments with approval on this 'web of kinship' among Asian traders as helping to move funds into the trade easily. She considers, however, that 'because of this it is doubtful whether the particular economy of scale, sometimes

[1] Anne Martin, *op. cit.*, p. 20.

obtainable where the large enterprise has easier access to credit, has a good deal of relevance in Uganda.'[1] It is likely that, with much superior communications and more advanced development, movement of capital in Uganda is less sluggish and trade more competitive, nevertheless this conclusion appears difficult to reconcile with the present writer's emphasis on the importance of control over the available supply of finance.

We may note in passing that the often-expressed view of Asians 'having a monopoly of trade' is a misleading one. It does not square with the economist's definition of monopoly, and we have in any case suggested that the important element of monopoly occurs at the merchanting level rather than the primary one, and this does not correspond to a racial grouping. Nevertheless it is interesting to note, in Tanganyika especially, a fairly well-defined racial division in trade. European enterprise tends to operate only at the exporting level, along with a few Asian firms; merchanting in up-country centres is Asian-dominated; and while primary traders are a more mixed group, Asians predominate. Arab traders tend to operate with rather less capital and are important in the more remote areas, where they survive due to their willingness to accept lower incomes and more trying conditions than most Indian traders. The concept of 'normal profits' the 'supply price of the entrepreneur' appears somewhat ambiguous in this context! Producers benefit greatly of course from the existence of groups with lower supply prices.

Efficiency of produce-buying in Uganda and Tanganyika

Having discussed to some extent the structure of the marketing system typical in Tanganyika, we shall attempt some appraisal of its efficiency. There is a long history of criticism of the marketing system in Uganda and Tanganyika, and we can now turn to a consideration of these criticisms which relate both to produce-buying and to distribution. The most frequent allegation has been that marketing has produced adverse effects on the quality of produce. Most commodities – groundnuts, sunflower seeds, maize, beeswax, gum – are affected by dirt, stones and other extraneous matter, often added deliberately. Drying of maize, for example, is generally badly done; mixed, rather than pure varieties of beans, rice or groundnuts are generally forthcoming, and sorting and cleaning is carried out only infrequently and reluctantly. By and large, responsibility for this state of affairs has fallen on the small trader rather than the grower or larger merchant. It is complained that traders have done little to encourage the marketing of good quality produce and have themselves been directly responsible for the adulteration of produce and the mixing of grades.

[1] *Ibid.*, p. 16.

In particular traders are held to have failed to offer premia for quality grades, so that farmers have had no incentive to improve their produce. The following is a sample of the sort of criticisms made in Tanganyika:

> ... with the exception of paddy in certain areas, I am unaware of any differential price paid by primary buyers in local markets for any other produce. Under such conditions, the producers see no point in making any improvement in the quality of the produce offered.

> ... we are once again up against the old problem of the primary buyers not passing on any premium for an improved quality.

> ... Because of the attitude of the Indian and Arab traders gum is being purchased at one price only in Nzega gum markets. There is no grading except for the rejection of dirty material and the sieving out of small particles.

Miss Martin has also recently found in Uganda that:

> Criticisms of the quality of Uganda's exportable crops, compared with world market standards, is a constant theme within the country.[1]

Such criticisms go back to the 1930's and have been made constantly with reference to the whole of tropical Africa. In explaining the imposition of regulated marketing in the pre-war period a prominent observer commented in 1939 that:

> Apart from the primitive methods and the lack of care on the part of the native producers, it has been primarily the shortcomings of traders, predominantly African in West Africa, Asian in East Africa, which have induced the Administrations to induce regulation and control. Many of these traders lack the nececessary knowledge and business morale to refuse produce of a low quality, and thus vitiate the efforts to improve native methods in the cultivation and handling of their crops and to build up a reputation for the country's exports abroad.[2]

This could still be taken as a representative of the views of those directly concerned with the administration of markets and marketing. The view has, however, been severely criticised by a number of writers, notably Bauer.[3] It is asserted that anxiety over the quality of produce is very often misplaced: it may stem from a confusion between technical and economic efficiency. What is relevant is *effective* demand for quality, that is, consumer demand backed by a willingness to pay cash for securing quality. If this willingness does not exist the trader will *inevitably* fail to offer a premium for a better grade: he does not pay a higher price because he cannot sell at a higher price. In this situa-

---

[1] *Ibid.*, p. 43.
[2] Charlotte Leubuscher, 'Marketing Schemes for Native-Grown Produce in African Territories', *Africa*, Vol. 12, 1939, p. 164.
[3] P. T. Bauer, *West African Trade*, C.U.P., 1954.

tion the imposition of minimum quality standards for marketability is likely to bring about a diminution in quantity produced, while some production for which consumers would have been willing to pay a positive price, however low, will not reach them at all, so that growers' incomes will be diminished. The same problem could be looked at on the supply side: there may be some effective demand for a superior product, but not sufficient to compensate for the additional costs which such a product entails. Taking demand as given, the only method of achieving an improvement in the product marketed is to reduce the cost of the better quality. Any arbitrary regulation which restricts the opportunity to market poorer qualities without reducing the costs of producing or marketing the better must mean a restriction in the total supply on the market and in the incomes of growers. This analysis requires the assumption that traders throughout are maximizing their profits, that they are charging as much as consumers are willing to pay for various products and grades of products. Because only then will traders always discriminate between qualities of produce whenever consumers discriminate between them, and when supply constraints do not prevent it. However, the assumption *does* seem justified, as profits calculations are made very closely, particularly by the primary buyer whose existence *depends* on their accuracy but who is most criticized. The trading community is certainly not characterized by excessive leisure-preference, and the contrary would not be compatible with the still more popular view of the middleman as an 'exploiter'. Although open to criticism, as we shall see presently, this is on the face of it a plausible argument. Unfortunately proponents of the view have been helped sometimes by critics' choice of case on which to build their argument. These are sometimes reducible to examples of a lack of effective demand for a superior product, or else the operation of genuine economic constraints at either the production or marketing level. We may note some of these possibilities to begin with.

There may first of all be rational factors operating at the production level inhibiting quality. Not a great deal is known in detail regarding the constraints effective on the African farmer. It may also happen that a product that is technically inferior has a higher yield or carries less risk. In Tanganyika the Agricultural Department, with the backing of exporters, has for years been pressing for growers to switch from the redskinned *mwitunde* groundnut, used mainly in the oil trade, to the higher-priced Virginia or Natal Common variety, used by the edible nut trade. The latter has turned out, however, to be prone to rosette disease and recent advice has been to encourage its production rather 'in those areas where the incidence of rosette disease does not prevent it'. The matter of the appropriate risk factor is a difficult one and even expert advice may alter.

The primary traders in particular are blamed for failure to sort or clean produce, or to reject very poor material: but this is perfectly reasonable where costs of sorting or cleaning exceed the relevant premium. It would be possible to quote innumerable cases in which, after a critical premium for sorted or cleaned produce had emerged, sorting and cleaning had taken place, to cease again when the premium disappeared. Similar immediate effects can be noted on those few occasions when exports have returned material as unacceptable. In the former cases the critical premium might actually be taken to *measure* the cost and inconvenience of sorting. Another point is that there may be 'economies of scale' in sorting or cleaning. The seed-bean industry in the Northern Province of Tanganyika, for example, caters for a rather discriminating market in Holland demanding a good and uniform product. Some 450 African women are employed seasonally in two factories in Arusha and Moshi for sorting, using machines operating with conveyor belts on lines similar to European canning industries. Similar equipment is employed in Dar es Salaam to sort groundnuts, again using African female labour, and machinery is used, for instance, in the cleaning of sunflower seed, this again depending on large-scale operations. The effect of these economies is of course that large firms will not offer premiums for sorted produce greater than their own unit costs of cleaning and sorting.

There may also be real economic constraints affecting the trader that are not immediately apparent but which have deleterious effects on quality. Taking the case of the hides and skins trade, we note that government efforts at establishing clearly defined grades have been in part frustrated by the practice of Arab and other buyers of buying 'unseen', that is, of buying hides in ungraded bundles without inspection. This practice is apparently widespread in Arab countries, but tradition here does not necessarily cut across economic motives. In the first place, buyers make their purchases over vast areas, often in small lots: buying unseen means faster transactions, wider areas covered, economies of time and transport, and larger turnover. Moreover, it must be realized that buyers are working with limited capital, and in the hides and skins trade, trade finance appears to be of even greater importance than in general produce, with loans out for much longer periods and renewed almost automatically. Under such credit conditions, with only a finite amount of finance available, the trader will attempt to turn this limited capital at as rapid a rate as possible.

Again, the deliberate mixing of two grades of produce by primary traders, which is sometimes strongly criticized, is in fact suggestive rather of a lack of effective demand for the pure superior grade. Traders might justifiably be criticized in failing to separate unsorted produce into grades: but where material is received in sorted condition, after incurring no cost or inconvenience of sorting, sloth is a less likely explanation. Moreover, when existing grades are such that a greater quantity of produce can be passed as superior grade by introducing a proportion of poorer material, it must be compatible with consumer demands to do so, and this quite in the interests of the producer.

The effect of our comments so far has been to discount some of the allegations made against the marketing system, particularly in respect of the role of the primary traders. Miss Martin, however, refers in her recent study to some aspects of the behaviour of the primary trader which may be responsible for deleterious effects on quality. Firstly, the existence of an oligopsonistic situation among primary buyers may prevent the emergence of price differentials for better grades:

> The groundnut buyers in Busoga are particularly insistent on the point that it is useless for one buyer to offer price differentials for quality; competition is so keen that his competitors would follow the price rise, applying it to all produce, even if it involved a temporary loss. They feel that compulsion is the only way of achieving the object without a ruinous price war....[1]

This example is not entirely convincing. It rests on the possibility of behaviour being misinterpreted: in fact grades are generally fairly well defined in this case, and of course buyers would not be prevented from offering discounts for poorer than average quality. The argument, however, is potentially valid: in the purchase of hides and skins in East Africa, which is dominated by a strong oligopsonistic group at the exporter level, rival buyers are alleged at times to offer disguised price rises to the primary trader by accepting as first grade hides those which would normally be classified as second, and so on. This is well-known elsewhere as non-price competition, and while it might be welcomed as introducing some competitive element and reducing the rigidity of oligopoly, the blurring of grades which inevitably results must act as a disincentive to quality production, probably to the eventual detriment of the trade as a whole.

Miss Martin also points to the practice of primary buyers of charging a specific rate rather than an *ad valorem* rate to cover their costs, as being detrimental to quality incentives:

> They (primary buyers) frequently buy on a flat commission of one per cent per lb or 100 cents per bag, irrespective of the produce bought, a procedure which has the advantage of simplicity, but gives the primary buyer no incentive to seek out the higher value produce.[2]

---

[1] Anne Martin, *op. cit.*, p. 44.
[2] *Ibid.*, p. 16.

Elsewhere she refers to other adverse effects produced by the tendency to charge flat rates:

> If, for example, the charges of intermediary buyers and transport operators amount to a constant of 5 cents per lb, a change in the Kampala price from 25 to 20 cents, i.e. of 20 per cent, will reduce the grower's price from 20 to 15 cents, i.e. by 25 per cent. This tendency to fixed distributive margins ... implies that when prices are falling it will pay the farmer to undertake more of the marketing functions himself.[1]

Again, in respect of co-operatives this time, she states:

> One deterrent to producers using their Society for a diversity of crops was discovered in Ankole. At least until recently, Societies were charging a flat rate of commission of 2 cents a lb, on all produce, whatever its final price ... It is, of course, absurd to leave it unchanged for crops for which it might represent 10 per cent or more ... and it is to be hoped that Societies will adopt the practice of charging a standard percentage commission on the selling price of the crop.[2]

Here there is probably a common confusion of principle involved in that there is approval of a fixed *percentage* commission being charged. But the common argument is that distributive margins should vary with the variable cost of the service rendered, not the value of the item. Actually, costs per pound of handling lower grade produce are unlikely to differ from those for a higher grade, and thus charging a fixed percentage rate, involving a higher charge on the latter, would depress its price to the grower, discouraging its production relatively. In the second example cited, farmers would be induced to do their own marketing when prices are *low* rather than high, for variable costs of marketing will not necessarily fall when the consumer price falls. Finally co-operatives would be advised to consider variable costs of additional crops they decide to market, which costs would likely be a good bit *higher* for perishable food crops for internal distribution as compared to cash crops sold to marketing boards for export. It would be reasonable to allocate overhead costs to the main crops, or to apply a rule-of-thumb such as proportional allocation. In the former examples too, the problem of allocating fixed costs, including the trader's normal profits, will arise, but this is merely the standard pricing problem. If a percentage mark-up is applied, the rate will in fact vary, not directly, but *inversely* with the value of the product.

Having considered these two aspects of price behaviour, we can return to the main theme of the argument of the 'free marketeers'.

---

[1] Anne Martin, *op. cit.*, p. 50, fn.
[2] *Ibid.*, p. 55, fn.

This argument was shown to depend on the pursuit of profit maximization by intermediaries. However, though small traders work to extremely small margins, for which they are prepared to assume considerable risks, by the nature of the case they are likely to take an extremely short-run view: in the long run they may not be in business! The government, on the other hand, would be justified in imposing a long view through regulation and restrictive measures against low quality production and sales, even at the cost of reduced profits and incomes in the short run. This argument must, however, be modified if it is to stand. The major part of exports in each of the East African countries passes through the hands of a relatively small number of large firms. These firms can afford to take a much longer view than smaller traders, their position in the trade being virtually assured for the foreseeable future. It seems plausible that the aim of these firms will be the long-run growth of their businesses, and that this will depend on expansion of the trade as a whole. And if the final intermediary discounts appropriately for long-run considerations, the profit horizons for earlier intermediaries will not be relevant: they will simply face price differentials which already reflect possible future repercussions.

Miss Martin, on the other hand, points out that as far as the majority of *minor* crops are concerned, exporters are 'in-and-outers', making profits as the opportunities arise, but not concerned with building up lasting market connexions. Here one would say that unless a government drive to develop a given crop was imminent this simply reflected the relative unprofitability of the crop, so that supplies were not forthcoming at a sufficiently steady rate to *warrant* improved organization. This is actually *supported* by her statement that:

Exporters' interest in minor crops is less than it was before the war, as instanced by the fact that one of the largest exporters in Uganda has now ceased to send out its own inspectors of groundnuts to the Eastern Province.[1]

Again the argument does not relate to the efficiency of the primary trader.

The argument that administrative action is required to prevent the 'spoiling of the market' depends, of course, on the extent of interdependence between operations in present and future; that is, the extent to which there is a *differentiated* market, with the existence and expansion of a market depending on its reputation for quality and reliability. Examples where markets have been lost can be cited, from East and West Africa. What is more difficult to assess, however, is the duration and reversibility of such damage, particularly when importers employ experts – coffee tasters for example – to appraise the quality of separate consignments. We can guess, however, that even in such cases

[1] *Ibid.*, p. 43-44.

there may be considerable market inertia, with importers 'geared' to a certain source of supply, some organization having to be built up, and some personal links developed.

The exporters themselves would in any event be the best placed to appraise the importance of this in any instance, and might thus be expected to incorporate this appraisal appropriately in their price differentials. A monopolist with an assured market, or marketing board, would be expected to do this, and it may be asked therefore if there is something in the oligopsonistic situation of the exporters to prevent it. In this case certainly unilateral action would be ineffective, and an oligopolistic agreement to preclude harmful short-run maximization might be difficult to attain, as was suggested in the case of hides and skins exports. We conclude that there may well be an argument for regulation here, according to the importance of the phenomena mentioned.

The most fundamental criticism of the Bauer argument is, however, that it assumes perfect competition or at least perfect knowledge. Yet there is clear evidence of the deliberate nature of the adulteration of produce, carried on by both producers and primary traders. Miss Martin refers to a case in Uganda of a miller rejecting a sample bag of groundnuts containing 30 per cent of extraneous matter.[1] Produce like maize is deliberately left badly dried for the sake of increased weight, subsequently causing serious deterioration during trans-shipment. Beeswax provides a ready medium for such deceits as the insertion of heavy stones or even more harmful matter within the wax. Locally consumed products like the dried fish of Tanganyika are equally susceptible, dirt and stones in this case quite often accounting for as much as 10 per cent of the weight. Clearly in these cases it pays for producers or traders to adulterate or to avoid simple cleaning of produce for the time being, since as a group they must lose. The poorer product must inevitably be penalized by a poorer price at the final consumer level, this price being carried back ultimately to the grower. At some point there is a divergence between immediate individual self-interest and ultimate group interest. It would not pay a monopolist to adulterate produce, yet adulteration takes place when produce passes through several hands. This must be where ignorance exists as to the exact character and quality of the commodity purchased by intermediaries, that is, where checks on produce are inadequate and knowledge is imperfect.

Whether regulation and control are therefore desirable, however, will depend not only on the extent of such abuses, but also on the cost of instituting effective checks for their prevention. This brings us into the realm of the practicability and expensiveness of control: and this

[1] Anne Martin, *op. cit.*, p. 43.

question may produce different answers according to commodity and to area. We can illustrate this with reference to attitudes towards itinerant trading and barter. Associated with produce market regulations in Tanganyika and elsewhere has been the discouragement of, and legislation against, itinerant trading with a view to eliminating exploitation, cheating and barter, or because it was held to constitute 'unfair competition'. Both itinerant trading and barter were also held to constitute a threat to improvement of quality. Attitudes are often apparently contradictory; while recognition has sometimes been given to the role of itinerant traders in opening up subsistence areas, acting as it were as 'outposts' of the market economy, itinerant trading may be restricted or completely prohibited in townships or minor trading centres. Not infrequently the criticism of the itinerant trader rests on a misunderstanding: one important example of this in Tanganyika is the discouragement of cattle-dealers by licence restriction from buying over larger areas. An argument here was that if buyers were free to make purchases as they liked in any locality where perhaps Africans were forced by some emergency to sell cattle, buyers would be in a position to exploit them. Yet such restriction must of course reduce the number of potential buyers and thus depress prices further. As far as the need for checks on quality, however, it must be accepted that these are impracticable in respect of produce purchased by itinerant traders. On the other hand, in the more remote areas with small and scattered turnover of produce the high cost, if not sheer impossibility of imposing controls, is fairly apparent. Barter is a function of certain economic conditions: it has in fact disappeared for the most part in the developed areas, though it is apparently still widespread in the remote parts, particularly in Tanganyika. Where it has not, it reflects the scarcity of traders' capital and in this case restriction of barter means restriction of trade. This is shown by the fact that the trader 'very often offers one price (cash) and a higher price if the seller accepts goods in exchange'.[1] Itinerant trading and barter in the remote areas is thus justified on the simple basis that some trade is better than no trade.

In the main areas of production, however, the balance of advantage is less obvious. But even here the difficulty of imposing effective controls on transactions has been a major factor behind the increasing freedom permitted in Tanganyika. First of all a very large proportion of total produce has been known to be passing outside the recognized channels. Secondly, success in altering standards has been comparatively limited, as far as is known. The occasional presence of the agricultural officer at the markets is not in any case likely to produce much

---

[1] An observation made by a government officer in Western Province, Tanganyika.

effect, while the busy proceedings at the markets might even be held to mitigate against checking of quality, and market clerks have never operated as produce inspectors. It is conceivable that more careful scrutiny is conducted of produce purchased illegally in the *dukas* (retail shops).

It is interesting that the largest produce-buyers in Tanganyika, merchants and exporters, have generally supported the system of produce markets and allied controls. For example one large buyer in the Western Province argued to the writer that traders sending up cassava from Kigoma should be compelled to use new gunny bags for packing. The argument that if there was sufficient wastage of cassava in transit better packed cassava might not be obtained by granting an appropriate premium was not appreciated. This has also been remarked by Miss Martin in Uganda who reports that:

> The exporters themselves tend to lay the blame for poor quality
> at the door of the intermediary buyer who, they say, is too
> rapacious or short-sighted to pay the grower an adequate differential
> for high grade produce.... They would prefer Government to
> forbid the export, or even the buying of the lowest grades, thus
> facing the grower with a choice between loss of his income from the
> crop of an improved product.[1]

Since a similar observation is made by Bauer with respect to West Africa, it can safely be assumed that this is a general phenomenon at least throughout tropical Africa and most likely in similar economies elsewhere. Bauer's explanation runs as follows:

> There seem to be several reasons for this *prima facie* unexpected
> attitude (of the large firms). Possibly the firms may not have
> appreciated fully the implications of the system. Moreover, though
> the firms are at a disadvantage in that the system has certain
> adverse effects on total supplies of produce, most of these costs,
> particularly the more obvious costs, are borne by the producers
> and the small-scale buyers. There are certain advantages in the
> system to the large firms. The responsibilities and the work of the
> local executives are to some extent diminished and administration
> and control facilitated; these are important considerations in view
> of the size and complexity of the large firms, and the problem of
> efficient control by overseas head offices.... Thus the absence
> of opposition by the large firms to compulsory inspection and
> grading is not altogether surprising....[2]

There may be something in Bauer's first point, as for instance in the case cited by the present writer, and it may be also that large firms prefer to be known as upholders of quality, particularly when govern-

---

[1] Anne Martin, *op. cit.*, p. 44.
[2] P. T. Bauer, *op. cit.*, pp. 372-3.

ment officers are known to be enthusiastic. If there is near-perfect competition among primary buyers, however, additional costs can hardly impinge on them and are much more likely to affect the large buyer in a non-competitive position. Finally the argument of administrative simplicity is not very convincing: exporters generally buy direct from merchants who have already bulked the produce anyway. It may well be that exporters hope that under control the government may indirectly be led to invest more in the marketing system in the preparation of markets or in storage provision, or in the supply of produce inspectors and clerks to relieve them of some costs of checking and sorting produce. We thus return to the consideration of administrative costs.

Economic attitudes and responsiveness of growers

Returning to the question of controls over the quality of African-grown produce, it must also be pointed out that the argument of the 'free marketeers' hangs on the existence of the reasonable economic responsiveness of growers, and this is somewhat less self-evident than that of those who depend for their living on receipts from trade. In the absence of this responsiveness it might be sound policy to impose restrictions, which might be more easily enforceable at the marketing rather than the production level. It is not without significance that the checking of grades and assessment of quality generally tends to be carried out mainly at the ports, the final and main bulking point in the marketing chain. Apart from this, the system of distribution itself has sometimes been alleged to have an adverse effect directly on the economic responsiveness of growers, in that small traders in particular have failed to offer a sufficiently wide and imaginative range of goods to the consumer.[1] Finally, some general comments on this subject may serve as background to other papers on the supply responses of African growers, and we consider now some aspects of growers' economic responsiveness.

An elaborate inquiry into alleged deficiencies in the retail trade in Tanganyika and Nyasaland was conducted in 1952 by Chalmers-Wright.[2] Despite his finding that by and large the range of goods stocked was simply a function of local demand, the view still has pre-

---

[1] A second effect was supposed to be that Africans were led to hoard cash, rather than spend it, and thus to waste resources and to hinder the development of a cash economy. The investigation referred to below did not reveal evidence of widespread hoarding, and in the present writer's view is more simply explained by the inaccessibility of, and lack of familiarity with, banks. Mead has also queried the harmful effects of such hoarding in a non-Keynesian situation. See D. Mead, 'Saving, Investment, and the Analysis of Growth', *Economic Development and Cultural Change*, October 1963.

[2] F. Chalmers-Wright, *African Consumers in Nyasaland and Tanganyika*, Colonial Research Studies, No. 17, HMSO, 1955.

valence among government officers that the absence of certain goods in the shops has reduced the incentives of growers to seek out cash incomes. The World Bank Mission to Tanganyika commented on the prevalence of this view, and suggested that there was 'a certain truth' in the argument.[1] Moreover, Chalmers-Wright qualified his analysis perhaps to a more drastic extent than he realized by suggesting that *certain* categories of goods, including 'housing equipment such as window-panes, window frames and shutters, door frames and shutters, door frames and panels, door locks, non-combustible roofing materials etc.'[2] were not being made sufficiently available to African buyers, since these are crucial items.

In fact, brief acquaintance with East Africa reveals wide variation in individual and regional ownership of 'superior' building components of this sort. Indeed local purchases of corrugated iron roofing, for instance, might serve as a useful index of the wealth of regions within East Africa, if such figures were available. The problem is, therefore, one not only of supply but of demand. In any case it seems *prima facie* implausible that the trader should fall down on the relatively simple matter of stocking the appropriate retail goods when the same trader, in buying and selling crops, is engaged in a trade which entails considerable initiative and ability to 'play the market'. Apart from variations in the cash available to purchase these items, however, there are definite local variations in the urgency of the desire for them. The 'demonstration effect', whereby the individual's pattern of wants is governed by those of the people with whom the individual is in habitual daily contact, is dominant in the strong social and tribal basis of African life. Africans whose lives are firmly rooted in the tribe will tend to have rather limited wants, while others, particularly those spending longer periods in the towns, may be attempting to emulate European or Asian consumption patterns, and have more flexible wants. This effect produces a vicious circle tending to preserve the existing static order of wants on a local or tribal basis, which will be broken down only slowly with the spread of basic education and improved communications. In all this the system of distribution cannot be expected to play any significant negative role; indeed we have already mentioned the important role of intermediaries willing to enter more remote areas in promoting the extension of the cash economy.

Lack of demand for cash incomes by Africans has also been ascribed to the demand for 'target goods'. We can quote for example:

The problem of Africa ... is that there is a discontinuity in the price range of the things men want to buy. There is nothing between

---

[1] IBRD, *The Economic Development of Tanganyika*, p. 72.
[2] F. Chalmers-Wright, *op. cit.*, p. 60.

the shirt costing 10s. and the bicycle costing £15, and nothing between the bicycle and the motor car.[1]

And again,

... the demand for money in a subsistence or embryonic exchange economy is derived from a demand for *specific* things for which there is a felt need. Once a limited objective has been attained, any further exertion to earn money would be meaningless ... the amount of labour or goods that members of such an economy are prepared to offer for sale in the market is determined by the target demand for exchange media rather than by price, cost and profit.[2]

The suggestion in the first case is that indivisibilities in consumption can operate as a major block to economic development. This seems rather dubious. Such is the poverty of equipment and other possessions in most African households, it is difficult to believe there is not a continuous range of articles available and in demand. This is evidenced in any case by the wide variation within households and within areas and regions in the stock of consumer goods possessed. If they exist, 'target goods' are in any case not attained simultaneously by all members of a community; and if some have attained them, others who have not ought to be striving harder to attain them.

The alternative concept of a target *income* is examined by Berg in a useful discussion of the concept of the 'backward-sloping supply curve of labour' in underdeveloped countries.[3] Here it should be stressed that *any* individual will have a high marginal valuation of leisure in terms of income at some level of supply of effort, and thus all supply curves of effort will become backward-sloping at some stage. It is significant when high marginal valuations of leisure exist over comparatively low *ranges* of incomes and with limited supply of effort. There will not, therefore, be a specific target *income*, though it might be a useful device to posit such. Berg refers to the confusion caused by the failure in discussing possible backward-sloping labour supply functions to specify *which* such functions are at issue, individual or aggregate. Aggregate functions may be normal when individual ones are not.

We can state here also that there is no necessary irrationality implied by a backward-sloping supply function of labour from villages to the market sector (plantations and town factories). Standard wage theory has always accepted the principle of the equalization of *net* advantages, incorporating non-pecuniary advantages. In the case of Africa, the

[1] W. Elkan, 'Incentives in East Africa', *H.R.H. The Duke of Edinburgh's Study Conference, 1956*, Vol. II, Background Papers, p. 124.

[2] S. D. Neumark, 'Economic Problems of African Agriculture', *Journal of Farm Economics*, February 1959.

[3] E. J. Berg, 'Background-Sloping Labour Supply Functions in Dual Economies – The Africa Case', *Quarterly Journal of Economics*, August 1961.

K

non-pecuniary advantages of a livelihood in the home region are strengthened by local and tribalistic ties and barriers which operate against other than temporary migration. Berg finds evidence plentiful that:

> The level of income derived from village sources, and changes in the level of this income are major influences on the supply of labour presenting itself for employment in the exchange sector .... [1]

Labour supply, he claims, is responsive to both an income effect, as when a bad harvest lowers village income, and a price effect, as when a fall in the price of a cash crop raises the effort price of income earned in the village. He cites considerable evidence of the importance of these factors and therefore of the economic rationality of the labour force.

However, Berg himself does not distinguish clearly between the supply of labour to *all* forms of economic activity *including* those within the village sector and to activities within the exchange sector alone. Berg is querying the existence of a backward-sloping labour supply curve in the latter case, whereas the present writer would consider that if its existence is dubious in this case it must be thought even more dubious in the former case which a good many of the critics have in mind. The clearest indication of high marginal valuations of leisure over all earned income is perhaps that there appear to be fairly well-marked differences between regions and tribes *within* East Africa in this respect, with some tribes having a reputation for more intensive effort. This also signifies that high valuation of leisure, as in the case of target goods, is a matter of underlying social attitudes, education and stage of development. There is not sufficient evidence, however, to show this could produce a *backward-sloping* supply function for labour as a whole, though it will be a factor making for a more inelastic function.

CONCLUSIONS

We can now attempt to summarize in brief some of our conclusions. The controversy over the efficiency of the marketing system, particularly as regards its effect on the quality of produce supplied, has been obscured by the fact that a good deal of criticism is genuinely misdirected in that it ignores a lack of effective demand or real economic constraints operating on trader or grower. In particular the criticism of the integrity and efficiency of the small trader has been misguided, though it remains true that the latter may be working in highly unfavourable conditions, including a lack of capital. Criticisms of the economic rationality of African growers were also examined, and narrowed down. The argument of the 'free marketeers', however,

[1] *Loc. cit.*, p. 480.

was shown to be inconclusive and evidence of the need for better checks on produce transactions cited. A separate issue is the cost of such checks, which might be very great in up-country areas and outside the main bulking points at the port. Large firms urging more supervision and control might possibly be underestimating these costs. There is also the question of feasibility *at any cost*, as evidenced by the active black market particularly in Tanganyika, and especially when checks are associated with the raising of revenue through produce cesses.

ERIC CLAYTON

Planning the
Development of Peasant Agriculture

*

The theme of this seminar is concerned, of course, with trade between the rich and poor countries of the world. The importance of trade in primary products to the developing nations is immense, a fact which is recognized by the considerable attention which has been given to problems in this field. However, it should be recalled that no matter how successfully we tackle the problems of *exchanging* industrial and primary products, far-reaching solutions will not be achieved if we ignore the problems of producing primary products. Furthermore, it is not only the production of those primary products which enter international trade that are important; of no less importance is the production of food and other crops which are domestically consumed. It is generally accepted that the contribution of export crops to the economies of developing countries can be significant, not only by contributing to a balance of payments equilibrium and as a source of scarce foreign currencies, but also as a dynamic growth point from which to stimulate sustained development. But the pursuit of increased efficiency in food production can be equally important if it leads to the release of land and other resources for increased production of high-value export crops. Food crops, because of their relatively low market value should not, therefore, be considered less important than cash crops and consequently ignored at the production and marketing phases. For example, a recent report by Anne Martin clearly indicates the immense benefits that can accrue from a serious economic study of the marketing of food crops in a developing country.[1] Thus, the economic problems of primary production and the planning policies which seek to solve them appear to be quite relevant.

When considering the planning of agricultural development in low-income countries, it would be generally agreed, I think, that the prime purpose should be to raise the productivity of resources in the peasant agricultural sector. Mellor[2] has neatly defined this problem as one of considering labour allocation as a transformation of leisure into goods

[1] Anne Martin, *The Marketing of Minor Crops in Uganda*, London (HMSO), 1963.
[2] J. W. Mellor, 'The Use and Productivity of Farm Family Labour in Early Stages of Agricultural Development', *Journal of Farm Economics*, August 1963.

which he subdivides into five intermediate transformations:

1. the transformation of utility from leisure into labour;
2. the transformation of labour time into agricultural output; this is affected by resource availability, technology and management;
3. the transformation of agricultural output into money;
4. the transformation of money into goods and services;
5. the transformation of goods and services into utility.

This paper is largely concerned with the problems of transforming labour time into agricultural output.

In discussing agricultural productivity it is customary, as a first approximation, to comment on the appropriate factor proportions required by a particular endowment of resources. For example, the liberal use of labour might be recommended in a land scarce/labour abundant situation and so on. Although this may be an instructive lecturing device, it is clear that a mere cataloguing of resource endowment does not take us far because factor scarcity must be related to the prevailing production function about which there is rarely accurate knowledge. It is important, for instance, to know whether rural underemployment is a year-round phenomenon or whether it disappears at peak farm-labour periods; for in the latter case, it assumes a *positive* marginal product and consequently a new status in economic resource – use reckoning.

Improved resource combinations leading to higher agricultural productivity cannot confidently be based on endowment generalization. What is needed here is detailed investigation and research. It is this reasoning that has led some economists to pursue the 'grass roots' approach as a means of promoting successful agricultural development planning. This point of view has been stated by Gordon Sitton, who says:

the micro-economic approach, which considers the actions of individual farms and manufacturing firms, is a more fruitful method of determining the procedures that will accelerate economic development than the macro-economic approach which considers agriculture as a unit. Agriculture as a unit makes no decisions and implements no policies. The individual farm, or the micro-economic unit which controls and commits resources in the productive process, is the decision-making unit.[1]

Problems abound of course at the macro- and micro-levels and both have to be tackled successfully if agrarian progress is to be achieved.

[1] R. G. Sitton, 'The Role of the Farmer in the Economic Development of Thailand', CECA Paper, September 1962.

A highly productive farm policy would founder if problems of land tenure, credit, extension or marketing were ignored.

To clarify the discussion, let us postulate the major ways of securing increased agricultural or farm productivity:

Firstly, output can be increased by a recombination or fuller utilization of existing farm resources. This could follow, for example, from more timely cultural operations, the use of better seeds (if these were supplied free of charge) and from better hygiene in dealing with livestock. Costless innovations, such as these, would increase yields without requiring greater inputs and, in the popular phrase, cause two blades of grass to be grown where formerly only one grew.

Secondly, the same output can be achieved with *fewer resources*. This process resembles the first category and is also based on a recombination or fuller use of farm resources.

Thirdly, a more valuable output can be produced from the *same* resources. This can be achieved by a recombination of enterprises. For example, the introduction of high-value crops, or, if these are already grown, a greater emphasis on them. Perhaps another example is the use of dry-weather fodder to improve the yield of dairy cows. The assumption here is that the value of extra output would more than compensate for the loss of some other product displaced by the fodder.

Fourthly, a greater output can be achieved by using *more resources* or inputs. For example, the introduction of more intensive farming systems, involving say double-cropping or the cultivation of previously fallowed land, where these innovations needed hired labour. Or, more capital may be introduced in the form of fertilizer, insecticides, irrigation facilities, mechanization and so on.

In practice, of course, these four categories are likely to overlap.

As the vital role of agriculture in the general development process has become increasingly realized, considerable thought has been given to the problems of raising agricultural productivity. But attention has centred mainly on the first, second and fourth categories, whereas the third category has been relatively neglected. This is seen, for example, in the many World Bank development reports which give serious attention to factor supplies – to the need for more fertilizers, better seeds, irrigation; to institutional factors such as land tenure and marketing arrangements; and to world market prospects for various farm products. However, they pay little or no heed to improvements in productivity that might follow from the recombination of enterprises. Of course, visiting experts find it difficult to procure the quantitative information and detailed knowledge of local agricultures which this approach requires. But this surely emphasizes why serious attention should be given to an important source of improved productivity, and it is my justification for considering the problem in greater detail.

I can best do this by referring to a recently completed regional study of peasant farming in Kenya which uses the large-scale linear programming technique.[1] The methodology employed here is briefly as follows. Typical farm situations were selected from the Nyeri District of Kenya's Central Province; positions of optimal resource use were then computed for these situations under a wide range of assumed factor endowments and technical ratios. The optimal solutions were inspected and compared and if recurring patterns and relationships were discerned, they were taken to be valid general characteristics of the agricultural region under study, on which policy decisions and recommendations could be based. By way of demonstration, I propose to discuss the sort of economic relationships that can be derived from this type of procedure and the relevance of these relationships to agricultural policy formation.

The study shows, for example, that on most of these typical family farms, *labour* and not *land* is the factor limiting increased production. In other words, assuming unchanged methods, the hiring of additional paid labour to supplement the efforts of the family is essential for net income to be increased.[2] It follows that, in these situations, land is relatively plentiful (fallow being frequently present in optimum solutions) and hence more of it (in the sense of a higher land/labour ratio) would not improve the income position. It is reasonable to generalize from this that, in some circumstances of intensive cash-crop farming in Kenya, the inability of family farms to employ hired labour will inhibit the raising of productivity and farm incomes.

The situation is, of course, the reverse of that commonly found in settled, peasant farming communities where land is the scarce resource which prevents agrarian progress. Where there is 'population pressure on the land', the lavish use of labour is required in order to maximize returns to land. And, by the same taken, where labour is limiting, the maximization of returns to this factor should receive prime consideration. That is why the existence of fallow land in optimal plans is perfectly consistent with a position of maximum profit. But the idea that idle land can be economic not only goes against the universal practice of the Kenya peasant farmer, it also contradicts the teaching of the agricultural department as embodied in their technical farm plans. In both cases, that is, the total arable acreage of a holding is cropped

---

[1] Eric Clayton, *Economic Planning in Peasant Agriculture*, Wye College, 1963, See also my *Agrarian Development in Peasant Economies*, Pergamon Press, 1964.
[2] Assuming the family is operating an optimal plan.

in both growing seasons. This I think illustrates how technical and economic efficiency can sometimes diverge.

Also shown is the *extent* to which family labour limits the economic expansion of production on the farms studied. This is seen to be substantial. For example the labour force has on average to be doubled by the employment of paid labour before it ceases to be limiting. But at this level, net income is almost *double* that which family labour alone can secure and the holdings are given over almost entirely to cash-crop production. Providing therefore the supply of hired labour is relatively elastic, it would seem desirable to encourage cash-crop specialization on many farms. This conclusion, based on research evidence, reinforces the wider notion, based on comparative cost doctrine, of regional specialization within the agricultural sector. This development has been retarded so far by the creed of mixed farming which implies farm self-sufficiency and which has dominated official policies. But as I have said elsewhere,[1] if true factor opportunity costs were allowed to determine the pattern and location of production, they would give rise to marked regional specialization of agricultural production, particularly between the food and cash-crop growing areas. In this way, the resources within agriculture would be put to their most economic use and would lead to the integration of the whole agricultural economy. In what are now called the areas of 'high potential', farmers would specialize almost entirely in the production of high-value cash crops – tea, coffee, pyrethrum, pineapples, etc. – appropriate to their location. Specialist food-producing regions would export their surplus output to feed the cash-crop specialists and urban dwellers. The consequence of this policy would be a large expansion in cash-crop production, a significant increase in rural incomes and probably an improvement in the country's external balance of payments position.

In a situation, where labour is the factor which limits the economic expansion of agricultural production, the substitution of capital (in the form of mechanization) for labour might well appear to be a sensible way of delaying the constricting effect of labour. But this of course will depend, among other things, upon how effectively mechanization can economize the use of labour and on the costs of mechanization itself. From the situation studied in Nyeri, it was found that although labour is invariably limiting on the family farm, mechanization[2] is not in all cases economic. This arises because the effective substitution of capital for labour, in the physical sense, is not always possible. In the context of Kenyan peasant agriculture the use of a tractor only econo-

[1] Eric Clayton, 'A Note on the Alien Enclave and Development', *East African Economics Review* June 1963.
[2] The use of a hired tractor for seed-bed preparations.

mizes labour during seed-bed preparation periods in the long and short-rain seasons. Hence, if restricting seasonal labour peaks do not coincide with these periods, which is possible in a mixed cash-crop farming complex, then the economic effectiveness of mechanization is almost certain to be reduced.

It was found on family farms in Nyeri that, in a few cases, tractor hire brings about substantial financial benefits; the maximum being a 20 per cent gain in net income over the hand-labour economy. In most cases, however, only modest increases in net income of between 3 per cent and 6 per cent flow from mechanization. And in only one of the situations studied is there no financial gain as between hand-labour and tractor use; that is, when mechanization is uneconomic. The additional employment of paid labour, however, changes this picture substantially for it rapidly causes mechanization to lose its economic justification. This is largely explained by the fact that an enlarged labour supply allows an expansion of the cash-crop acreage to take place. And this reduces the physical effectiveness of the tractor which, in general, is not used on the cash crops.

It might be thought that a significant cash gain alone justifies mechanization from the farmers' point of view. But this need not be the case. For even when mechanization shows no financial advantage over the hand-labour alternative, it does enable a given income to be made with less physical effort. In the case of a family farm, mechanization will here be desirable since it makes life easier for the family which yet suffers no loss of income. But where paid labour is employed, it is not necessarily of economic advantage to the farmer to ease the physical burden of his workers. However, if paid labour that is released by mechanization can be put to productive use or can take over tasks previously done by the family, the farmer will no doubt prefer to hire a tractor.

The programming study of Nyeri also shows that in some family-farm situations, where no cash gain arises from tractor use, mechanization nevertheless induces a fall in the fallow acreage, a rise in cropping and thus an increase in the output and variety of arable products including milk. The tractor, that is, makes a better family diet possible, which is nutritionally desirable, with no loss of income. Here again, the sole use of economic criteria is not enough to assess the desirability of mechanization. So long as it involves no loss of income[1] (cash), a home-grown balanced diet is clearly worth while since it obviates the need to purchase and transport home the dietary deficiencies. Or if this is not contemplated, the risk of family malnutrition is reduced without cost to the farmer.

[1] I.e. if mechanization does not reduce net income below that attained by the hand-labour economy.

If therefore, in addition to the economic test, nutrition and the manual effort of the family are taken into account, the occasions when it would be an advantage to hire tractors are considerably increased. As far as Nyeri is concerned, the study makes it clear that government policy should foster mechanization (based on hired tractor services) on farms with a land/labour ratio exceeding 2·5 : 1 in all but one of the ecological zones. This is likely to apply to most family farms (except the tiniest) where arable cropping is important (cash cropping becomes dominant at much lower land/labour ratios). In particular, farmers near the town should be encouraged to hire these services, where farm labour is likely to be scarce, and also those situated in the pyrethrum zone where mechanization provides the greatest financial benefit. Only in the zone where tea is the sole ecologically feasible cash crop should mechanization not be encouraged. Here tractor use is uneconomic even with a land/labour ratio as high as 5 : 1.

The Nyeri study further revealed a situation where economic resource use on the farm might conflict with the optimum pattern of the agricultural sector as a whole. On all but one of the family farms studied, the optimal plans which have no cropping restrictions produce a relatively large dairying enterprise. It follows that if similar farm families were encouraged to adopt these plans (which at the micro-level maximize their incomes), it would give rise to a new, peasant milk-producing industry. This would almost certainly result in the domestic overproduction of milk and raise the difficult problem of finding external markets (for butter of course) and maintaining minimal standards of dairy hygiene. Indeed, experience suggests that tropical, peasant butterfat producers would find it difficult to compete with the highly organized and experienced temperate exporters. But even if Kenya could compete on the world dairy produce markets (in terms of price and quality), the costs of processing and transport would lead to reduced ex-farm gate milk prices. And the effect of these lower prices would be to reduce the importance of the dairy enterprise in the optimal plans.[1] From a national point of view, therefore, there is a definite need to limit the size of the peasant dairy industry. This means that when computing optimal farm plans, intended to serve as blueprints of agrarian development in Nyeri, a ley restriction should be incorporated limiting the acreage to that necessary for fertility maintenance only.[2]

I hope this discussion has helped to make my point that improved enterprise combinations can be an important source of increased

---

[1] A fairly small fall in milk prices would achieve this.
[2] This refers only to leys carrying dairy cows. A different answer might result from leys stocked with beef cattle or sheep.

agricultural productivity.[1] Of course, the sort of answers given by this approach are no more than approximations, but at any rate they should avoid the gross misuse of scarce resources which can often arise out of the process of purely physical planning.

If I may again use the example of Kenya, the agricultural planners there have undoubtedly been guilty of some misdirection of resources. They have, for example, used scarce investment funds to develop the *pastoral* areas by means of ranching schemes, water development and so on. Inevitably, this has slowed down the tempo of development in the much more productive *arable* areas. Contrary to Myrdal's attitude on balanced regional development,[2] I believe that equal development, though desirable, is a luxury which few low-income countries can afford to pursue. Another example concerns the misuse of investments within the arable areas. Over the years, substantial funds have been used to establish a number of *settlement schemes* none of which have proved economic ventures.[3] They have not relieved rural congestion, one of the declared purposes, and they have been costly and of low productivity. Clearly, the funds used here could have been more pro- ductively employed to reinforce the gains already made in the 'high potential' areas. A final example relates to the uneconomic land-use patterns, within the areas of *high potential*, which are the result of physical planning. Although cash crops are the major creators of wealth, nevertheless, undue encouragement has been given to food crop and livestock production. The consequence of this has been that the great potential of Kenyan agriculture, to contribute to general economic development, has not been fully exploited.

I am sure that a systematic approach to the problems of raising agricultural productivity, which gives due weight to economic vari- ables, would avoid the inefficiency and waste of the examples just cited.

As for the limitations of economic planning methods, these are numerous and often forbidding. As far as export-crop peasant economies are concerned particular difficulties are associated with product price fluctuations,[4] declining secular terms-of-trade and the risks of specialization. For example, research evidence (as well as comparative cost doctrine) suggests that a policy fostering extreme

[1] See also, Dean and Benedictas, 'A Model of Economic Development for Peasant Farms in Southern Italy', *Journal of Farm Economics*, May 1964.
[2] Gunnar Myrdal, *Economic Theory and Underdeveloped Regions*, Duckworth, London, 1957.
[3] This does not refer to settlement of African farmers in the areas previously called the White Highlands.
[4] Sir John Crawford, 'Problems of International Trade in Primary Products', *Progress*, 1/1964.

regional specialization, between the food and export crop areas in Kenya, is desirable and economic. But the evidence for this is based on a linear programming exercise which assumed certain relationships. Should these change, through for instance a fall in coffee price, which has in fact occurred over the last year or so, does the policy of regional specialization become no longer valid? And will a new policy, using current price relationships, have to be devised? This may be so, but there are strong grounds for supposing that the policy of regional specialization is firmly based, even for the longer period and for quite large price changes. For one thing, the much-vaunted claim of secular declining terms-of-trade between poor and rich countries has not, according to Haberler, been proven. If anything, world prices of primary products tend to fluctuate about a fairly constant trend. Hence a specialization policy initially valid on economic grounds may well continue to be so in the longer period. Even in the shorter period, changes of policy need not be necessary for the type of agricultural sector I have specified. In the first place, it is shown in an important article by Sydney Caine that fluctuating primary product prices, far from adversely affecting rates of economic growth, probably lead to higher rates of saving and investment.[1] Incidentally, although Kenya coffee prices fell over £50 a ton in 1963, export receipts for the period increased by half a million pounds. Secondly, in the study already referred to, probable supply responses to changes in coffee prices were computed and these indicate a low supply elasticity. Very large price falls are required before reduction in output becomes economically justified. The desirability of a short-run policy fostering export-crop specialisation is clearly reinforced by both these points.

It may be of interest to give some details of the exercises undertaken into supply response relating to coffee. Optimal acreages were computed for two typical peasant holdings (with land/labour ratios of 2·8 and 2·7 acres to 1 man respectively) for a range of coffee prices. The first farm could grow both coffee and tea, the second farm coffee only. The results were as on page 157.

From the figures it can be seen that the 'normative' supply responses of coffee farmers to changes in coffee prices are markedly different, depending upon whether they grow coffee only or coffee and tea. On the dual cash-crop farm, the curve showing output response to price change is on the whole very *elastic*. Coffee growing ceases to be profitable, relative to other alternatives, when the farmer receives less than £200 a ton for this product. By contrast, on the single cash-crop farm, supply is completely *inelastic* over a very wide price range. In other words, between £325 and £150 a ton, the farmer has no economic

[1] Sir Sydney Caine, 'Instability of Primary Product Prices', *Economic Journal*, September 1954.

| | Farm 1 | | Farm 2 |
| price/ton | coffee & mulch | tea | coffee & mulch |
£	acres	acres	acres
350	1.5	1.1	1.3
325	1.5	1.1	1.2
300	1.5	1.1	1.2
275	1.1	1.4	1.2
250	.4	1.7	1.2
225	.4	1.7	1.2
200	.4	1.7	1.2
175	—	1.7	1.2
150	—	1.7	1.2
125	—	1.7	1.1
100	—	1.7	—

inducement to alter his coffee acreage. Only when he receives less than £150 a ton is it economic to reduce his acreage and at £100 a ton production of coffee is no longer worth while.

The relative elastic supply curve for farm 1 is obviously associated with the alternative tea crop. Indeed it illustrates the point that factor opportunity costs in peasant production become relatively high when more than one high-value cash crop is grown. In this case, the opportunity costs of coffee are related to the foregone tea crop. However, the number of farms situated on the ecological margin, where both coffee and tea can be grown, are relatively few, hence supply response here has little practical importance for policy. The single cash crop farm is the more typical production unit and the inelastic supply of farm 2 arises from the fact that the alternative opportunities to coffee relate solely to low-value food crops.

These programmed supply curves cannot, of course, claim to predict producer's actual response to price changes with certainty. That is why they are referred to as 'normative' curves, indicating what *ought* to be the response of the producers, at given prices, in order to maximize profits. The extent to which normative and positive responses will diverge, will vary according to circumstance. But obviously the smaller this divergence the more useful the normative curve will be for prediction purposes. With regard to the supply curve relating to farm 2, it has been shown that, because it relates to perennial tree-crop production, the convergence of the normative and the positive is likely to be close, giving it operational value for policy-making purposes.[1]

The kind of economic planning that I have been discussing is only one facet of the process of raising agricultural productivity which overall bears on wider sectorial issues such as capital availability, land

[1] *Op. cit. Economic Planning in Peasant Agriculture.*

tenure, crop processing capacity and extension resources. Indeed, in certain situations, concern with enterprise combinations can only have a minor role to play in the quest for higher productivity. But, in the case of the high-value cash-crop economies, it is likely to be of preponderant importance.

ALI AHMED SULIMAN

Stabilization Policies
for Cotton in the Sudan

*

Cotton in the Sudan contributes about 70 per cent of the Sudan's exports (as seen in Table 1) and 13 per cent of the Gross Domestic Product, but it definitely contributes a greater percentage of that part of the Gross Domestic Product which is exchanged for money. There is nothing yet published on the size of the subsistence and barter sector in the Sudan. However, without going into subtle refinements, one may estimate that part of the Gross Domestic Product which is produced and consumed within the subsistence and barter sector to be about 35 per cent (1956). Thus cotton seems to contribute approximately 20 per cent to money incomes generated in the Sudan. With the future agricultural and industrial development of the Sudan this percentage will fall, but will certainly remain important for a long time to come.

The Sudan produces only about 5 per cent of the world's cotton. A rapid expansion in output is envisaged over the next decade with the completion of the Managil Extension to the Gezira Scheme, but as other countries' output will also rise, the Sudan will remain a relatively small world producer.

It may be argued that about 90 per cent of the Sudan's cotton is extra-long staple cotton, so making the Sudan the producer of 20 per cent of the world's total supply of extra-long staple cotton – as seen from Table 2 – and this may give the Sudan some bargaining power. This can only be true if the rate of substitution between the extra-long staple cotton and the long-, medium- and short-staple cottons, on the one hand, and the man-made fibres on the other, is zero or very small. However, it is considered that such a rate of substitution is large and will be even larger as a result of advances in both textile machinery and in the quality of man-made fibres in the future. Moreover, it has already been proved that the correlation co-efficient between the prices of American Middling, a short-staple cotton, and the prices of Sakel, an extra-long staple cotton, was 0·8 for the period 1922-36, and that both prices changed in the same direction in thirteen cases out of the fifteen studied.[1]

In this paper we shall attempt to discuss the meaning of stabiliza-

[1] Gamal El Din Mohammed Saeed, *Egyptian Economics*, Nahada Press, Cairo, pp. 87-88 (in Arabic).

tion, to see how far the Sudan supply of cotton is price-elastic, and then examine some problems of stabilization. We intend to indicate what variables are to be stabilized, why there has been a need for stabilization, and how it can be attempted. Finally, we shall look into methods of stabilization.

Stabilization is defined here as the reduction of short-run fluctuations around the long-run trend. This really means just narrowing the range of changes in the variable(s) concerned and not necessarily fixing it or them at one given level. The general principle of pure stabilization[1] is very simple. Stabilization of price or income has to be achieved by setting off successive seasons or years against one another; the surplus of good years is set aside and distributed back to producers when conditions are unfavourable. Thus over the long run the prices received by the producers would normally be the same as the world price and only differ from it through greater stability, being higher when the world price was low and lower when it was high, assuming that supply is inelastic.

Stabilization of price or income in practice may mean merely setting a floor or minimum price, or minimum income, or it may mean reducing fluctuations to a definite range so that price or income can only fluctuate so much above and so much below the average, or it may mean just reducing the change in price or income from one year to another. It should be clear in our minds that stabilization policies are intended for the solution of short-run problems and that they are not supposed to interfere with the long-run trend. However, the long-run is actually made of short-runs and it is rather difficult to differentiate between a short-run change and a long-run trend. There is still a difference, though, between a policy intended to affect supply or demand in the long-run in order to raise or lower price or income, and a policy intended to smooth out fluctuations in income or price.

Elasticity of supply

Before going into any discussion of stabilization for the cotton sector of the Sudan, it may be worth while examining how far the Sudan supply is elastic, because elasticity of supply has an important part to play in shaping the policies to be followed for stability.[2]

About 90 per cent of the Sudan cotton is produced in schemes with fixed area and rotation. Thus, in this way, supply tends to be quite unresponsive to changes in prices. However, there are other factors

[1] I.e. stabilization which does not involve any income redistribution.

[2] For definition and measurement of elasticity, please see J. T. Ward, 'A Note on Price Flexibility of Supply', *The Farm Economist*, Vol. X, 1963, and for some of the problems of measurement, please see G. T. Jones, 'The Response of the Supply of Agricultural Products in the United Kingdom to Price', Parts I and II, *The Farm Economist*, Vol. IX and X, 1958-61 and 1962 respectively.

to consider. Although the area may be fixed, the effort of the tenant and his family is variable and one expects it to be influenced by changes in price of cotton. It is difficult to find out statistically how far the tenant varies his effort with price. Besides the natural factors which affect yield, some of the tenant effort goes into increasing the yield per feddan and some of it goes into improving the quality of the cotton. The lustre, colour and cleanliness of cotton depend to a large extent on the effort of the tenant. It is not possible, however, to find out how much of the tenant's effort goes into increasing output and how much goes into improving quality. On top of all this, natural factors influence yield per feddan very much, thus distorting the relationship between supply and price and making it very difficult to make any measurement of the elasticity of supply of the Sudan cotton. However, the fact that only about 10 per cent of the Sudan cotton is produced by small farmers who can shift some of their land and labour from or to cotton makes one tend to conclude that the Sudan cotton supply is fairly inelastic. But it seems that *big* changes in price tend to influence supply. A large price fall, which makes cotton production unprofitable reduces cotton production significantly. If a price rise takes place, on the other hand, it is unlikely to influence cotton production unless it is sustained for a considerable period. Factors of production are not mobile in the Sudan. Cotton production is labour-intensive and for a number of economic as well as social reasons labour is immobile. This lack of mobility is particularly true of the tenant who is a semi-owner of the land. He is bound to his land by family and tribal ties. The tenant and his family offer the bulk of the labour required for cotton, and the production of cotton is, to them, not merely a way of earning an income but a way of life as well. Thus the tenant tends to stay where he is. On the other hand, as far as changing or substituting cotton for another crop is concerned, this is rarely possible. A very large percentage of the Sudan's cotton is produced in schemes with fixed rotation, so that the tenant can neither vary his crop (cotton) nor the area under cotton. He can only vary the effort or labour that he puts into the cotton production. Moreover, in the private sector, although it is easy to give up a cotton scheme, it takes a long time to obtain a grower's licence to establish one and it takes an even longer time to prepare the land for cultivation. On the other hand, the cotton producers (whether tenants or farmers) on the land already used for cotton usually put some regular effort into that crop. They are a part of a well-integrated society from which it is very difficult to get away. It is not easy, therefore, for the cotton producer to put more time and effort into his cotton production, although it may be easy for him to cut down his cotton production, and time and effort devoted to it, and 'invest' more time in his social life. As long as cotton is profit-

L

able he will continue to devote his usual effort to it but as it becomes unprofitable, or almost unprofitable, it is much better for him to enjoy more leisure, more social life and devote a minimal time to cotton. All this means that cotton production in the Sudan is *fairly inelastic except when price falls very much, or rises very much and stays there for two or three years.*

We are unable, unfortunately, to make a more accurate measurement of the elasticity of the Sudan's cotton supply than this. Comprehensive statistics of cotton supply and cotton prices for the whole Sudan are not available, while there is little information on how the average annual cotton prices which are available for some schemes are compiled. A year is a long time. A price which is low for eleven months and then rises in the last month has a different effect on supply from a price which is high for one month at the beginning of the season then falls and stays low for the rest of the season. Area is most probably determined by the level of price at the time of sowing, while effort or the amount of labour put into cotton is determined by the level of price throughout the season. Most probably, in the Sudan, the price level has a more important impact on the output of cotton at the picking season. If price is reasonably high, cotton is picked to the last bit; but if price is *very* low, some cotton may be left hanging to the trees. Most likely the cotton prices which are available for some schemes and areas for some years are actually sale prices. As one expects, most sales take place in the middle of the following season as it takes time to transport cotton to collection centres, gin it and send it to markets. It is highly doubtful that the average actual sale price is the same price which has influenced the cotton producer to decide how much land to put under cotton production, how much effort to put into looking after the cotton while it is growing and how much of it to pick finally. For all these reasons perhaps it is safer to depend on one's own understanding of the structure and organization of the cotton sector and the mobility of factors of production in the Sudan for determining the elasticity of the supply of cotton, rather than to depend on inadequate statistics with no guide as to how they have been compiled.

The variables to be stabilized

The variables[1] of economic interest that may change with the world cotton price (export price) seem to be:

1. Local cotton price paid to the producer (producer's price).

2. Money income of the cotton producer (producer's income).

3. Real income of the cotton producer.

[1] A. I. Macbean, 'Problems of Stabilization Policy in Underdeveloped Countries', *Oxford Economic Papers*, Vol. XIV, 1962, pp. 261-2.

4. Revenue of the government (both as taxes and profits).
5. Output (specially with a big drop in price).
6. Terms of trade.
7. Regional income.
8. National income.

The Sudan – as a producer of only about 5 per cent of the world supply of cotton – cannot influence the world cotton price in any way. It may only be able to do so through international agreement which has the support of the producers of most of the world's cotton. However, such an agreement is difficult to bring about – mainly because the United States, the world's biggest cotton producer, is reluctant to join. Without the support of the United States it may not be possible to have a big enough slice of the world cotton under the agreement and, moreover, the finance of such an agreement would be difficult. On the other hand, international agreements tend to be static, and it may not be very desirable for the Sudan to join and thus sacrifice all the possible expansion in its cotton production. Finally, cotton is not homogeneous and differences in grades and qualities may make agreement rather difficult to obtain.

Thus it seems that international action in the form of stabilization of the cotton export price is yet in the realm of discussion and may not be a reality for some time to come. Therefore, the Sudan, if it is seeking stability, must assume that fluctuations in the cotton export price are inevitable and try to devise appropriate corrective domestic action which can reduce the undesirable effects of such fluctuations.

There are several variables (as we see above) which are feasible and desirable to stabilize. But perhaps the two most important variables are income derived from cotton and cotton price. It is a controversial question whether to stabilize income or price. Some economists support income stabilization, e.g. Bauer and Paish,[1] while others[2] are mainly concerned with price stabilization. We are going to discuss this question in relation to the Sudanese economy, and the method of cotton production in the Sudan and its problems. We do not intend to discuss stabilization in the abstract or theorize about it. We are merely trying to find some practical solution to the problems of instability in the Sudan, which is, at the same time, feasible. It is much better to devise a less ambitious policy which can be implemented

[1] P. Bauer and F. W. Paish, 'Fluctuations in Incomes of Primary Producers', *Economic Journal*, December 1952.

[2] J. C. Wells, 'Price Stabilization of Nigeria's Export Crops', *The Nigerian Journal of Economic and Social Studies*, Vol. IV, No. 1, March 1962; and J. Gourdriaan, 'Comment', *Kyklos*, Vol. XI, 1958.

rather than a policy which promises much but which is very difficult, complicated and expensive to carry out.

If a country produces the bulk of a world crop and the world demand for this crop is rather stable, then changes in its supply are offset by opposite price changes and gross income or proceeds from that crop will tend to be stable in spite of the fluctuations in its supply. But this is not the case with the Sudan. The Sudan is a very small producer of cotton and at the same time the world demand for cotton is not at all stable. As far as the relation between price and supply is concerned, we have already mentioned that supply is rather inelastic unless price either rises very much and stays there for a considerable time or drops markedly. For instance, when prices fell in 1958 by about 30 per cent production declined in all cotton schemes in the Sudan. In the Gezira Scheme yield per feddan fell from 6·759 to 1·505 kantars.[1] How much of this decline in output was due to price fall and how much was due to natural factors is not easy to say. It is not, however, unrealistic to assume that such a sharp fall in price had an important impact upon the output and perhaps upon quality too. If such a reduction in cotton output and perhaps quality – which is necessarily a waste of economic resources – is to be prevented, policy should be devised to prevent sharp and excessive reductions in product prices. On the other hand, we need not worry about a rise in prices. We should, instead, let it have the full effect in expanding output so that the Sudan can obtain the highest possible proceeds, even though one does not expect such an expansion to be of any importance unless prices stay high for three years or so. At the same time, we are suggesting income stabilization which in the end may indirectly reduce all price fluctuations. Therefore our concern is to reduce the large downward changes of cotton prices. The simplest way of doing this, which is within the reach of the Sudan, is to build a national buffer stock by not selling if prices fall below a certain level. As soon as the price rises from that level stocks can be cleared, and as changes in the Sudan's cotton supply are not expected to affect the world price in any way, output retained in a 'bad' year could be sold a year or two later at higher prices. This policy, as a matter of fact, was tried in 1958 but it could not be maintained because the Sudan's foreign exchange reserves were exhausted and there was considerable pressure to import. Thus the Sudan Government had to sell cotton at low prices in order to maintain supplies of imported goods. A small quantity of 1958 cotton which was retained, however, fetched a higher price in the following year, 1959. Therefore to make a national buffer stock successful, the Sudan needs to build up foreign exchange reserves. There are already reserve funds for almost all the cotton producers in the Sudan.

[1] Feddan = 1·038 acre: kantar = 99·05 lb = 44·93 kg.

But they are not enough and, moreover, they may be required for income stabilization. A reserve fund can be built gradually by charging the cotton producers an annual premium as an insurance against wide falls in cotton prices. Once a reserve from cotton proceeds is accumulated a national buffer stock can be initiated. The aim behind such a national buffer stock is not only to keep the cotton in store until it can be sold at a higher price in a year or two, but also to guarantee a minimum price to the cotton producer at the beginning of each new season.

The question is, how is this minimum price to be determined in advance? Perhaps the best way to solve this problem is to use a moving average as an indicator of the level of cotton prices. At the same time, to avoid the problem of paying a higher price than that actually received by the agency, and to avoid the problems of deficits as well, it may be wise to give the producer a price a little lower than the moving average. Moreover, this derived minimum price must be adjusted to the size of the buffer stock. If the stock is growing or decreasing continuously, it may mean that the minimum price is not in harmony with the long-run trend of world cotton prices. Although tying the guaranteed minimum price to the size of the buffer stock has the advantage of helping the Sudan's supply of cotton to adjust itself to demand in the long run, it may be argued that it makes it easy for speculators to take advantage of the fund. If the size of the stock reaches a certain high level they know that the minimum price will be lower in the following season, and if the size of the stock diminishes very much, they will know that the minimum price will be higher in the following season. Even though such an argument seems attractive, it cannot be true unless the demand and supply of cotton in the following season remain the same as in the former season. With highly fluctuating supply and demand, the price in the following season is very difficult to forecast and thus speculators cannot take much advantage of the fund unless there is some indication of changes in world demand due to certain world crises, or of changes in Sudan supply due to expansion in large cotton schemes. However, the same difficulty of forecasting prices for the next season will be facing the agency of the buffer stock. Wrong forecasts of price may lead to de-stabilization of price and income.[1] Thus because of the difficulty of accurate price forecasts and the inadequacy of trained staff in the Sudan, it may be advisable to refrain from price forecasting. Price can be calculated from a moving average for a period of a few years, ending at the time of sowing in every new season. Then the minimum should be announced and should remain fixed for the rest of the season in order to give the producers some security. If the minimum price is frequently adjusted downwards, it may cease to be effective. It is always better

[1] P. Ady, 'A Comment', *Economic Journal*, Vol. LXIII, 1953, p. 601.

to determine it rather low (but not very low), and maintain it there, than to determine it initially rather high and then to lower it during the season. Once the cotton producers lose faith in the minimum price it will be good for nothing and it will take a long time to regain its acceptability.

We have already explained that the aim behind price stabilization through a guaranteed minimum cotton price is to reduce the fall in output of cotton production in years of very low prices and to reduce the waste of resources. Another equally important aim behind the stabilization of the price of cotton is the stabilization of the income of the cotton producer. But will the stabilization of price stabilize the income[1] of the cotton producer in the Sudan?

Price stabilization will automatically lead to income stabilization if production is stable while price is the fluctuating variable. But this is not the case in the Sudan. Income is the product of the area under cotton, the yield per feddan and price. The area under cotton in the cotton schemes is quite stable. But the yield per feddan fluctuates widely. From Table 3 which refers to the Gezira Scheme we notice that the yield of cotton per feddan in the period 1950-59 has an average annual rate of fluctuation (fluctuation from year to year) of 57 per cent while the price per kantar of sakel has an annual rate of fluctuation of 22 per cent. This indicates that the average rate of fluctuation in yield in those ten years is more than twice the average rate of fluctuation in price. Thus the stabilization of price alone is *not enough* to create stable income for the cotton producer in the Gezira Scheme or in the Sudan as a whole. As fluctuations in yield per feddan are due to natural factors, some of which are impossible to interfere with, e.g. temperature, sunlight, winds, amount of rainfall, etc., *it becomes necessary to try to smooth the fluctuations in income directly.* Since the Sudan is a small cotton producer, with world demand for cotton fluctuating very much and with the yield per feddan fluctuating even more, the relationship between the price of cotton and the income from cotton is very weak. In one year, price may fall but income from cotton may rise because of higher yield per feddan, or price may rise but income from cotton may fall because of lower yields. For example, Table 3 shows that in 1953-54 price fell from Ls. 13·5 to Ls. 11·5 but the tenants' income rose from Ls. 5·1 to Ls. 6·5 millions, while in 1954-55 price rose from Ls. 11·5 to Ls. 14·6 but the tenants' income fell from Ls. 6·5 to Ls. 5·1 millions because of lower yields . . . and so on. In the period 1950-59, as shown by Table 3 only in four years out of ten were changes in yield per feddan offset, to some extent, by changes in price. Thus price stabilization in most years of the period 1950-59 would have resulted in destabilization of the cotton producer's

[1] I.e. Gross money income from cotton, as we shall explain later in this paper.

income. We do *not* wish to imply by this that cotton supply in the Sudan moves in an opposite direction to price or that price stabilization will always destabilize income. Whether or not price stabilization in the Sudan for any span of time will lead to income stabilization depends upon the movement of cotton prices, which are controlled by changes in the world supply and demand for cotton, and also on changes in yield per feddan. If yields and cotton prices move together for most of the period under consideration, then price stabilization will lead to income stabilization, but if they move in opposite directions, price stabilization will destabilize income from cotton. It is impossible to forecast for the coming ten or fifteen years whether cotton yield per feddan and cotton prices will move in the same direction or not for most of the years. All we want to prove is that there is no direct relationship between cotton prices and income from cotton in the Sudan, and that *price stabilization does not necessarily stabilize income*. It is feasible and desirable to stabilize the income of the cotton producer directly through using a moving average and also a reserve fund. Such income stabilization will take care of upward fluctuations in price (if they affect income) and fluctuations in yield. The long-run trend of cotton prices is expected to decline but at the same time productivity in the Sudan is increasing because of the spread of education, agricultural research, etc. Thus cotton income may be expected to be steady over the long-run and therefore the use of a moving average for smoothing out short-run income fluctuations is not going to be faced with chronic deficits or surpluses.

Now we turn to consider briefly some of the other variables. The advantages of stabilizing the export price seem to be the reduction of fluctuation in foreign exchange earnings, the stabilization of government revenue from export taxes and perhaps the stabilization of the terms of trade. This last advantage turns really on the relative movement of import prices. In the case of both prices of exports and imports rising and falling together, the stabilization of any one of them may lead to the destabilization of the terms of trade for the country concerned.

Stabilization of the real income of the producer is a big problem because it does not depend only on the movements of the price of his produce alone, but also on the prices of the goods he buys. As such a policy needs extensive administrative machinery and adequate statistics, both of which are absent in the Sudan and in other underdeveloped countries, we feel that little can be achieved in this direction.

Government revenue is probably destabilized if it tries to stabilize cotton prices and income directly through taxation and subsidy. But fluctuations in government revenue are not as serious as they seem. They can easily be smoothed out through some method of averaging. However, the stabilization schemes we have suggested here do not destabilize the government revenue because they are mainly independent, being financed by the tenants and the cotton producers themselves. The instability in the government revenue will continue, however, because of the fluctuations in its share of cotton profits (in absolute terms) and also in receipts from taxes, especially export duties. The government can and must stabilize public expenditure at an average level of revenue over a number of years rather than spend at the current level of revenue. In fact, the Sudan Government did attempt such a policy. In 1949 a Revenue Equalization Account was established with the object of stabilizing government revenue in order to avoid drastic reductions in government current expenditure in years of low revenue. The major credit to this account was made from a budget surplus of high export proceeds in 1951-52. A substantial part of this account was used to finance an irrigation project. Since 1951-52 no additions have been made to the account. It was a good policy to establish such an account, but unfortunately it was used for the wrong purposes. Such an account should have been used for the stabilization of government revenue in low years (e.g. 1958-59) and not for extraordinary development projects.

Arguments for stabilization of income and/or price

So far we have argued the case for stabilizing price and income. We have suggested a guaranteed minimum cotton price under a national buffer stock as a way of stabilizing the cotton price in the Sudan. This is a very modest way of stabilization. This method of stabilization, besides being desirable from an administrative point of view because of its simplicity, is mainly desirable because it reduces the waste of the Sudan's productive resources.

If cotton becomes unprofitable or almost unprofitable tenants on the various schemes will not find it attractive to put any substantial effort into production in that season, and the small cotton farmer of the Nuba Mountains will definitely reduce both the area under cotton and the effort that goes into cotton production. Most probably the tenant puts a certain money value on his labour, and if cotton prices fall to such an extent that he does not get what he expects for his labour, he will definitely prefer to have more leisure and less cotton. Assuming that more cotton or a higher income is better than more leisure for the tenant, price instability can lead to waste or to a loss of productive resources which could have been utilized in more cotton production and could perhaps have led ultimately to a higher rate of growth for the Sudan. However, if such a value judgment about the preference of the tenant for higher income and less leisure cannot be accepted, there is still some waste of economic resources in the sense that the tenant cannot use his labour or effort in the best possible way (or in the case of Private Cotton Pump scheme, the owner cannot allocate his investment in the most profitable way) because of cotton price fluctuations. At the beginning of any season it is quite possible that the cotton price may drop drastically and remain low for most of the season or perhaps until the cotton is picked. Cotton production thus becomes unprofitable or almost unprofitable and therefore the tenant may decide to reduce the effort that be devoted to cotton, though the area under cotton remains the same due to rotation. Towards the end of the season, or after the cotton is picked, world demand for cotton may increase and cotton prices may rise considerably. Then the tenant would find it too late to increase his cotton production or improve its quality for that season; and the opposite is equally true if prices are high during the season and fall sharply at the end of it. The tenant cannot allocate his effort or time between leisure and cotton production in the most satisfactory way because of cotton price fluctuations and his inability to forecast such fluctuations. Thus over the years the tenant's satisfaction or well-being can be greater with a more stable price which is guaranteed at the beginning of the season, even if he does not produce any more cotton.

In the case of the cotton farmer of the Nuba Mountains, who is free to use less land and less labour for cotton, the possibility of growing some other alternative crops reduces the economic waste. However, as the prices of most agricultural products move together, and the total area under all crops may tend to fluctuate too, one can still detect some waste of productive resources.

It may be worth while here to summarize the advantages of the stabilization scheme operated by an agency of a national buffer stock:

(1) Because it is a modest and simple scheme, it does not require a huge administrative machine.

(2) By putting a floor to price fluctuations it prevents waste of productive resources.

(3) By carrying cotton stocks until world prices rise, it gives the Sudan and the cotton producers higher prices, higher output and even higher cotton proceeds.

(4) By adjusting the minimum guaranteed price to the size of the stock and by allowing prices to fluctuate above the floor it does not choke the price mechanism and thus it does not isolate supply from demand conditions in the long run.

We have already mentioned that price stabilization may not necessarily lead to income stability. But income stabilization is important for certain economic and social considerations.

Wide fluctuations in the incomes of the cotton producers (whether tenant or farmer) may create great hardships. Small cotton producers and tenants are unlikely to have the self-restraint and foresight to set aside in good times a part of their incomes as a reserve to cushion the effects of bad times. It seems clear that the social factors must be put in the forefront of those which affect the making of national policies stabilization. The social objective of these policies, in view of the wide income fluctuations, is social justice, through action by the state. This social aspect is much more important in the production of agricultural raw materials than in the exploitation of mineral resources. While the former is generally carried out by many small producers whose income is relatively low and who have no means of countering its fluctuations, the production of minerals is usually concentrated in the hands of large companies which are often themselves in a position to devise an adequate policy to iron out fluctuations. When income is generally low, any downward fluctuations in it can cause very great hardships for farming families. However, it is difficult to stabilize the farmers' income in the subsistence sector for economic and administrative reasons.

Foreign direct investment has not, and is not, likely to finance any significant proportion of the Sudan's future developments. As to international aid, this evades any chance of prediction as it seems to depend largely on political factors rather than on economic premises. It appears, then, that the Sudan will have to rely on self-help, at least in the early stages of its development. The first possibility here is the borrowing from the public, or mobilization of savings. Thus every possible means should be attempted to increase domestic savings. By stabilizing the income of the cotton producer through a moving average, or, in effect, by forcing him to save in the short-run when his income rises, we may make him save more voluntarily in the long-run. A more regular income, besides reducing his hardships, helps him to organize and plan his consumption and this may lead to more saving in the long-run. When incomes are rising from a bad year to a good year it is easy to increase consumption, but when income falls it is not as easy to cut down consumption and cotton producers may find it necessary to borrow in an attempt to maintain the same standard of living as before.

Fluctuations in expenditure, resulting from changes in cotton incomes met by an inelastic home supply of food materials while imports are changing after a lag, can easily lead to general instability. This is actually accentuated in the Sudan by the fact that cotton boards deposit all their surpluses with commercial banks. At the end of December 1959 advances rose by Ls. 10·8 million, financed to the extent of Ls. 5·8 million by the increase in the deposits of cotton boards.[1] This shows clearly the importance of the role played by the surpluses of

---

[1] *Bank of Sudan*, Annual Report, 1960, Khartoum, March 1961, p. 26.

cotton boards in the creation of advances in the Sudan, though 1959 was not in any way a year of exceptionally high cotton proceeds. In years of high cotton proceeds, in which both national income and demand are high, banks, because of the surpluses of cotton boards, are able and willing to expand advances, while the opposite is true in years of low cotton proceeds. Wide changes in the size of advances lead to more fluctuations in expenditure and add to the general instability of the economy.

Another interesting aspect of cotton production in the Sudan, which may have some bearing on transmitting instability from income derived from cotton to the whole economy, is that the cotton is produced mainly by Sudanese capital and labour, although about a quarter of the hired labour in the Gezira in 1958-59 came from Nigeria and French Equatoria. Private owners of cotton pump schemes, especially the small ones, may borrow capital on short-term bases for running their schemes. Some of this capital used to come from foreign banks in the early 1950's before the Ministry of Finance and Economics made available to such people some loan facilities; later in 1960 the Agricultural Bank was established for this purpose. As the whole private sector produces much less than 20 per cent of the Sudan's cotton, and a small fraction of that is financed by foreign capital, it seems that the bulk of the cotton income goes into Sudanese pockets. Though this has the advantage that the Sudanese alone enjoy almost all the fruits of their land, it has the disadvantage of making them bear alone the full burden of fluctuations in cotton income, while the foreigners who help them in the production of their cotton get a very stable income in form of profits, wages and interest.[1] The conclusion is that the stabilization of the income of the cotton producers in the Sudan is absolutely essential for the stability of the whole Sudanese economy.

On the other hand, wide fluctuations in the income of the cotton producer may lead to waste by demanding structural changes in the economies of the producing country because of making hired labour fluctuate between the agricultural or the cotton sector and the industrial sector. When cotton producers receive high incomes from cotton, especially those who have small families or are old, they cut down some of their labour, substituting it with hired labour, and take more leisure. The tenancy in the cotton schemes of the Sudan, whether government or private, is designed with the view that the tenant and his family supply all the necessary labour for the production of cotton. There is a certain amount of permanently hired labour, but this constitutes a *very small percentage* of the total labour force engaged in

[1] J. V. Levin, *Export Economies*, Harvard University Press, Cambridge, Mass., 1960, pp. 302-304.

cotton production. Changes in this hired labour force do not have any important effect on the supply of cotton in the Sudan because, besides the fact that the size of the hired labour force is only a very small percentage of the tenant labour, it is also complementary when the incomes of the tenants become high. Tenants who are old or have a small family cut down their labour and substitute hired labour when their incomes become high. Though these changes in the size of the hired labour force are not important as far as the cotton sector is concerned, they are important for industry and the economic development of the Sudan. Such permanent hired labour is the only potential supply of labour for all industries in the Sudan. It is, however, made unstable through the instability of the cotton sector. When cotton income is low, and wages are low in the cotton sector, the labourers, or some of them at least, move to industry, and as soon as wages rise in the cotton sector because of higher incomes they move back. They are not getting high enough wages to keep them in industry because industry is still in its infancy and its productivity is very low. These shifts of the labour force will certainly reduce the efficiency of industry, through the lack of specialization, and may discourage investment in industry due to the uncertain supply of labour. In such conditions it is difficult for anyone to estimate the most probable level of profits. Therefore, when we stabilize the income of the cotton producer, we do not only stabilize his consumption of goods and increase his savings, but also regularize his work and leisure, and ultimately reduce shifts of the labour force and create conditions more favourable for general economic development.

The means of stabilization

While some countries use *ad hoc* methods, other countries have made a determined effort to work out a set approach to price or income fixing. There are, possibly, two main reasons for this. One is that it reduces the farmer's feeling of insecurity to know exactly what factors enter into the price or income fixing process. The other is that it reduces as much as possible the area of political pressure and corruption, or, at least, controversy and arbitrariness.[2] The choice of any definite formula or set approach for fixing the level of price or income is an arbitrary one in itself, but it is much less arbitrary than leaving all current decisions on price or income levels to be made on an *ad hoc* basis.

[1] We cannot go more fully into this problem because we are mainly concerned with the partial analysis of instability of the cotton sector rather than with the general analysis of economic growth in the Sudan.
[2] Food and Agricultural Organization, 'Problems of Agricultural Support and Stabilization in Asia and the Far East', *Monthly Bulletin of Agricultural Economics and Statistics*, Vol. VII, Nos. 7/8, pp. 3-4.

There are different formulae for stabilization but the income formula seems to be most comprehensive. However, the net income formula runs into the difficulty of relying on a concept which is difficult to pin down statistically. Apart from the conceptual difficulties, a considerable margin of error is liable to enter into the calculation.

In the Sudan cotton is produced either by tenants in cotton schemes, or by small farmers using rather primitive methods. In the case of the tenant, the income he gets is mainly for his labour, as all the expenses on the capital goods, fertilizers, pest-control chemicals, etc., are paid for from the share of the board and government. The small farmer, on the other hand, does not incur such expenses because of his simple and primitive methods. In such cases there is little difference between net and gross money income from cotton. To avoid all conceptual problems and excessive costs incurred in compiling information on prices and costs in order to compute a net income for the cotton producer, it is much better if we use a *gross money income* concept.

Before leaving the discussion on the formulae approach, or the set approach, it may be worth while to discuss a directly linked and interesting problem. We have already suggested the use of a moving average for smoothing out income fluctuations. The choice of the length of the period over which the producer's income is to be averraged out is an important problem. This questions brings out *the essence of income stabilization which is really a compromise between efficiency and equity.* Any decision made as to how long the period should be is arbitrary, but we can say that if the period chosen is very long, say ten years, then production may become detached from the conditions of demand, and, on the other hand, if the period chosen is very short, the hardships created by a fluctuating income are not reduced sufficiently. Thus a compromise has to be made and perhaps a period of three or four years may be suitable.

Finally we come to discuss how actual stabilization policies for the cotton sector in the Sudan can be carried out, or implemented in different ways. So far we have discussed price stabilization through a national buffer stock, and income stabilization through the use of moving average together with the use of a reserve fund. However, there are three other methods, or groups of tools for the stabilization of price and/or income, the *physical measures, fiscal policy* and *control.* These can be used with the above-mentioned measures to create greater stability in price and income for the whole Sudan, or can be used alone. Price and income fluctuate because of changes in supply and demand. The Sudan cannot change or influence the world cotton demand or supply, but she can take certain measures to affect or regulate the flow of her supply of cotton, not in order to influence the world cotton supply and price, but merely to reduce the fluctuations in the cotton yield per feddan and ultimately smooth out some of the income fluctuations of her own cotton producers; and we have already seen from Table 3 how far the cotton yield per feddan fluctuates from year to year. Perhaps the most effective measures in this respect are the regulation of the flow or supply of water by replacing rainfall by perennial irrigation through the use of dams and reservoirs on the Nile and other rivers, further research to find more effective pest controls and pest-resistant cotton plants, the training of farmers and tenants and perhaps diversification. A major difficulty about making more extensive use of such physical measures is their cost. In general the cost of such measures falls on the government, and to shift the emphasis of stabilization from buffer stock, reserve fund and fiscal policies to physical measures may mean, in the Sudan (and other underdeveloped countries), that a heavy economic burden is transferred from the cotton producers to the treasury and taxpayer. This may be more equitable in developed countries where taxes are graduated with incomes and where farmers fall into a lower income group than the rest of society. At the same time, however, such physical measures cannot be ignored completely in the Sudan (or any other underdeveloped country). The other type of stabilization tool is fiscal policy. Taxation can stabilize both income and price and may be used with or without subsidy.

The use of export taxes as an effective means of stabilization has been a controversial question in the literature of fiscal policy. Some economists, notably Buchanan and Ellis,[1] and W. A. Lewis,[2] strongly advocate the use of export taxes for economic and political reasons; while some other economists, such as Professor Nurkse,[3] recommend the use of general taxation instead of export taxes. Charles E. Staley[4] concludes that 'export taxes should not be regarded as stabilization devices' in the case he studied, and supports the view of Professor Nurkse. But what are the merits and demerits of export taxation?

Export tax has one important political advantage and that is that it is easy to hide from the general public or to persuade them that such a tax is borne by the foreign buyers.

The economic effects or the economic advantages and disadvantages of export taxes depend on the one hand on the incidence of the tax which in turn depends on the elasticity of supply and demand of the

[1] N. S. Buchanan and H. E. Ellis, *Approaches to Economic Development*, New York, 1953, pp. 316-17.

[2] W. A. Lewis, *The Theory of Economic Growth*, Homewood, Illinois, 1954, p. 291.

[3] R. Nurkse, 'Trade Fluctuations and Buffer Policies of Low Income Countries', *Kyklos*, Vol. XI, 1958, pp. 152-154.

[4] Charles E. Staley, 'Export Taxes in Ceylon 1948-52', *Public Finance*, 1959, p. 264.

taxed export crop, and on the other hand on the expenditure of the revenue collected from the tax. If importer demand is inelastic and the export supply is elastic, the tax is shifted forward, and if the demand is elastic and the supply inelastic, the tax is shifted backward. As the Sudan produces only about 5 per cent of the world supply, the demand for its cotton is more elastic than the world cotton demand. Though the Sudan is mainly a producer of extra-long staple cotton, the high rate of substitution between the different types of cotton makes the demand for the Sudan cotton rather elastic and therefore the export tax is expected to be shifted backward, to the Sudanese producer. But in a boom such as the Korean Boom, most probably the demand for raw materials like cotton becomes very strong and inelastic for all the producing countries and, in such a case, the export tax is shifted to the foreign buyer. If all the tax is shifted to the foreign buyer, then it has no stabilizing effect on the income of the cotton producer. It merely increases the total proceeds of the Sudan from cotton. The cotton producer would have the same income while the government would have more revenue. If the government spends that revenue in the boom then it may lead to increasing the pace of inflation which may have already gone very far. If the export tax is borne by the exporting country, then there is a number of possibilities for sharing the incidence or the burden of the tax. It is possible that all or a part of the burden of the tax is borne by foreign firms in the exporting country depending on the part they play in the export crop. As the profits of such firms are usually sent abroad, the effect of such a tax on the instability in the export country will only be to the extent that it affects retained and invested profits. But in the case of the Sudan, as foreign firms play no direct part in producing the cotton and a small part in exporting the cotton (which they usually do for a commission as buying agents), it seems that the effect of such a tax cannot be important in this respect. The bulk of the tax burden will be borne by the indigenous producers, the tenants, the boards, the Government and the owners of the pump schemes. In such circumstances it will stabilize their income and may reduce their consumption or investment. It is not highly probable that all or most of it will be shifted to the workers because the size of the hired labour employed for the cotton production is small and a considerable part of it is used during the picking season and there is always a great labour shortage during that season. In 1961 and 1962 the government had to call students and the army to help in the cotton picking in the large schemes.

However, as future price fluctuations are likely to be fairly moderate such as those of 1955 and 1959, rather than that very strong boom of the Korean War, it is possible to have a reasonably effective and progressive export tax which can help to stabilize the income of the cotton producers of the Sudan. But such a progressive export tax may have disincentive or misallocation effects. This depends partly on the use of the revenue collected from the tax. If the revenue from the export tax is used to subsidize the cotton producers in bad times, then most probably there will be no movement of capital and labour from the cotton sector as income earned in the cotton sector will simply be stabilized at the same level, while an export tax without a subsidy means income stabilized but at a lower level. At the same time, if the export tax proceeds are used to finance public expenditure which benefits all the sectors of the economy rather than the cotton sector, then there may be disincentive effects associated with the export tax.[1] In the case of the Sudan, the government already takes a certain percentage from the cotton producers (except the Private Cotton Pump Schemes) for providing any special services to the cotton scheme or area. So any increase in the export taxes on cotton in the Sudan – under the present system of percentage sharing and marketing of cotton – will mean an increase in the government revenue and more expenditure on all the sectors of the economy and ultimately means income redistribution in favour of the other sectors of the Sudanese economy, benefiting people such as all government, firms' and banks' employees who do not pay any income tax and perhaps no other direct tax. As the *per capita* income of a considerable part of the cotton producers in areas such as the Nuba Mountains, the Zandeland, Gash, etc., is much less than the bulk of such employees, it seems very unfair from an equity point of view that such an income redistribution takes place. Furthermore, it may be argued that though export, taxes may accomplish their goal of stabilization of cotton prices, they may encourage the cotton producers, especially in remote areas, to move into the subsistence sector.[2] Though stability of income and prices of the cotton sector is very desirable, equity and efficiency of the economy cannot be completely sacrificed for it.

If the export tax is to be effective as a means of stabilization of the income of the cotton producer, it has to be *progressive and high*. But at the same time the effect of such a tax on the expansion of the cotton or any export crop cannot be ignored. Professor Nurkse quotes the case of Argentina as an example of how a high export tax can harm the export sector, reduce export supply and damage the country's major source of foreign exchange.[3]

But, in spite of these demerits, an export tax has important adminis-

[1] J. V. Levin, *Export Economies*, Harvard University Press, Cambridge, Mass., 1960, pp. 271-280.

[2] John F. Due, *Taxation and Economic Development in Tropical Africa* M. I. T. Press, Cambridge, Mass., 1963, p. 146.

[3] R. Nurkse, *op. cit.* p. 152.

trative and economic advantages which make it very attractive to use. It is very easy to administer in the first place. Elaborate accounting is not necessary; evasion is rather difficult.[1] In the second place, it can tap increases in income as soon as they arise. Most of the under-developed countries suffer frequently from export-induced inflation and a progressive and high export tax can be very effective for the pre-vention of such inflations, or at least can reduce them to a great extent. As a matter of fact, no other tax in the Sudan at present can tap so effectively an increase in income of the export sector as soon as it rises or be so easily administered. If the land tax is to be used for such a purpose it will entail great administrative work and cost, while the Business Profit Tax only touches the owners of the private cotton pump schemes who form a small percentage of the total cotton pro-ducers in the Sudan. Indirect taxes cannot be used until the rise or fall in the income of the export sector is generalized throughout the economy. But before that, no higher indirect tax can be used without making all the people in the non-export sector suffer. If, therefore, in the Sudan, where there is no income tax, we accept Professor Nurkse's suggestion of using general taxation rather than export tax and of using some indirect taxes because they are easier to administer, we can only stabilize the income of the cotton producers or the export sector after we let instability spread to the whole economy first, or sacrifice equity!

However, taking into consideration the fact that the instability in the income of the cotton producer in the Sudan arises from fluctua-tions in the yield per feddan as well as from the price of cotton and that the fluctuations in the yield per feddan are greater than the price fluctuations, *using progressive export tax which acts on export price alone may not lead to consistent stabilization of the income of the cotton producer*. In one year the cotton producer may have high prices but very low yields and vice versa in another year. Perhaps a progressive income tax can be more consistent because it operates directly on income rather than upon just one of the variables that makes income.

In the past, prior to 1953, the Sudan cotton was sold directly to foreign buyers. The Sudan Plantations Syndicate used to export and sell its cotton on the Liverpool Cotton Exchange. During the war years and until 1953 the Sudan Government, mainly representing the cotton boards, sold cotton directly to the United Kingdom Raw Cotton Commission and to the Indian Government. In the case of such direct sale of cotton from the public schemes, the government, the boards and the tenants were the exporters. As export taxes have been included in the joint cost accounts of such cotton schemes, the Sudan

[1] K. J. Rothwell, 'Taxes on Exports in Underdeveloped Countries', *Public Finance*, Vol. XVIII, Nos. 3-4, 1963, pp. 311-312.

M

Government had to pay about 44 per cent of the export taxes by one hand in order to get the revenue from them by the other. Also if the export tax is shifted backward to the producers, the Sudan Government may bear 44 per cent of it. Thus export tax on cotton was not particularly popular with the government and was not taken seriously as a tool of stabilization.

Control can be used as a means of price stabilization, but, besides affecting only price, it can only be exercised within the national boundaries. Cotton, being an export crop, makes its price outside the Sudan Government control. Only when the time comes when the Sudan's cotton is processed and consumed in the Sudan can control be an effective tool for the stabilization of cotton price. However, control, besides interfering with the price mechanism and allocation of resources, may require huge administrative machinery to carry it out and at a great cost; and, in any country which does not have enough trained staff and citizens with sense of civic responsibility, control may lead to corruption and bribery.

In conclusion, we must note that the decision to produce other crops rather than cotton in general, or extra-long staple cotton in particular, does not depend only on the movement of prices of cotton in relation to the prices of other export crops that can be produced in the Sudan, but on the margin between price and cost. Prices of cotton – or extra-long staple cotton in this case – may have a downward trend, *but cotton still remains more profitable than any other export crop in the Sudan.*

TABLE 1 The percentage shares of cotton, gum, sesame and groundnuts in the Sudan's exports, 1949-59.

year	cotton %	gum %	sesame %	groundnuts %
1949	72	6	Nil[1]	2
1950	72	8	Nil	1
1951	78	6	Nil	1
1952	70	6	2	3
1953	62	7	3	4
1954	56	9	4	3
1955	62	10	4	5
1956	64	9	2	6
1957	45	9	6	9
1958	51[2]	12	5	8
1959	60[2]	8	4	5

[1] Less than 1 per cent.
[2] Cotton, excluding seed and scarto, for 1958 to 1959.

Source: Calculated from *Annual Foreign Trade Reports*, Department of Statistics, Sudan Government.

TABLE 2 World production of extra-long staple cotton and the share of the Sudan, 1957-58 to 1960-61 in 000 bales.

Country	'000 bales			
	1957-58	1958-59	1959-60	1960-61
U.A.R.	847	1185	1078	1045
Sudan	167	535	560	485
	(13%)	(26%)	(30%)	(26%)
Peru	107	129	120	144
U.S.A.	80	82	69	67
Others	50	56	80	72
Total	1251	1987	1907	1813

Source: International Cotton Advisory Committee, *Cotton: Monthly Review World Situation*, November, 1962, p. 4.

TABLE 3   Average annual prices of sakel per kantar and average annual yield per feddan and their percentage changes 1949-50 to 1958-59

Season	(1) average annual price	price change	(2) average annual yield	yield change	(3) tenants' income
	L (Sudan)	%	kantar	%	L (Sudan) (millions)
1949-50	15·5		4·586		5·8
		41·3		47·9	
1950-51	21·9		6·782		18·1
		5·9		54·3	
1951-52	23·2		3·100		6·9
		43·1		51·9	
1952-53	13·5		4·710		5·1
		15·4		4·2	
1953-54	11·5		4·690		6·5
		30·0		8·7	
1954-55	14·6		4·284		5·1
		13·7		13·6	
1955-56	16·6		4·865		7·3
		3·6		43·3	
1956-57	17·0		6·759		8·3
		23·5		77·7	
1957-58	13·0		1·505		0·9
		23·1		213·0	
1958-59	10·3		4·710		5·9
Total	195·6		514·5		
Average annual rate of fluctuation		21·7		57·2	

Source: (1) *Capital Formation and National Income of the Sudan in 1955-56*, Department of Statistics, Sudan Government, p. 29.
    (2) and (3) Gezira Board Headquarters, Accounts Office.
Note: Change in price and yield, taken as the difference between two years and then calculated as a percentage of the first year.

J. J. MACGREGOR

Development of
African Primary Products
and International Trade in Timber

*

An assumption that the planning of the forest industry in any country was part of the general land-use policy and that the allocation of the land resource among competing users was judged broadly on a costs-benefits analysis type of approach would bring comfort and joy to many economists. To foresters it would also be welcome because they are aware that the indirect benefits of their activity – general protection against erosion, desiccation, loss of fertility, and so forth – often appear to be overlooked in policy decisions. It is perhaps not surprising that forest policies are usually worked out in a national context where the main question appears to be how far each country can meet its own requirements and contribute to international trade now and in the future. Satisfactory solutions thus point to surveys of resources, to timber trend studies, to assessments of demand and to estimates of the potential demand and supply of wood in other countries, particularly in the same region.

The claim is often made that systematic forestry can only be practised satisfactorily in areas set aside for this purpose. Estimates have put the area of forest reserves – i.e. demarcated forests – in tropical Africa at 50 million hectares and the *FAO Africa Survey*[1] urged that the area should be doubled – i.e. to the size which is now used there. In 1962 Africa had 17 per cent of the world's total forest area (but only 9 per cent of the area is used), only 7 per cent of the total forest removals and only 1·5 per cent of the industrial wood output. In certain selected areas, particularly in the montane country of East Africa and in the rain forests of West Africa, there are areas of high productivity in timber growth and there is considerable scope there and elsewhere for raising productivity by bringing more forest land into use by growing more on existing land and by making better use of forest products.

There are certain pre-requisites for the formulation and implementation of a reasoned forest policy, especially forest resource inventories and timber trend studies, but I realize that many programmes have been formulated on much less. However, inventories using aerial photography have greatly speeded up some of the survey requirements. Measurement of demand is obviously important in the long-term planning which is associated with land use policies and one appreciates how much of FAO's activities are involved in timber trends studies but it will be many years before Africa will be covered by such investigations.

Even the most casual acquaintanceship with this vast continent makes it quite clear that forestry is carried on in a great variety of environments. For convenience three main forest types were distinguished in the foregoing survey[1]: (1) Closed rain forest; (2) seasonal (deciduous) forest, open woodland, *miombo* and *mopane* woodland; and (3) shrub and thorny savannah and acacia-commiphora woodland. This classification excludes specific reference to possibilities of growing coniferous trees in the montane areas of Africa and there are other special areas where tree-growing is economically productive. Foresters often suggest that increases by the first method would seem to depend on getting away from 'selective' methods either by favouring the growth of the economic species by suitable silvicultural techniques or by wider use of the 'secondary' species. Already, however, the consumption of secondary species has gone a long way and those who have had experience feel that reliance will have to be placed on increased productivity which, more often than not, implies plantation techniques – even in high forest zones.

An example of forest development which involves plantations and higher productivity is described for Gabon, where:

it was realized that as supplies of okoume are vital for the maintenance of future production at the present level, it is necessary to carry out a planting programme. Okoume plantations are being established at the rate of 2000 hectares per year, based on a target yield of 300 tons per hectare in a 60-year rotation which would provide 600,000 tons of okoume annually. Furthermore, naturally regenerated okoume stands subject to silvicultural improvement operations give a yield of 50 tons of timber per hectare per rotation, against 10 to 15 tons per hectare in unimproved natural forests.

The price of timber determines what can be spent on its extraction and this (often about 70 per cent or more of total cost) varies with species and relevant markets. For this reason improvements in the infrastructure and equipment have an obvious and direct bearing on the extent of the zone within which timber can be commercially handled. It is clear enough that the high extraction costs will limit the use of natural forest crops for pulp and paper.

For the second type of forest it is pointed out that their multiple use raises some difficulties, such as the competition between private agriculture and forestry. There is scope for the economic use of the forest and woodlands, and especially for establishing plantations, particularly of exotic species such as eucalyptus and pines; and these could be attractive to private commercial enterprises. The report mentions that the best indigenous woodland can supply an average of 20 tons per hectare on a 20 years rotation compared with the exotic species in a 30 years rotation producing 8 to 10 times as much. Not only could these plantations supply structural, mining and fuel needs; they could also be the basis of pulp for paper if supplies could be planned on a regional basis to meet the minimum raw material volumes necessary for an efficient mill.

In this type of forest, in the open woodland, trees carry out a variety of protective functions, but in many areas they are also potentially, if not actually, productive. The importance for the economic development of many African countries by improved use of these forest types was recognized by the FAO Forestry Commission during its first session (Ibadan 1960) when it set up an *ad hoc* working party to examine existing work and to make recommendations.

Close integration of forestry and grazing requirements is described as essential in the third forest type and also in the miombo woodlands. Later burning, associated with grazing, is inimical to the growth of trees and it was urged that the conflict would have to be resolved by sound land-use planning. Three different requirements were distinguished for (*a*) those areas where grazing had priority; (*b*) areas where close integration implied controlled or early burning, and (*c*) areas where forest reserves – with productive and protective functions – had priority and here burning had to be prohibited. An associated part of the recommended policy is the protection of the wild life of the area; it is again of interest that the African Forestry Commission (1960) also set up a working party on wildlife management.

Development of forest industries

Variety in the needs of the rural and urban populations and in the growing demands are likely to be associated with increasing incomes and populations make it desirable to examine briefly the characteristics of the different forest industries and then to judge what part they may play in development.

Processing industries using wood as their raw material vary widely in their capital and labour requirements and this may set limits to their suitability for development in given districts or regions. The extent to which they are capital intensive, subject to economies of scale, require skilled technicians or require imported raw materials have obvious bearing on their opportunities for given situations. The extent to which they are likely to be attracted will depend on the quality and quantity of supplies in a given area. The report on *The Role of Forest Industries in the Attack on Economic Underdevelopment* comprehensively reviews this important function implied in its title.[6]

Wood is the traditional building material in Africa, but often in the peasant agricultural areas the demand is for poles rather than for sawn wood and in the savannah there are shortages of suitable poles. Industrial and urban areas create the main demand for sawn wood which, near the west coast, is met from the rain forest belt and elsewhere from dispersed pockets and partly from softwood imports. Heavy sawmilling is concentrated on the west coast. Inter-regional trade is of minor significance in tropical Africa. The western trade produces a surplus for export – with most going as logs for the plywood and sawmill industries particularly of Western Europe. For the Ivory Coast, Gabon and the Congo (Brazzaville) sawn-wood exports are less than 3 per cent by volume of the log exports and for Nigeria they are 11 per cent.

Prospects have been described in *FAO Africa Survey* as follows:
With the approaching exhaustion of areas being 'salvage-felled' for agriculture in West Africa, it seems probable that West African timber removals and production will decline in the future in some of the major producing areas, unless production from reserves coupled with improved silvicultural techniques can make up for the deficit. It is significant that in Nigeria it is even now being forecast that within the next two decades or so the export trade in timber will have virtually ended. The situation will undoubtedly direct attention to secondary timbers now in poor demand, and also to hitherto somewhat neglected areas, such as Liberia and Eastern Nigeria. It is also certain that a larger local demand will develop as a consequence of the rising living standards of a rapidly increasing population, and that this will lead to an increase in local sawmilling. On balance, however, there is some prospect of the volume of exports being maintained for some time to come.[1]

There is an active, efficient, plywood industry on the west coast where there are logs of fine veneer quality. If a shortage developed local supplies could be maintained by diverting logs from the export trade. The production has increased to 97,600 cubic metres in 1959 – a sevenfold increase from 1950. There are only two other smallish plywood mills in other tropical regions south of the Sahara and outside the west coast suitable material is scarce. Although there has been a fairly rapid increase in the consumption of fibreboard and particle board in Africa in individual countries the demand is not sufficiently high for establishing these industries – but the raw material should be plentiful enough and, again for economic reasons, plantations are likely to be the sources.

Paper consumption has also been growing rapidly and it seems likely that some countries may start manufacturing in the near future. In 1962 the only two relatively small-scale mills producing paper in tropical Africa south of the Sahara were in Southern Rhodesia where pine plantations provide the raw material supplemented by waste paper and some imported pulp. The possibilities of having modern mills are more likely to be achieved on a regional, rather than on a national, basis if obvious difficulties of organization and politics can be overcome. Technically there is no difficulty about pulping tropical African hardwoods and the long-fibre requirements in paper making (20 to 25 per cent of total) could be provided by coniferous plantations on selected sites. It should be possible to grow plantations of suitable conifers for producing long fibres in most African countries.

Current problems of supply and demand

An introduction to the current problems in Africa is to be found in *African Timber Trends and Prospects* (1964), which is the first stage of a comprehensive study for Africa as a whole. It covers most of tropical Africa and is divided into six country groupings.

East Africa. If we take the east group of countries first: in each of these countries, Kenya, Tanganyika and Uganda, FAO has carried out wood consumption studies[7] – and is thus better served than in the other five groups. It was expected that a break-through of industrialization in forestry was imminent and the demand projections for the main groups of forest products – both in East and West Africa – are summarized in relation to 1960 in Table 1.

While there is likely to be difficulty about supplies of saw and veneer logs for the 1980 level of demand, this may be met by careful pre-planning; greater economies in sawn-wood uses and greater reliance on secondary species and on wood-based panel products. Kenya's plantations could meet the expected paper (newsprint excluded) and paperboard needs and the small roundwood needs for fibreboard and and particle board needs should also be readily available.

The prospect for 1980 in East Equatorial Africa is thus summarized as holding promise for a substantial expansion in its sawmilling and plywood industry, for installations of a particle-board industry and of an integrated pulp and paper enterprise. By 1980 exports of sawn hardwoods may decline slightly but it was also thought that there would be an offsetting decline in sawn-wood imports and virtual elimination of plywood imports. If the particle board industry develops, the fibreboard imports would also be expected to decline. Newsprint is likely to be the main import of value even with an integrated pulp and paper industry installed. Yet for the area as a whole by 1980 export and import values of wood products should be in balance; in 1960 import values were four times those of exports. After that time there will have to be reliance on an expansion of plantations of both exotic and indigenous species.

West Africa. In the ecological sense the five groups of West African countries are divisible into two zones: (*a*) the savannah – a wood deficit zone, and (*b*) the tropical high forests – which are wood surplus areas.

Sawn wood in the savannah areas is not used much – partly because saw-logs are scarce and partly because incomes are low and consequently import prices are too high. Construction in this zone depends much on poles and branchwood which are regarded as adequate for foreseeable needs. However, there are bound to be local shortages which can be met by planning conveniently-sited pole plantations and, for this, research could be effectively diverted to site and species requirements. Imports meet about 40 per cent of sawn-wood consumption and it is likely that reliance on West Africa will continue after 1975, as it will for veneer logs. Only in Senegal is it thought likely that local demand would be sufficient to justify the establishment of a particle-board industry. For pulp products the small market seems likely to rule out economic production although in Senegal production, supplemented with imported long-fibre pulp, might be possible for small-scale production of certain paper grades.

The position of the savannah countries was summed up in the Economic Commission for Africa's report[2] which estimated that the demand expected in 1975 should offer 'interesting' trade prospects to the wood-surplus countries of West Africa – with the possible exception of pulp products. A conclusion is that, in spite of the difficulties, efforts should be made to increase output of raw material by plantation in order to meet the expansion of demand and growth in the period beyond 1975. It was thought that saw-log rotations should be adopted even if high-grade logs could not be expected.

The second group – the wood-surplus countries of West Africa – includes Commonwealth, French-speaking, Spanish and Portuguese countries. These are associated with tropical high forest and with the traditional export timbers. Between 1950 and 1960 log exports from these countries increased three and a half times.

Substantial rises in demand for the domestic market by 1975 are expected, but the ability to meet these demands for veneer logs without eroding the basis of the export potential is questioned. A more concentrated attack on the forest could help to reduce extraction costs, and perhaps could widen the range of species acceptable in the export market; but some weighty effort will have to be made to convince the trade about these possibilities. Potential European demand for veneer-grade logs is likely to advance steeply in 1975, but it is not thought that this demand can be met from the traditional species: half of the existing volume is confined to two species – okoume and obeche – and 90 per cent to eleven species. If there were a gradual transfer of EEC plywood factories to the raw material areas in West

Africa these would enable a wider range of species to be used. The preparation of veneers in West Africa for export to European plywood factories is a possibility and any improvement in communications would be helpful in expanding log-production.

Sawn-wood exports are likely to move more slowly than those for veneer logs. It is thought that the greatly expanded sawmill industry which will be necessary to meet the heavier domestic demand should have little difficulty in meeting overseas needs for high-grade material. Other wood-based panel products (fibreboard and particle board) should have an expanded demand similar to that for plywood. By 1975 the demand level for these products should be sufficiently high to justify the establishment of competitive production units in some of the surplus countries (Congo-Leopoldville and Nigeria) and the raw material basis should be ample.

Expansion of paper and pulp demand is expected to go beyond that for wood-based panels and should increase by threefold the 1960 levels by 1975. Here, again, Congo-Leopoldville and Nigeria are likely to be most suitable for economic production of pulp and paper products, but the possibilities for small-scale industries in Ghana, Ivory Coast and within the Equatorial Customs Union should not be ruled out. It would still be necessary to import the long-fibre pulp needs but the rest could be obtained from natural or planted broadleaved species.

The broad inference from all these assessments is that the prospects for Africa are substantial and the existing industries (sawmilling, plywood, veneer and blockboard) are likely to be supplemented by such new industries as particle board, fibreboard, and pulp and paper products. In view of the expected and continuing expansion of West African timber demand and the problem of how best to meet the demand for veneer-grade logs, it is felt that much more information about the forest and its content will be required for extension of economic exploitation. In other words, the supply position will have to be elucidated. A conclusion that can be applied to the African forests as a whole was:

For the longer-term prospect, beyond 1975, to meet the even
heavier demands that will then arise, competent personnel with
adequate technical qualifications will be needed to serve the
forest estate and to promote the usage of a far wider range than is
now the case. The best methods of improvement of the natural
forests will have to be sought and applied, and plantations of exotics
such as teak and gmelina and of native species should be expanded
to the limit of economic feasibility. Suitable ground for the planting
of coniferous species should also be assiduously sought out.[2]

Much concern is felt about the position after 1980 and it is perhaps not sufficiently emphasized by the policy makers that action should be taken now if supplies are to be assured.

International trade in forest products

In 1961 the value of the world trade in forest products was about 5 per cent of the total.* In relative terms the forest product trade of the developing countries has grown faster in recent years than the world trade in this commodity and also faster than the developing countries' trade in all commodities; yet the growth in these exports is little more than sufficient to keep pace with forest product imports.

The net trade deficit is explainable by the fact that the exports are mainly unprocessed while imports are mainly processed. Because most forest products are not 'portable' in the economic sense many items, such as fuelwood, rough poles, pulpwood and pitprops hardly enter into international trade. Most of the trade is, in fact, inter-regional, e.g. inside Europe and inside North America. The percentage entering world trade has been shown as 2, 11 and 16 for unprocessed roundwood, processed wood, and pulp and paper products respectively. However, the weight-losing effect has not always been the most decisive explanation for the location of forest industries; indeed, the population distribution and potential demand distribution do not coincide readily with the raw material distribution. Economic efficiency dictates that the siting of pulp-industries – which find their most suitable raw material in coniferous species – is largely in the northern hemisphere. However, the FAO view is that there will be a steady, but distinct, movement away from existing positions and the change will provide opportunities for the developing countries. Over 70 per cent of all the trade is between 'advanced' countries, of which one-third is between U.S. and Canada and one-half between European countries. In recent years it is known that two main streams of international trade have developed from Asia to Japan and from Africa to Europe.

Not only is the expansion of trade limited geographically, but it is also concentrated on unprocessed roundwood especially on hardwood logs. What little pulp and paper comes from the developing countries to the 'advanced' countries comes from North Africa. Europe is still the main market for forest products exported from the developing countries (especially from West Africa) and absorbs more than half of the total. Japan has become an extremely important market for hardwood logs, with North America presently ranking next in importance.

By 1975 it was reckoned in the report on prospects[3] that the develop-

* These introductory remarks are based on 'Prospects for Expanding Forest Products Export from Developing Countries'.[3]

ing countries could raise their earnings in Western Europe from tropical woods from 150 to 400 million dollars as a minimum but, if all were processed in developing countries, the level could be 750 million dollars. Theoretically, the 750 million dollars could be raised to 900 million dollars by fully processing all the existing log trade – this would, of course, have a direct effect on the existing processing industries in Europe. It would be reasonable to expect that processing to veneer and plywood stage and even to the furniture stage might be feasible in the developing countries if political and other hindrances could be removed.

Coniferous trade is small at present from developing countries, but in the East and South-east African exotic pine plantations there is a potential opportunity for expansion. Many of the tropical areas have soil and climatic advantages which would enable production to reach 15 to 30 cubic metres per hectare a year on short rotations compared with 2 to 7 in the natural softwood forests in the north-temperate zone.

The importance of a regional approach to forest development in African countries can be inferred from the following passage:

Of the 11 million dollars in forest product exports within African countries, over one-half were in sawn wood and plywood, with most of the remainder in pulp and pulp products. The bulk of the sawn wood was of broadleaved species which was exported from Ghana to South Africa and other African countries, and from the Congo to Nyasaland.

The presently low levels of trade in forest products between the developing countries (both intra- and inter-regional) and the growing dependence on imports from the developed world noted above are in fact related phenomena. Considerable efforts have been made since the war, especially in Latin America and parts of Asia, to establish domestic forest industries and reduce national dependence on imports of processed wood. Almost invariably, however, these efforts have been conceived within the narrow frame of import substitution at the national level. Countries have been obsessed with the 'dollar saved equals a dollar earned' approach in its crudest form. Confronted by the dilemma of narrow national markets on the one hand and very pronounced economies of scale on the other, countries have established many import-saving – but uneconomic and high-cost mills which have required continuing high protection instead of seeking to resolve the dilemma through effective regional and sub-regional collaboration. The result has been that in the countries where mills have been established, the further development of the forest industries has been retarded or frustrated, while neighbouring countries which might have drawn their supplies from an efficient plant within the region have had to look to the developed countries for rising imports to meet their rising domestic needs.[3]

In studying the trade of the developing countries it is necessary to look at their imports, and to note that in all the regions wood requirements will rise sharply by 1975 – a position which many feel can only be met by expansion of plantations. Some developments are foreseen in broad terms:

Thus by 1975 the developing regions will require annually about 3 billion dollars worth of forest products over and above their current (1959-61) needs.* This is additional to the imports (well over half a billion dollars) they are currently receiving from the advanced countries. Regardless of the important prospects already noted for expanding exports to the developed countries, their own rapidly rising requirements offer opportunities for a rapid expansion of forest industries which, if properly directed, will enable them to ensure the establishment of efficient units, taking full advantage of wider markets and the complementarity of their forest and other fibre resources. An industry securely based on a secure domestic and local market is much better poised to enter the arena of inter-continental trade than one which has no such base on which to gain experience and from which to expand.[8]

It is clear enough that there will have to be very large imports of capital if the desired expansion of forest products is to be achieved in the developing countries.

In examining features of the African export trade I have drawn heavily on the *Report on the Trade in Tropical Wood in Europe up to 1962*.[4] Europe, as a highly industrialized area, is one of the chief markets for timber entering international trade – and as it takes about 90 per cent of African exports the European data can give a useful picture of current trade development.

The growth of the export trade from Africa

Up to the end of the nineteenth century only a few specialty woods such as mahogany, teak and ebony, etc., entered into the world's hardwood trade. Expansion began as exploitation of African forests grew especially for mahogany and gaboon – species which went mainly to Europe and to North America to meet some marginal requirements in the plywood, veneering and sawmilling industries. Before the first world war, Germany and France were the most important importers, and the economic depression of the early 1930's hit the trade very hard, and recovery was slow. Just before the second world war, Europe's hardwood logs were imported in the following percentages: Europe

* Calculated on the basis of world average import (c.i.f.) prices in 1959-61.

(39); North America (7); U.S.S.R. (2) and Tropical areas (52 – mainly from West Africa). On the other hand the sawn hardwoods came mainly from temperate zones, and Europe, itself, provided half of its total import needs.

It has thus been clear that the well-being of the tropical hardwood trade has depended on the economic conditions in the industrialized countries. The introduction of improved slicing and peeling machinery plus mass-production techniques has meant that light-weight tropical species such as gaboon and obeche could be processed technically more efficiently than European woods. This advantage has offset the heavy freight costs which represent about one-third to one-half the import prices. As the more accessible sources were used up logging had to be more efficient and in this the extension of mechanization – always dependent on European initiative – was a big influence as were improved port facilities. Apart from the peeling and slicing qualities, the tropical hardwoods were favoured because of their attractive appearance.

By 1960, in Europe as a whole – the main importer in the world's international trade – the net import of hardwood logs was about 4½ million cubic metres, of which only part came from the tropics. In this year softwood net imports were only 1 per cent of the total whereas with hardwood the percentage was 14. It is clear enough why the tropical hardwoods accounted for over 90 per cent of Europe's growth in hardwood log requirements; they had the advantages of being shipped in large and predictable quantities; they had large, straight, cylindrical boles, even grain, stability and density. This made many of them suitable for the automated and mass-producing plywood and veneer industries and the large number of species provided the variety which the increasing living standards demanded.

Some of the more important features of the trade with Europe can be inferred from the following tables. Table 2 shows the relative importance in the 10 countries responsible for 97 per cent of Europe's tropical timber imports; it also shows the predominance of African sources, the relative decline in Britain's share, and the growing importance of Western Germany, France and Italy – whose increase had been responsible for 85 per cent of the total change between 1950 and 1960. In 1950 Britain and Germany had 'artificially' high and low positions respectively because they each had limited hard foreign exchange which meant that the former had turned away from dollars to sterling area sources – particularly West Africa. Table 3 shows that Italy, Denmark and Portugal had substantial amounts of their total trade in the Asia/Pacific and the Latin American regions. Nearness to main markets was one big influence on the trade flows: over 90 per cent of African exports went to Europe; 73 per cent of Asian Pacific exports went to Japan, and Latin America sent mainly to North and South America. Italy had come relatively late into the market – one explanation for her greater reliance on non-African sources – but when, for example, the log trade in Ghana was nationalized she was able to take advantage of the hesitancy of Ghana's traditional buyers.

According to the 1963 ECE Timber Committee's *Report*[4] the tropical logs of many species imported into Europe can be shown in three categories:

(1) The largest category includes lightweight logs for peeling and slicing in the manufacture of plywood and non-luxury veneers.

(2) Saw logs for medium quality sawn timber: these are often second quality of the species listed under (1).

(3) The third category, though much smaller by volume, has higher average prices than the two previous categories. It includes logs of selected qualities of the two previous categories as well as such species as afrormosia, ebony and wenge from West Africa, and teak and Brazilian rosewood from Asia. Since they are widely used, for example, in the furniture industry for decorative veneers and high-quality sawn wood, they are the most subject to changing tastes. It was expected – although this is often doubted – that an increasing number of species would win acceptance in Europe as more of the established species became harder to obtain in adequate quantities. The data in Table 5, showing the percentage of main species imported into five European countries, make clear that gaboon was just ahead of obeche.

It was difficult to compare prices between different countries because of differing specifications, but recent trends for French, Dutch and British purchases showed that between December 1959 and mid-1961 the first had increased by 20 per cent, the second by 12 per cent and the third by 30 to 50 per cent. Abura prices showed the only price decline in the period.

Tropical sawn hardwoods

Although in Europe imports of sawn hardwoods played a marginal role in 1961 – about 4 per cent of total requirement – they had risen by about 25 per cent to about a half million cubic metres sawn, or at a faster rate than imports of sawn softwood. In quantitative or proportionate terms, the post-war increase in Europe's sawn hardwoods was small in relation to hardwood logs, and thus the general tendency for semi-manufactured goods such as softwood and pulp to replace raw materials like softwood logs and pulpwood did not apply to hardwoods. The reasons for this situation were explained by the fact that

Europe's veneer and plywood industries needed special qualities of logs and that panel products had been replacing sawn wood since the war especially in the furniture industry which was the main consumer of sawn hardwood. In Scandinavia the manual skill and emphasis on design enable some of these countries to develop a comparative advantage in furniture making although it meant importing tropical hardwoods. France, Rumania and Yugoslavia were important European exporters of sawn hardwoods (76 per cent of total in 1960). Much of the sawnwood is consumed in the expanding furniture and building industries and architects and designers often specified tropical species because of their greater variety in grain, pattern, aesthetic appeal, extreme hardness and dimensional stability (e.g. teak and afrormosia) and homogeneity (e.g. ramin and keruing).

Table 6 – covering 90 per cent of total European imports – shows that the United Kingdom imports more tropical sawn hardwoods than the rest of Europe. The United Kingdom has not had the same problems as some other countries have had in finding its sizes and specifications, for in Africa many of the firms have been British and in Asia the strict grading rules earned the trust of the purchasers. France has tended to trade almost exclusively with its own former overseas territories, but Britain has done little trade with these countries.

Tropical sawnwoods can be divided broadly into three groups: (1) general-purpose timbers with excellent machining properties, such as keruing and ramin, which compete directly with some European species in both price and quality; (2) hard timbers, such as teak and afrormosia; and (3) timbers with outstanding aesthetic appeal, including teak and afrormosia above, and others such as mahogany and utile.

An interesting feature of the 1960 sawn hardwood imports was that 60 per cent of Dutch imports were of Asian species whereas the United Kingdom imports were 50 : 50 Asian and African; and Denmark, in 1955, had teak forming 83 per cent of its imports.

Tariffs on tropical hardwoods

In the 1950's many European countries imported tropical hardwood logs free of import duty, but important exceptions were France and the United Kingdom, where preference was given to their colonies or ex-colonies. In France the *ad volorem* duty ranged from 10 per cent on hardwood logs to 15 to 20 per cent on roughly squared wood, and to 18 to 20 per cent on sawn wood from the 'external' countries. The United Kingdom rates on logs and sawn wood were 10 per cent.

One of the effects of the EEC, EFTA and recent GATT negotiations has been to reduce, or to 'level up' (within EEC) the rates of protection. Recent negotiations have led to a general suspension of protection on

N

tropical hardwoods, in EEC and the United Kingdom, for two years from January 1964, and it is thought likely that the suspension will be made permanent. Thus non-Commonwealth countries will compete in the United Kingdom market on equal terms, as will the associated and non-associated countries. The Common External Tariff of the EEC countries on the listed tropical species is unlikely to come into force. On the other hand, as the ECE Timber Committee's *Report* (1963) points out, exporters of temperate-zone hardwood species to Europe, such as Canada, U.S.A., Japan and Australia, as well as European exporters themselves, will face stronger competition from tropical sources.

CONCLUSIONS

(1) One must not exaggerate the importance of the forest industry in the national economies of individual countries but it is clear that many of the African territories have substantial advantages in timber production over at least limited areas of their land surfaces and that the forests have protective as well as productive functions.

(2) For some of the more capital-intensive industries, e.g. pulp and board, development will be associated with plantations of fast-growing species. This, in turn, means that planning of timber production would have to start at least 10 to 15 years ahead of the processing factories. Raw material has to be in prospect in reasonably concentrated form in order to attract industrial capital.

(3) One of the very real problems is to assess the future potential and to get the essential backing to plan for its realization. Systematic forestry requires security of tenure and such policies have to be based on comprehensive exploration of timber and other resources. In the past the long-term development of the forest resources has often been handicapped by the lack of finance in Forestry Departments.

(4) Development of forest industries, as of other industries, is likely to be carried out best on a regional rather than on a national basis. This implies that national plans will have to be co-ordinated and phased.

(5) Favourable prospects for the expansion of tropical timber output are related to the dynamic characteristics of the demand for forest products and to the fact that in many of the advanced countries raw material supplies are becoming 'strained' as in Europe, Japan and North America. There is scope too, for encouraging bilateral and multilateral trade-and-development arrangements and for making use of the technical assistance programmes of the international agencies. Aid will have to be more 'trade orientated'.[5]

(6) There is scope for the organization of the demand in developing countries in such a way as to favour the use of domestic forest products.

(7) Over 90 per cent of African international trade in timber normally goes to Europe and the discussion on trade is accordingly very largely related to European statistics.

(8) Tropical Africa, in common with some other developing areas of the world, has a net financial deficit on its timber trade with other countries and the reason is that unprocessed products are exchanged for processed. The industrialized importing countries of Europe and elsewhere could help to reverse this position if they were prepared to reduce some of their tariffs on finished products.

REFERENCE DOCUMENTS

1. *FAO Africa Survey*. Report on The Possibilities of African Rural Development in Relation to Economic and Social Growth. Food and Agriculture Organization of the United Nations, Rome, 1962.
2. *Africa Timber Trends and Prospects*. Preliminary Report on Western Africa and Equatorial East Africa. (Prepared in collaboration with FAO) Economic Commission for Africa, Sixth session, Addis Ababa, 19 February to 3 March 1964. (E/CN/14.272 14 January 1964).
3. *Prospects for Expanding Forest Products Export from Developing Countries*. Prepared by Forestry and Forest Products Division, Food and Agriculture Organization of the United Nations in cooperation with the Regional Economic Commissions of the United Nations, February 1963.
4. *Secretariat Report on the Trade in Tropical Wood in Europe up to 1962*. Economic Commission for Europe, Timber Committee (TIM/Working Paper No. 71, 9 September 1963.)
5. *United Nations Conference on Trade and Development*. Second Committee. Statement by Mr. J. C. Westoby (FAO) on item 2 of the agenda, 13 April 1964.
6. *The Role of the Forest Industries in the Attack on Economic Underdevelopment*. FAO, Rome, 1962.
7. Report to the East African High Commission on *Present Wood Consumption and Future Requirements in Uganda* by S. LeRoy Pringle and J. E. M. Arnold, No. 1287, FAO, Rome, 1962.
8. Report to the East African High Commission on *Present Wood Consumption and Future Requirements in Kenya* by J. E. M. Arnold, M. F. E. De Backer and S. L. Pringle, No. 1503, FAO, Rome, 1962.
9. Report to the East Africa High Commission on *Present Wood Consumption and Future Requirements in Tanganyika* by M. F. E. De Backer, J. E. M. Arnold and S. L. Pringle, No. 1536, FAO, Rome, 1962.
10. *Some Economic Problems of Forestry in Western Nigeria* by J. J. MacGregor, Department of Forestry, University of Oxford. October 1959.
11. *The Natural Resources of East Africa*. Edited by E. W. Russell. East African Literature Bureau, Nairobi, 1962.

N*

TABLE 1 Index of estimated demand changes for East and West African
countries (1960=100)

	East Africa in 1980	West Africa in 1975	
		savannah	wood-surplus countries
sawn wood	120	165	210
plywood	150	165	260
other panel products	230	—	260
wood pulp products	180	170	300+
poles and branchwood	—	110	—

Source : Compiled from text of *African Timber Trends and Prospects* (1964)

TABLE 2 Tropical log imports into ten European countries by regions of origin – 1950 to 1960 (thousand cu.m.)

tropical exporting regions

selected European importing countries	Africa		Asia/Pacific		Latin America		Total		change 1960-50
	1950	1960	1950	1960	1950	1960	1950	1960	
Western Germany	124	1545	2	27	5	8	131	1580	+1106
France	226	904	1	10	1	2	228	916	+302
Italy	11	487	3	150	1	1	15	638	+4153
United Kingdom	373	361	32	13	12	9	417	383	−8
Netherlands	56	203	8	5	10	8	74	216	+192
Belgium-Luxembourg	45	155	0·3	0·6	0·3	0·2	46	156	+239
Switzerland	28	130	—	2	—	0·3	28	132	+371
Denmark	3	81	0·3	21	—	2	3	104	+3367
Portugal	6	59	—	—	13	21	19	80	+321
Sweden	18	27	—	5	—	0·5	18	33	+83
total (10 countries)	890	3952	47	234	42	52	979	4238	+333
percentage change 1960-50		+344		+398		+24		+333	

TABLE 3 Tropical log imports into ten European countries – the percentage share of the three tropical regions – 1950 to 1960

importing country	Africa		Asia/Pacific		Latin America	
	1950	1960	1950	1960	1950	1960
	%	%	%	%	%	%
Western Germany	95	98	2	2	3	0·5
France	99	98	0·5	1	0·5	—
Italy	73	76	20	24	7	—
United Kingdom	89	94	8	4	3	2
Netherlands	76	94	11	2	13	4
Belgium-Luxembourg	98	99	1	1	1	—
Switzerland	100	98	—	2	—	—
Denmark	100	78	—	20	—	2
Portugal	32	74	—	—	68	26
Sweden	100	82	—	16	—	2
total (10 countries)	91	93	5	6	4	1

Source: Report on Trade in Tropical Wood in Europe up to 1962.

TABLE 4 Imports of tropical hardwood logs by the six main European importing countries from main West African exporting countries in 1955 and 1960 (thousand cu.m.)

importing country	Cameroun		Ivory Coast		Gabon and Congo (Brazzaville)		Ghana		Nigeria		Congo (Leopold-ville)		total	
to	1955	1960	1955a	1960	1955b	1960	1955	1960	1955	1960	1955	1960	1955	1960
Western Germany	27	67	63	280	306	545	160	336	110	255	80	60	746	1543
France	27	29	113	323	258	542	—	6	—	—	—	1	398	901
Italy	—	20	—	80	13	14	74	284	15	77	—	2	102	477
United Kingdom	4	1	2	5	36	26	78	126	166	175	1	1	286	334
Netherlands	13	34	8	41	56	72	24	32	6	16	—	—	108	196
Belgium-Luxembourg	4	12	4	25	16	52	4	24	1	10	24	31	53	154
total	75	163	190	754	685	1251	340	808	298	533	105	96	1693	3605

a Former French West Africa.
b Former French Equatorial Africa.
Source: Report on Trade in Tropical Wood in Europe up to 1962.

TABLE 5 Percentage breakdown by species of tropical log imports into five European countries

1955 (actual year)

Western Germany		France		United Kingdom		Netherlands		Switzerland	
species	%	*species*	%	*species*	%	*species*	%	*species*	%
Okoume	28	Okoume	57	Obeche	27	Okoume	38	Limba	38
Limba	27	All others	43	Mahogany*	22	Mahogany	11	Obeche	23
Obeche	23			Abura	18	Limba	6	Okoume	19
Makore	6			Sipo	5	Teak	4	Abura	4
Ilomba	4			Tola	4	All others	41	Fromager	4
Ramin	4			Sapelli	3			Tola	4
All others	8			All others	21			All others	8
Total	100	Total	100	Total	100	Total	100	Total	100

1960 (actual year)

Western Germany		France		United Kingdom		Netherlands		Switzerland	
Obeche	45	Okoume	52	Mahogany*	23	Okoume	30	Obeche	37
Okouma	18	Sipo	13	Obeche	18	Mahogany	14	Limba	31
Limba	8	Niangon	7	Sipo	15	Obeche	12	Oboume	11
Makore	5	Mahogany	6	Abura	12	Azobe	11	Tola	7
Mahogany	5	Obeche	6	Sapelli	5	Kokrodua	5	Abura	3
All others	19	All others	16	Tola	4	Doussie	4	All others	11
				All others	23	All others	24		
Total	100	Total	100	Total	100	Total	100	Total	100

* Includes Okoume.
Source: *Report on Trade in Tropical Wood in Europe up to 1962*

TABLE 6 Tropical sawn hardwood imports into ten European countries by regions of origin – 1950 to 1960 (thousand cu.m.).

selected European importing countries	Africa		Asia/Pacific		Latin America		total		change 1950-60 thousand (cu.m.)
	1950	1960	1950	1960	1950	1960	1950	1960	
United Kingdom	176	226	133	223	20	14	329	463	+134
Western Germany	—	32	1	36	—	1	1	69	+68
Netherlands	2	21	7	35	4	3	13	58	+46
Denmark	—	7	2	36	—	—	2	43	+41
Belgium-Luxembourg	5	16	2	23	11	—	18	39	+21
France	6	22	4	8	—	1	10	31	+21
Italy	—	13	1	6	—	—	1	19	+18
Norway	8	11	2	8	—	—	10	19	+9
Sweden	1	4	3	13	—	1	4	18	+14
Switzerland	1	3	—	1	—	—	1	4	+3
Total (10 countries)	199	355	155	389	35	20	389	764	+375
percentage change 1960-50		+78		+151		-43		+96	

Source: Report on Trade in Tropical Wood in Europe up to 1962.

Index

*

O

O*

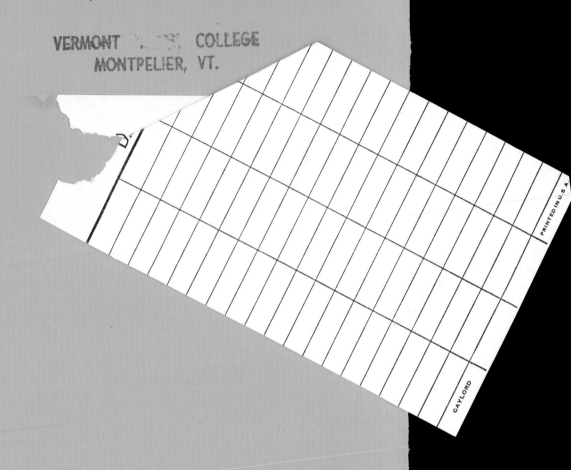